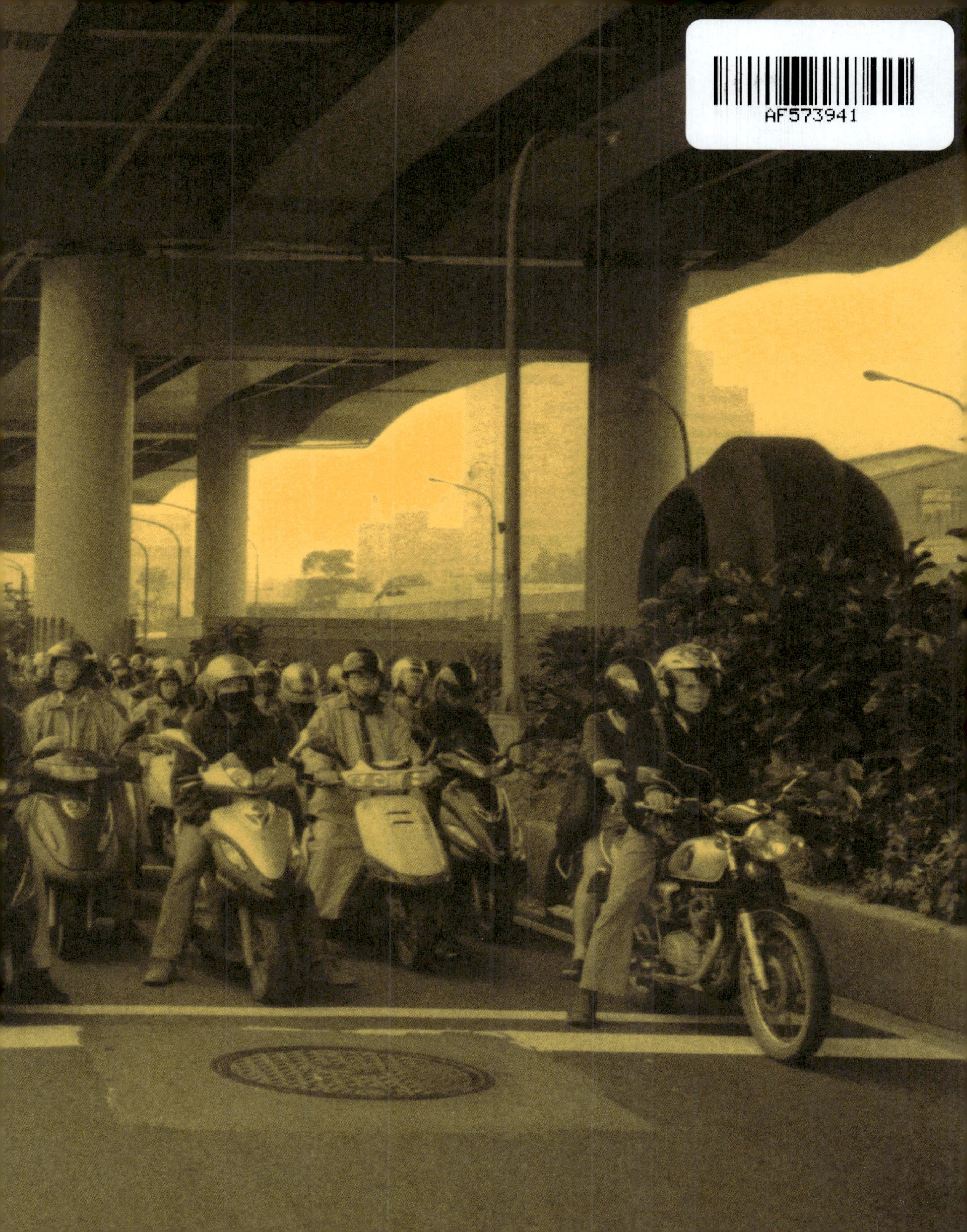

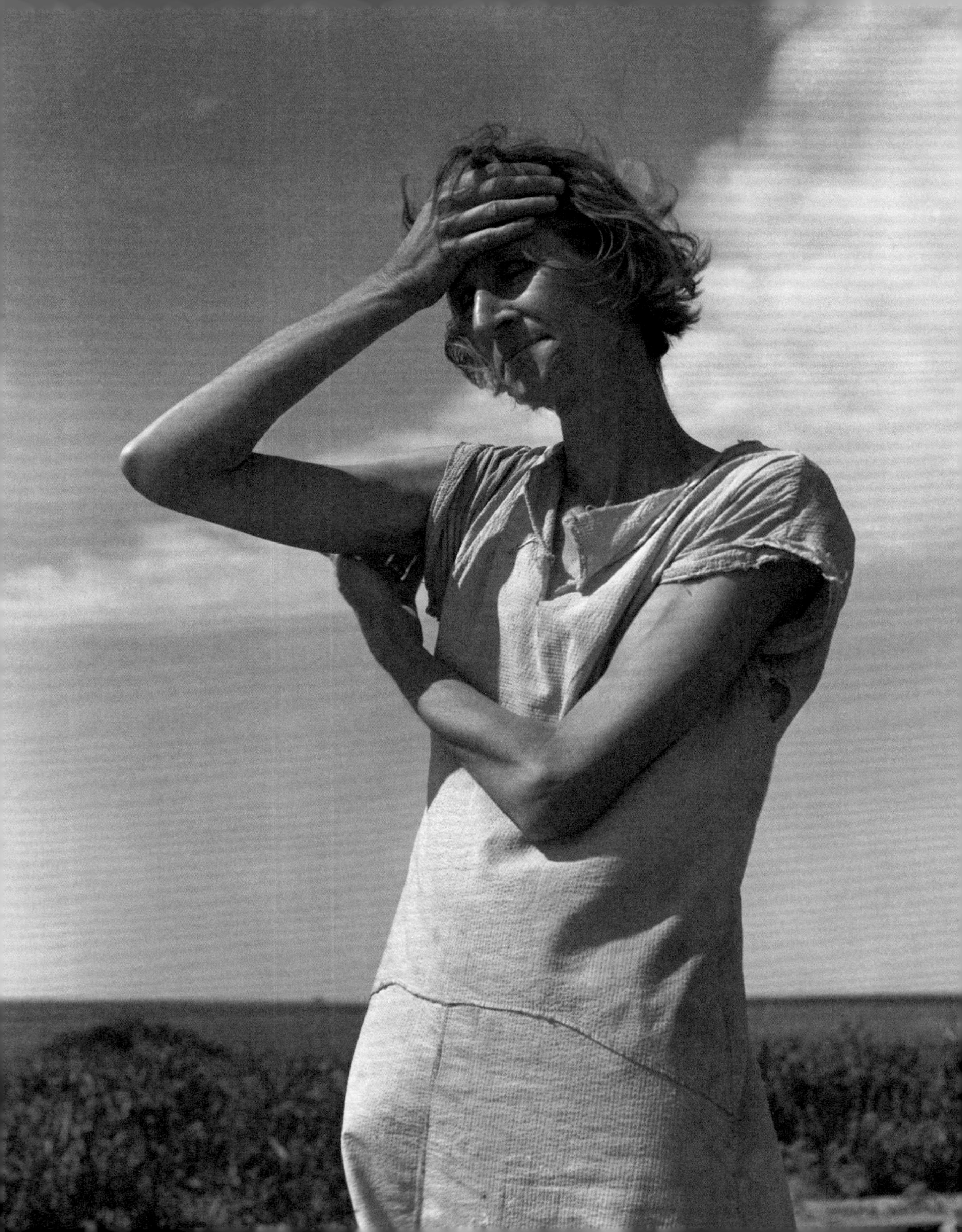

PHOTO**ESPAÑA**2009

LA FABRICA EDITORIAL

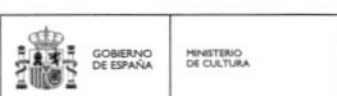
GOBIERNO
DE ESPAÑA
MINISTERIO
DE CULTURA

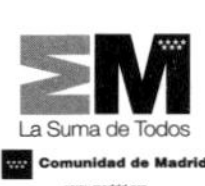
La Suma de Todos
Comunidad de Madrid
www.madrid.org

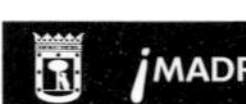
¡MADRID!

# The Everyday

Sérgio Mah

# Senses of the Everyday

The theme chosen for the programme of PHotoEspaña 2009 is centred around the idea of *The Everyday*. The aim of such a choice is to give special emphasis to artists and visual works that show a particular relationship with the experience and perception of what happens to us and surrounds us in the course of our day-to-day encounters and our most intimate and most common gestures. In fact, the theme directs our attention to the prodigious diversity of daily and ordinary life: the instants and the events, the figures, places and objects. It is a field offering a broad spectrum of subjects, meanings, forms and actions that are both accessible and recognisable, and, in this context, everyday life can be understood as the measure of all things, the understanding (or rather the misunderstanding) of social relations, the use that we make of the time in our life (banal, trivial and repetitive). As Henri Lefebvre remarked, in one of the stages of his colossal *Critique of Everyday Life*, "The Human World is not defined simply by the historical, by culture, by totality or society as a whole, or by ideological and political superstructures. It is defined by this intermediate and mediating level: everyday life."[1]

This is a fertile terrain for our perception, imagination and reflection about the modes and experiences of reality, a terrain filled with micro-knowledge that allows us to discern social, cultural and political trends. Everyday life is, therefore, the level of reality in which there is a dialectical confrontation between nature and culture, history and present, or, in other words, it is the quintessential domain of transitions, resistances and fragmentations. Consequently, both thinking about and representing everyday life implies regarding it as a diverse and complex domain, open to all types of potentialities, weaknesses and opportunities; a domain of practices, combinations and (re-)inventions that tend to avoid the logic of categorisation, and, as such, their understanding requires an analysis of its own, because it implies knowledge and qualities that lie outside institutional and specialised contexts, immune to previous descriptions and standardising classifications.

Far beyond being just a concrete theme, everyday life is proposed here as a reference that is capable of determining an area of current and opportune reflections, where some of the most decisive questions of our time converge and diverge. Therefore, neither does the theme seek to limit the possibilities for the acceptance of works, nor should the exhibitions be preferentially understood as illustrations of a given theoretical stance in relation to the theme. PHotoEspaña does not seek to be a context of aesthetic and moral authority. Above all, it is intended to be a space that is open to the great profusion of sensibilities, motivations and behaviours that currently shape the panorama of our image-making practices. As such, this interest in everydayness also fits in with the call for a series of visual proposals which, because of their aesthetic, perceptive and speculative qualities, make it possible to define a particular culture for the photographic in its peculiar forms of representing and examining reality.

On the other hand, this theme was also chosen because of its pertinence and opportuneness at the present moment in time. Our idea is to highlight and reflect upon recent trends in contemporary culture and the visual arts, namely by pointing to a renewed interest in images that reproduce and reshape everyday life. In fact, in recent years, in the fields of photography, documentary cinema and video art, but also in the spheres of television and the Internet, it has been possible to detect a proliferation of proposals and visual objects that focus on and explore the banal and routine movement of day-to-day situations. In a certain sense, it can be said that we are faced with symptoms of a new demand for something genuinely trivial, recognisable and "true".

1. Henri Lefebvre, *Critique de la vie quotidienne*, Fondements d'une sociologie de la quotidienneté, Paris, L'Arche, 1961; *Critique of Everyday Life, vol. 2, Foundations for a Sociology of the Everyday*, John Moore (trans.) London and New York, Verso, 2002, p. 45.

In a world that is inevitably marked (and tending towards homogenisation) by the effects of economic and cultural globalisation and by advanced forms of spectacular communication, it is both symptomatic and revealing to witness the growing number of artists who clearly prefer to resort to simple and immediate languages in their approach to reality. It is a discursive front that is founded on individual experience, on the artist's capacity to share situations, experiences and concrete relations, and, in this way, it may be regarded as a privileged channel for research and for reinventing alternative and significant forms of being and living. It is a matter, here, of enhancing what Maurice Blanchot suggested in "La Parole Quotidienne" when he wrote that "every individual carries in himself a set of reflections, of intentions, that is to say reticences, that commit him to an oblique existence." [2] The obliqueness is the space, the gap, through which the individual escapes from the (self-)controlled side of life.

These are therefore artistic trends that seek to revisit histories and construct stories that are clearly distanced from (and critically reject) extraordinary, heroic and spectacular narratives – persistently conveyed through the discourse of television, advertising and politics, as well as through some art – just as they also dispense with the logic of contemporary culture, as determined by the virtual autonomy and immateriality of digital technology. Hence, there is a certain impetus to mobilise a sensitivity, in fact an affectivity, that is defined through the practices and ideas of everyday life, in such a way as to (re-)present an accessible and common world, one that is sometimes monotonous and trivial, but, despite everything, profoundly pregnant with meaning. This means that the expressiveness and knowledge emanating from the banal do not inevitably result in banal works. On the contrary, this *return to the basics and to the essential*, seems to arise from the following challenge: the everyday is the original and legitimate terrain for constructing an extraordinary and necessarily elaborate set of mental images, based upon the ordinary. Basically, it is these images that draw our attention to a subjectivity based on simple, common and familiar gestures, which testify to impulses, idiosyncrasies and relations of proximity with the everyday that is to come.

It seems evident today that, for many artists, everyday life is, despite everything, a sufficiently authentic, democratic (and liberating) terrain for encouraging a spontaneous and genuine creativity, free of disciplinary and institutional constraints. In this context, everyday life is reconfigured from the idea that art may be illuminating and, at the same time, reveal freer and simpler, yet nonetheless highly significant, forms of experience and conviviality. Everyday life provides that basic level of original and intuitive fermentations and derivations – which is why this is such an attractive (and natural) field for artists.

In this way, the recent changes in direction towards an artistic practice linked to everyday life also represent an attempt to rediscover the roots of a creativity that is based on spontaneity and intersubjectivity, in order to bring about the *despecialisation* and *respecialisation* of artistic practice. Essentially, it is an art that is being constantly reconstructed and reclassified, and which, consequently, calls for the adaptation of aesthetic and conceptual protocols to more direct and understandable modes of reflecting upon the appearance of reality, or, if we wish, the reality of appearance. Everyday life is therefore a territory that is open to all types of incursions, allowing for all manner of gestures that are susceptible to examining and reconverting the meaning and role of the visual arts.

Proposing this theme for an event that is preferentially linked to photographic practices also means acknowledging that this shift in the focus of the visual arts towards everydayness has implied a

2. Maurice Blanchot, "La Parole Quotidienne", *La Nouvelle Revue Française*, no. 114, Paris, 1969; republished in English, "The Everyday Speech", Susan Hanson (trans.), in *Yale French Studies*, no. 73, Yale University Press,1987, p. 12.

reassessment of what we might consider to be photographic. It is known that, throughout its history, photography has been regarded as a privileged medium for the representation and perception of everyday life, to the extent that this idea has slowly taken root as one of the central themes in the panorama of the genres and historical lineages of photography since its invention in the first half of the nineteenth century. First of all, it is important to bear in mind that, in the midst of its ontological, aesthetic and mundane characteristics, the act of photographing has gradually established itself as an act that it is capable of affording importance and meaning to the most diverse and unpredictable subject-matters. This means that the distinctiveness of what is photographic also derives from photography's specific ability to induce formal, communicational and conceptual significance into the most irrelevant and unexpected subjects. Between its specialised uses and its "amateur" uses, the chronology of the photographic is a fertile terrain for statements, narratives and commentaries about themes from everyday life, themes drawn from the most simple and trivial life led by anonymous people, at any moment and in apparently irrelevant places.

In this way, it may be said that one of the most evident features of photogenics derives from that quality of being able to discover (*reproductively*) the peculiar in the indistinguished, the extraordinary in the trivial. Thus, the challenge of the relationship between the photographic and the everyday is not the management of similarities, but the management of the differences between things, the gaps between ourselves and others. Furthermore, this is also a way of constructing a legitimacy for the photographer: he lives, looks and feels like all other individuals. Hence also its political dimension: to draw people's attention to the level of everyday life. It allows us to perceive, imagine and think, at a basic level, about the consequences and effects of social structures and the action that power systems can inflict on people's lives.

Notions such as "making visible", "historical awareness", "counter-knowledge" or "counter-information" are different aspects of the expectations of truth and criticism that have accompanied photography throughout its history and which have determined most of its unique characteristics. All of these aspects simultaneously make up the archival and counter-archival side of photography. Indeed, let us not forget that there are abundant examples in the history of photography of photographers being committed to displaying the clandestine themes of social reality, just as there is a constant insistence on confronting it with the dominant discourses, which, in some way, also represent the individual's response to the erosion of his freedom and individual autonomy. In this sequence of logic, the question of everyday life not only has to do with a question of artistic attitude, but also with the photographer's ethical involvement as a social actor.

Another aspect that we should like to stress in the context of these incursions into everyday life is a certain revival of documentary models and styles and a reformulation of the parameters of the image, which are both inherent in the photographic. Within this scope of understanding, we are interested in reflecting upon the persistence and updating of a culture of the image that, in the course of history, has established a relationship of significant proximity with the simple gestures, events, experiences and routine objects of everyday life.

The documentary refers to modes of representation that give special privilege to formal simplicity, to stylistic, emotional and dramatic restraint. As a genre, the documentary is first and foremost based on an attempt to (re-)present reality and, in this way, its expectations are linked to concepts such as realism, reproduction, truth, factography, testimony, etc. The idea of an image-document and a documentary style are consubstantial to photography in ontological, epistemological and historical terms. Throughout modernity, this genre gradually set itself up as the reserve (or the enduring residue) of the historical combination between the arts and the sciences, to which, with its familiarly overwhelming effects, photography added the uncommitted modes and unexpectedly prosaic themes of social, popular and "amateur" practices.

We may therefore say that, above all, the documentary defines a singular ethos: an image-making practice that creatively reconciles the values of description and factuality with aesthetic, poetic and emotional values; a *culture of framing* that mixes together features, conventions and lineages from photography, painting, cinema, video and the most recent technologies of image production. But it is important to bear in mind that this is a model for an image-making practice that has been successively reformulated, that has been gradually updated in the light of the different historical conditions and specificities. So that, nowadays, the documentary includes characteristics and meanings that are increasingly relative and ambivalent: a genre, a method, not strictly descriptive and testimonial, increasingly aware of its own values and limitations; a field of essentially paradoxical images, which combine reproduction with construction, a mixture between the real and the mental, between the representation of histories and stories, with it being generally recognised that both aspects belong to the same system of truth. This means that we are now faced with a model of authorial representation that mobilises different ways of understanding and gauging reality, operating between the truth of the facts and the real value filled with the fictional experience that is intrinsic to the projective, narrative and speculative possibilities of the image. It is also on the basis of this same rhetoric of ambiguity that many artists have embraced documentary forms, because they regard them as one of the ways of renewing aesthetic languages and reinvigorating the social dimension of art. A genuine "*back to the basics*".

In this context, the thematic programme of PHE 2009 seeks to define a diversified range of photographers and visual works. Taking part are roughly 40 photographers from different generations, geographical origins and aesthetic and conceptual tendencies. The programme of exhibitions is preferentially centred upon their most recent production – and on their multiple derivations upon the theme – but it also attempts to highlight historical moments, such as the 1930s and 1970s, in which this connection between the photographic and the everyday acquired a special preponderance and whose principles and features still prevail in certain current practices.

Once more, we should like to stress the aim of defending an open and eclectic platform about the images of everyday life, through a heterogeneous group of practices that branch out into different identities and forms: from the poetics of proximity to critical realism; the reformulations and updated versions of documentary strategies and styles; the practices of appropriating and using images from private and public archives; from the confessional modes to the informal aesthetics generically related to the unspecialised practices of photography; cinematic and videographic works, with particular emphasis on the use of long takes and images in real time; these are some of the trends that we were interested in bringing forth and which have gradually begun to stand out in the present-day artistic and communicational landscape.

Consequently, this is a group of artists who are involved in the reformulation and reinvention of the visual arts in the context of a renewed faith in the art that both bears witness and is committed to social reality, or, in other words, these are image-making practices that call upon the conventions of the history of art and photography, and which, at the same time, open up a space and channel our attention towards individual experiences, asserting their differences, singularities and idiosyncrasies. In short, in everyday life, everything is expressed and reinvented – even everyday life itself.

José Manuel Cuesta Abad

## The Quotidian Gaze

To think of the everyday leads to the experience of concealment: evidence of the invisible lying in wait in every apparent immediacy. Levelled by the mirage of equality, the days pretend to retract time into a recurring event, and wakefulness tends to become confused with a cyclical dream that endows life with the thickness of the unreal. The everyday belongs to the order of the imaginary, and what its images simultaneously hide and display is the defection of the most visible under our gaze, engrossed in the memory and expectation of its own hypnosis. "The aspects of the things that are most important for us are hidden because of their simplicity and familiarity," Wittgenstein reminds us (*Philosophical Investigations*, § 129). Reality loves to hide itself, and the most hidden things are surely those that are always before our eyes as if, in a renunciation of their own clairvoyance and focusing only on the dark inertia of what has been foreseen or the sudden glow of the unusual, they become refractory precisely to what is closest and most accessible, to what is most important to see or to everything that daily threatens their anaesthetising automatism, an automatism that, overcome from without and within, and "mentally" or "politically" imposed, seeks the opacity of what is real to favour an everydayness that cannot be distinguished from the mechanics of habit, the sclerosis of the gesture or the miniaturization of existence into the ideal mode of a peaceful, unalterable familiarity. As a form of modern life, a mediocre utopian construct of a bourgeois conscience for which the urban environment is an abbreviation of the world, the everyday represents the permeability if not the erasure of the boundaries between the interior and the exterior, the private and the public, the domestic and the social.

Needless to say, daily existence is not limited to the desirable comfort of the home, to the sordidness assumed by force of habit to be placid, or to the satisfaction or fatigue that personal activity and daily tasks may bring. The everyday is *being (as if) at home*, wherever one may be. Existential philosophy discovered in everyday life, *Alltäglichkeit*, the latent imminence of anguish. In Heidegger's analysis, anguish is something more than the basement whose gloomy void sustains the home and daily activity of those residing therein. It is the invasion of the uncanny and sinister, *das Unheimliche*, into the calm lethargy expected of the familiar or requested of the customary. The "being at home" (*Zuhause-sein*) thus suddenly becomes "not being at home" (*Un-zuhause-sein*), which Heideggerian interpretation considers the oldest phenomenon of our "ontological-existential" condition (*Being and Time*, § 40). Wherever one is, *one is nowhere*, in an exterior indistinguishable from a house where anguish, rummaging through the buried foundations of ordinary life, has opened devastating breaches in an entirely alienating exterior that now invades the everyday, infiltrating its cracked walls. A defence mechanism against the basic emptiness brought forth by anguish, the everyday turns against whomever observes it too closely just as a mirror image turns against those who believe they have discovered in their own features a growing similarity to those of someone dead or detested.

Superfluous and necessary behaviour, a small individual rite and collective practice, an idiosyncratic and morally accepted code of behaviour, a space to frequent and time subject to serial patterns, the everyday is also – and because of all of that – a mechanical predisposition, alienating praxis, a sophistication of the conditioned reflex and the ethics of an automaton. Therein resides the interest Freud shows in *Psychopathology of Everyday Life* in tracking the symptoms of breakdown and interruption in the semiconscious economy of verbal and behavioural habit: forgetfulness of names or words, linguistic errors, ambiguous associations, chance and faulty acts... Taking into consideration the Freudian decoding method, it is not hard to predict in these erratic signs small tears in the surface tension of the everyday through which disperse fragments of a repressed libido appear. Everyday life reappears as a way to conceal a reality in whose depths the continuous undertone of anguish resounds or some unconscious desire jerks in momentary spasms. How can we fail to recognise in the everyday the most persistent way of concealing anguish or sublimating repression? But if this concealment and sublimation occur daily and are daily exposed to breaches and crises due to the constant pressure that symptomatic drives exert on them, then anguish and repression would be everydayness itself masked by a translucent screen that confirms – and dissimulates – the radically everyday nature of what it covers up. Even so, the everyday continues to be concealment, not of what is distressing or repressed, which as an elusive presence even in the most banal routine always remains there, a shadow in need of the light of day, but of *everydayness itself*, of each day as another day that hides something from the gaze, which time, even when procrastinating, never ceases to initiate: the unique nature of each instant, the singular character of each object, the newness that can accompany each event.

Maurice Blanchot warned that "The everyday: it is the hardest thing to uncover," and at the end of his reflection added an idea that should be emphasised: "The everyday is our portion of eternity: the eternullity *(l'éternullité)* of which Laforgue speaks" ("La Parole quotidienne", in *L'Entretien infini*). Daily life becomes a parody of eternal life, the fallacious promise of a lasting, comfortable, undisturbed existence for the armoured optimism of the bourgeois mentality, which due to its anxiousness for "eternullity" and avid need to store one more day every day – "Time is money" – sooner or later will have to pay a price of boredom, fear and neurosis. In any event, the secret (if there is one) of the everyday has to do with the experience of time. The equational, iterative logic of the day: every (*quot*) day is all (*quot*) days; every day is ideally the same and in reality similar or comparable to any other by virtue of the "every", the Greek *katà*; in other words according to its recurrent consent to an existing order or a pre-established model. It could be said that daily activity prolongs duration so that the greater the routine nature of movements, feelings, gestures and actions, the longer temporal experience reposes or stagnates. It is not that time passes slowly in comparison with the accelerated rhythm usually imposed on the *durée* by unusual or extraordinary events, or that it is slowed down by attempts at repetition; it is that "nothing is going on." Here is the slowest and fastest duration and ultimately it is neither slow nor fast: it *eternullizes*. The perfect image of the everyday is that nothing happens (not even the hours, which are now always in circular suspension), that every day is too fluid yet at the same time coagulated, that every event happens so that nothing will happen, like a dike that offers resistance to the real future and its potential, unforeseen, anomalous and exceptional events. The day loses the match as soon as it begins, sunk in a yesterday that seeks to equal itself to today and tomorrow, and temporal experience gives itself away indifferently, insignificant in the defunct succession of its periodic phases.

In this insignificance of the everyday, however, one glimpses the retention of life in the image's absent gaze. Strictly speaking, there is no imagination in everydayness, regardless of how, as we said, it is recorded in the sphere of the imaginary. It only forms part of this sphere as a phantasmagorical return of the what has been that is projected not by the incantatory fantasy of a malign genius but by the repetitive impersonal mechanism of an artefact. It only comes from the imaginary as an amnesic substitute, degraded to absurdity, of a condemned mythical life (Sisyphus, Tantalus, the Danaides, eternal return...) within a demystified world. The image of the everyday and the everydayness of the image spring from our gaze, which when transferred to things turns them into effigies that look at us without being able to see us. In *The Invention of Morel*, Bioy Casares tells the prodigious tale of a fugitive who, hidden in an apparently uninhabited island, does not take long to detect the presence of a group of visitors or tourists. From then on, the main character dedicates himself to the surveillance and furtive observation of these "intruders", who little by little become familiar to him, a sort of distant company, friendly in their everydayness, so much so that he falls in love with one of the women in the group, named Faustine, until he eventually discovers that his beloved and all the others are images recorded by a strange machine that repeatedly projects the same figures, the same places, the same events, the same time sequence. Let's consider the meditation that this character writes in his notes:

> "A rotating eternity may seem atrocious to an observer, but it is quite acceptable to those who dwell there. Free from bad news and disease, they live forever as if each thing were happening for the first time; they have no memory of anything that happened before. (...).
>
> Now that I have grown accustomed to seeing a life that is repeated, I find my own irreparably haphazard. My plans to alter the situation are useless. I have no next time, each moment is unique, different from every other moment, and many are wasted by my own indolence. Of course, there is no next time for the images either (they are all equal to the first).
>
> Our life may be thought of as a week of these images – one that may be repeated in adjoining worlds."

There is no other time, a time totally other: either each instant is unique and unrepeatable – and this would be the real, beyond abstraction, cataleptic memory, subjective time – or else each instant is "once-again-the-first- time", the vicarious moment of a past, returning from one time to the next, in which case every day reabsorbs in its fugue of equal instants, *rotating eternity.* For the lead character in Bioy's tale, all of life is reduced to a week of repeating images. The fable would be trivial if its meaning were exhausted with this conclusion, if it were not that the fugitive, the solitary and ignored observer of an everyday alien to him has been prohibited forever access to the phantasmal life he contemplates, if the images populating the island did not conceal a truly deserted space. The half-longing, half-desperate gaze with which this character pursues Faustine's image reflects to a certain extent the imaginary nature of the everyday: gazes may cross but the eyes of the image cannot see the unknown lover they appear to look at and he who looks in the eyes of the beloved image can only see in them *his own* everyday emptiness.

The everyday returns to us the gaze that we fix on reality, a hologram or a spectral countenance whose fixed and seemingly absent expression turns inexpressive. It is this imaginary rigidity, the effect of the entrenchment of real life and temporal experience, that leads us to consider the close relationship, easily confirmed in history, between everydayness and its artistic representation, and that poses a question about the representability of the everyday's power of concealment. It is known that among the modern artistic forms that have paid increasing attention to capturing the everyday, photography undoubtedly plays an exceptional role. The reasons for which photography – "the art of modern life" –has shown a preference for massive recording of ordinary life's figures and spaces are well known and diverse enough to refrain from enumerating them here. We would only point out that such a preference has been partially conditioned by the instrumental, political, technical, domestic, commemorative and documentary functions that photography has had from the start. Nevertheless, to what extent is the photographic image the privileged reproduction medium for the (in)essentially everyday or, to go even farther, to what point can photography be conceived of as the art par excellence of everydayness, capable of revealing the inessential reverse side of the *quot-*?

Photography of the everyday has usually been identified with the realism that rescues from oblivion and lack of attention details of the intimate and the mundane with a *costumbrismo* that idealises or caricatures ordinary daily activities and situations with the picturesque local colour that accentuates the specific, eye-catching aspects of people, objects, places or trades that represent the marginal, ordinary and popular. But all of this is not what is "essentially" everyday. Realism, *costumbrismo*, local colour and picturesque popularisation are all aesthetic and ideological values that have been assigned to everydayness. Photography frequently tends to aestheticise, mystify or make a fetish of the everyday. In this way it faithfully responds to the clear investitures of everydayness, initially inseparable from a routine implementation of the basic needs of human existence by means of urban planning and regulations, the economy and its lucrative laws, work and its obligations, technique and its impersonal powers. To a certain extent, when photography reproduces these dimensions of the everyday it becomes transparent, a transparency that upon tearing open the membrane of monotonous appearance reveals particularly all the insignificance and neutrality of the everyday. In this reproduction, things and human beings wear the death masks that images stamp out in series on their real models. Photography shares with everydayness certain varieties of a compulsion to repetition: an obsessive fixation no longer on the ephemeral and what is usually overlooked but on individuals and objects that, sunk in an abulic recurrence or on the fringes of abandonment and margination, are already really tortured by the paralysis that the image corroborates and enhances. There is no authentic event in the *interior* of the day by day (as painful or dramatic as this may seem to someone observing from the outside); and photography's uncontrolled drive toward mass production of images interferes in this interior emulating – deliberately or not – the apathetic repetition that rules in everydayness. Carried to a compulsive extreme, the "everydaying" of the photographic image is equivalent to its erasure: a second degree obliteration of illusory reality by the imaginary. Photography, if it has to put what is hidden from the gaze into play, must make of the everyday an experience in the order of the imaginary that communicates with the real. And to do so, it has to capture the moment of uniqueness and disaster accompanying experience of the everyday; it has to preserve the everyday by lifting off the protective scab covering its wounds and defeating the powerful apathetic and aestheticising force of its reproductive obsession by means of an unintentional deautomatisation even less appalling due to its artifice.

Beyond daily existence there really is nothing. Nothing more than the desire, trapped in fear or indolence, for a life that is "somewhere else", for a time of unmutilated freedom, an impossible redemption of dead things. The image of an image, a photograph can only show the everyday revealing in it the cloudy vision that transforms reality into a grey "ideality", sordidly unimportant, resisting any possibility of "enchantment". *Enchantments of reality* is the paradoxical formula that Samuel Beckett took from the sickly Proustian adherence to habit. For Proust, habit as second nature, stops us from knowing the first, of which it has "*ni les cruautés ni les enchantements*". In reference to this idea, Beckett points out the following: "When the object is perceived as particular and unique and not merely the member of a family, when it appears independent of any general notion and detached from the sanity of a cause, isolated and inexplicable in the light of ignorance, then and only then may it be a source of enchantment" (*Proust*). These words are also applicable to the everyday as a photographic motif. The camera is photosensitive and receptive, but it is obvious that, strictly speaking, *it cannot see*, only imagine (to make an image, *reimaginise*) that toward which the lens is pointing. The camera's gaze, like that of the faces we see in photos, looks at us without being able to see us; it limits itself to making images of what we "really" cannot see. And the photographer's eye needs that of the camera to imagine or reimaginise, what he in turn cannot see, that which normal perception conceals, the unique and ungraspable instant of the *enchantment of reality*. Such an enchantment is not the curse that petrifies life closing it in the narrowness of immutable regularity and custom. Everydayness has much of pure abstraction, the anonymity of a law somatised by the individual mind and collectivised in the social body. Today, the "enchantment of the everyday" has come to be a pandemic, standard modality of the epochal nature that Weber called *Entzauberung*, a disenchantment with the world, the all-embracing predominance of science and technology, a cult to an absolutised rationalism and to a universal mechanicism. In contrast, the enchantment of reality that photography can make intuitable confronts a certain "cruelty", to use the Proustian term, the harsh reality that shines in the everyday's glassy gaze when images are able to glimpse within it its unapparent power of incantation.

Instants of this enchantment were "imagined" by one (not the only) of the great photographers of the everyday: Eugène Atget. From the first years of the nineteenth century until well into the second decade of the twentieth, Atget dedicated – whether on assignment or on his own initiative – a large photographic series to scenes of the modern *Vieux Paris*: a Paris that was "anti-Haussmannian" in great measure and in which, like someone who is determined to preserve the remains of a ruinous house, Atget portrayed petit bourgeoisie interiors and street scenes, façades of slightly decrepit buildings and establishments, marginal urban locations, heaps of second-hand objects and merchandise, fair stalls and attractions, commercial avenues with their shops and shop windows and *petits métiers*: street vendors, road workers, street musicians, bootblacks, junk dealers, prostitutes, etc.[1] After his work was discovered by Berenice Abbott and experienced the enthusiasm that it immediately inspired in Man Ray, Atget was considered a Balzac (or perhaps even more a Baudelaire) of photography and a forerunner to the surrealists. Subsequently, his legacy has influenced various generations of photographers of a recognised "avant-garde audacity". The historical importance that Walter Benjamin attributes to him in *Short History of Photography* and in *The Work of Art in the Age of Mechanical Reproducibility* is lies specifically in having freed photography from the decadent aura that characterised fin de siècle portraiture and in having recorded the streets of Paris in 1900 in their empty aspect ("peopleless": *in menschenleeren Aspekten*), as if they were a crime scene where the evidence of what had happened must be found. Evidence of a historical disaster that Benjamin, with his lucid perspicacity, finds in the disturbing desolation of deserted streets – to which Atget's "peopleless" and melancholy rooms have to be added. In this desertisation it is possible to glimpse the imaginary reverse side of the everyday, indifference among streets full of people and the solitary streets of a city that in full daylight appears abandoned. It is a deserted panorama that enables us to sense the enchanted reality of those streets in the everyday void *that fills them*.

In a poem from *Alcools*, "La maison des morts", Apollinaire compares a cemetery mortuary in which the bodies rest on display within showcases to the shop windows of the *boutiques de modes* behind which

1. Atget's photographic work is compiled in the excellent four-volume edition by John Szarkowski and Maria Morris Hambourg. The urban photographs of Paris to which we refer appear in volume IV of *The work of Atget (Modern Times)*, London, Gordon Fraser, 1985.

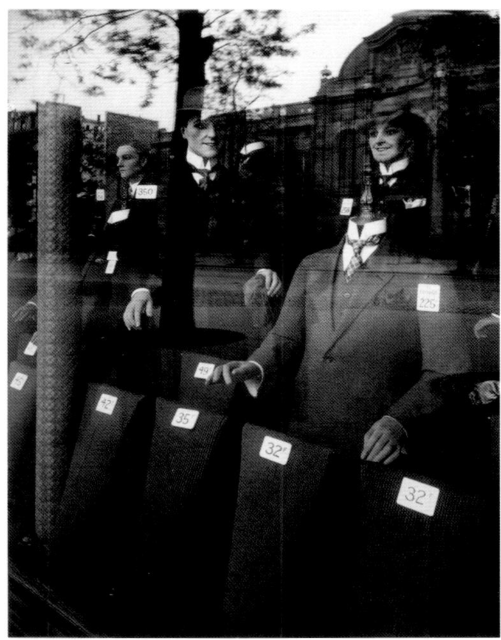

**Eugène Atget** *Men's Fashions*, 1925. Printed by Berenice Abbott in 1925 from a negative by Atget. Courtesy George Eastman House, International Museum of Photography and Film. © Eugène Atget

manikins stand eternally simulating expressions ("*Les mannequins grimaçaient pour l'éternité*"). Among the photographs that made Atget an icon of surrealism those depicting commercial streets with shop windows full of manikins with fearless, sinister smiles (*Magasins du Bon Marché, Avenue de l'Observatoire, Avenue des Gobelins*) are outstanding because of their rare visual irony, not far from Appollinaire's black humour. In many of them the window glass spookily reflects pieces and perspectives of the outer buildings so that these, due to a catoptic effect, appear as the "real" backdrop against which the manikins pose like impeccable citizens, elegant ladies and gentlemen who walk through the streets of Paris. It is not just that the exterior penetrates in the interior of the shop windows and vice versa but that these photos merge the reality of the urban landscape with the unreality of an affected scene of dolls. Atget's manikins are the cruelly paradoxical humanity of modern daily life and there is something in them that suggests the inverse counterpart of the *flâneur*: individuals who stroll through a small multitude without taking a single step, who cannot see those who look at them fleetingly without recognising their own faces in those of these servile and inert FANTOCHES that daily make the same grimaces at the sad eternity of each day. To photograph the everyday – perhaps Atget's brilliant lesson is only this – is to imagine the enchantment of the real hidden in the empty gaze that our own images return to us: evidence of the invisible for the multitude that moves daily through the streets of a deserted city.

Christoph Ribbat

# Stay Clear of Propellers at All Times: Photography, Daily Life, and *William Eggleston's Guide*

Here's a complicated issue. We usually think of William Eggleston as one of the greatest artists of the everyday. Generations of photographers have admired him, walked in his footsteps, enthused by the way his color shots reflect the banality of our world. Consider now, though, how far the subjects and places he shows really represent everyday life on this planet. This is going to sound moralistic, but it is a real intellectual problem. Look at the hunger, poverty, military conflicts that people are facing day in and day out (and were facing, back then, in the 1970s), then look at the documentary photography in the Eggleston tradition, and you will find that the photographs we used to think were particularly helpful, brilliant, inspiring in making us understand people's day-to-day existence are actually images depicting a perfect world: a quiet, good place. This isn't everyday life. This is heaven.

Take *William Eggleston's Guide* (1976), for instance, perhaps the most influential photobook of the last four decades. Touch the dark, textured cover, look at that tricycle parked on a suburban street. Go on and on and you will find that this is a visual narrative whose subjects, in contrast to the real experience of countless men, women, and children, seem entirely safe from harm. Again and again, we're looking at scenes of perfect safety or rituals of (over-)protection. There's a picture showing an upbeat middle-aged man in a business suit on a small airfield, a hangar in the background, and a sign to his right on which red letters ask people to "stay clear of propellers at all times." There's a boy we imagine to be walking home from school down this street in pastoral suburbia, and not only is he guided by an older friend or big brother, there's even a dog running ahead, protecting the bigger boy protecting the smaller boy who really, we feel, doesn't need protection at all. And, in a picture we might find problematic these days, this white Southern gentleman is standing next to a car, amid the trees in a small wooded area, and his black valet is there in a perfectly white jacket, standing slightly behind him, gazing in the same direction as if he were watching over him, again performing an overly protective gesture. Sure, there are hints of sadness and loneliness in some of these photographs. For the most part, however, they contain the promise of a safe, peaceful, elegant world. The essence of this can be found in Eggleston's gorgeous still life of an evening meal shot in Sumner, Mississippi, and its array of vegetables, steak, salad, biscuits, baked potato, ice tea and enormous ice cubes that anyone who's ever felt real hunger or real thirst will probably read as a really well-photographed version of paradise on earth.[1]

This, in fact, is what makes for the beauty of the new American color photography and it may be the reason behind its success and its impact on contemporary photographers. Whether we're looking at Eggleston's pictures or at the chronicles of Stephen Shore's travels across America, we like to think that we are being transported to the heart of ordinariness (the motel, the diner, the parking lot) – but it is a light-filled everyday that seems marvelously pleasing, warm and rich and smooth. (Yes, sure, there is a famous Stephen Shore picture of a clogged toilet, but look at the rainbow he saw over the Horseshoe Bend Motel, Lovell Wyoming, July 16, 1973, look at the pancakes, the melon, the glass of milk at Trail's End Restaurant, Kanab, Utah, August 16, 1973,[2] and you'll catch the drift of this reading). So there's something wrong with the standard narrative of late 20th century photography. We used to think that Shore and Eggleston portrayed the everyday (your neighbor and his beer can) with everyday

1. In his preface to *William Eggleston's Guide*, John Szarkowski claims that the people Eggleston photographed "seem to live surrounded by spirits, not all of them benign" (John Szarkowski, Preface. *William Eggleston's Guide*. 1976. New York: Museum of Modern Art, 2002. 7). That sounds like an odd reading, not so much because we don't really believe in spirits any more (this may have been different in the 1970s), but because the spirits in Eggleston's world are all benign – and there's no question about it.

2. See Christy Lange, Michael Fried, Joel Sternfeld, *Stephen Shore*. London: Phaidon, 2007.

3. Martin Parr and Gerry Badger, *The Photobook: A History, Volume I*. London: Phaidon, 2004. 119.

tactics (color photographs that look like your neighbor shot them), prompting generations of photographers to explore their own vernacular worlds. This history may be misleading.

The issue would be marginal if the world of photography hadn't changed so much in the last few decades of the 20th century. In the 1960s and 1970s a new "hierarchical value system" (Badger) organized photography. With the medium's growing acceptance by the museum, audiences began to separate photojournalism from documentary photography, now considered documentary-as-art.[3] As a result, the tradition of engaged, humanistic photo-reportage (think of W. Eugene Smith) was now seen as middlebrow at the most. Smart viewers of photography wanted the everyday plus the colors (Eggleston, Shore), though minus the suffering. Susan Sontag's *On Photography* (1977) painted the representation of war and violence as problematic ("the medium," Sontag wrote, "which conveys distress ends by neutralizing it"[4]) and thus legitimized the marginalization of concerned photography. This helps explain why Western photography audiences now like their documentary work tame and civil, colorful and just a wee bit grotesque – while the true crises on this planet remain largely invisible.

The problem sketched here isn't photography's problem alone. It's familiar to students of literary realism wondering whether all these supposedly critical middle-class novels didn't just cement the very social differences the bourgeoisie depended on for its survival. Ben Highmore, editor of *The Everyday Life Reader*, calls the term 'everyday life' "vague and problematic," and sketches how it is used and misused as a quick formula to identify "people like us, lives like ours" and thus imagine our day-to-day lives as being "haunted by implicit 'others', who supposedly live outside the ordinary the everyday".[5] So clearly, this is an extremely problematic concept that looks inclusive at first glance and then excludes all those not partaking in our particularly privileged everyday existence.

These reservations prompt the question, of course, of how any photographer could produce pictures addressing our everyday provincialism without making his works seeming provincial in themselves. How do you, to paraphrase Highmore, denaturalize everyday life in photographs?[6] Eggleston, notoriously anti-theoretical, isn't a likely candidate.

Usually, scholars of these issues turn to Jeff Wall of Vancouver, Canada, as the paragon of a smart kind of art photography that manages to do both: depict the everyday in its seemingly banal sketchiness and construct the complex connections to the historical and ideological contexts of our world – which is a challenge instinct-driven photographers like Eggleston and Shore are often too lazy to take on. As all photography enthusiasts know, Wall finds that the chaos of the real doesn't make for flawless photographs and thus diligently reconstructs scenes in the studio and on outdoor sets. John Roberts, in his 1998 study *The Art of Interruption: Realism, Photography, and the Everyday*, argues that Wall's choreographed images connect the "semiotic to the *objective dynamics*" of the world we live in, thus revealing the "secret and not-so-secret pathologies" of everyday life by and by colonized by capitalism.[7] There is a "realist commitment" in Wall, Roberts proclaims, and also the "continuing intellectual vitality of the avant-garde appropriation of the photographic archive."[8] Linking Jeff Wall's work to Heidegger's and

4. Susan Sontag, *On Photography*. London: Penguin, 1977. 108.
5. Ben Highmore, "Introduction: Questioning Everyday Life." *The Everyday Life Reader*. Ed. Ben Highmore. London: Routledge, 2002. 1 (1-34).
6. Highmore 28. (There's an uncanny echo here of the "spirits, not all of them benign" that Szarkowski finds in Eggleston's photographs.)
7. John Roberts, *The Art of Interruption: Realism, Photography, and the Everyday*. Manchester: Manchester University Press, 1998. 197.
8. Roberts 215.
9. Michael Fried, *Why Photography Matters as Art as Never Before*. New Haven: Yale University Press, 2008. 63.
10. Fried 352.

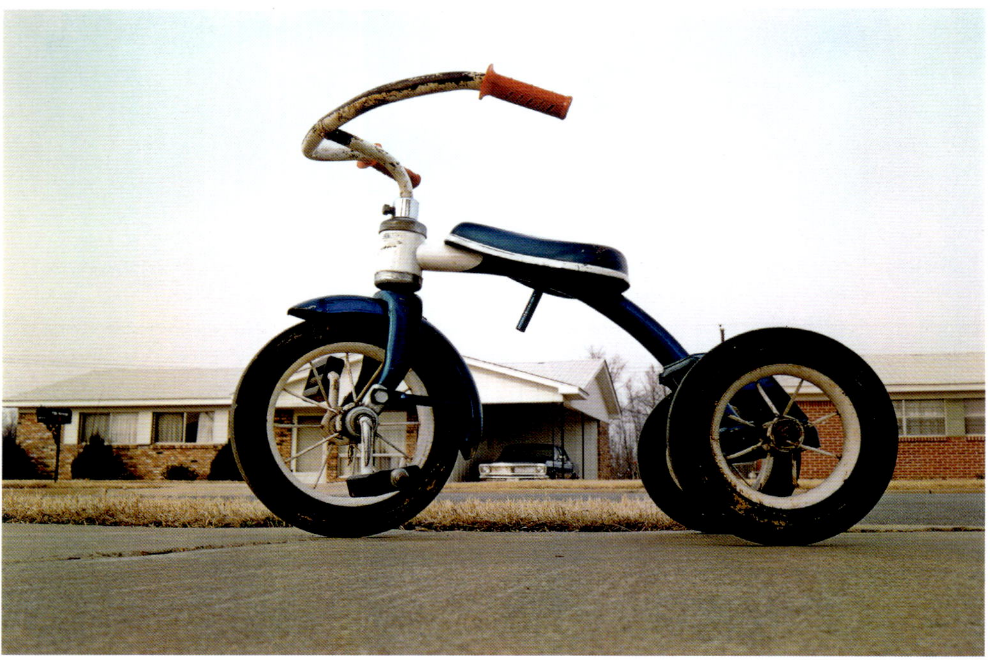

**William Eggleston** Untitled (Memphis), 1970. Courtesy Cheim & Read, New York. © Eggleston Artistic Trust

Wittgenstein's theories of the quotidian, eminent art historian Michael Fried makes similar observations. Though not a straight photographer, Wall, according to Fried, has been constantly involved with "the worldhood of the world"[9], producing the "hauntingly antitheatrical pictures"[10] Fried admires. (He finds them particularly pleasing, though, when they are exactly in line with his own theoretical writings). Reading most scholarly explorations of Wall's oeuvre, one can almost hear the gasps of relief by elite art historians that finally, at long last, a photographer has severed the ties to the vernacular. Wall's references are to Courbet and Manet rather than to the usual street photographers by the hot-dog stand and that, obviously, secures his position in the art world.

It's hard, though, to love Wall's controlled panoramas of the mundane – so much harder than falling for Eggleston's sketches. It's similarly hard to tell whether Wall's work will last, partly because he abandons the energies that have kept photography alive for more than 150 years. There is something thoroughly quaint about the fashion in which Wall partakes, over and over again, in the conventional rites art photography performs to repress its vernacular foundations. As Geoffrey Batchen argues, snapshots, tintypes, and coffee mugs featuring children's photographs constitute "the popular face of photography, so popular it has been largely ignored by the critical gaze of respectable history."[11] Batchen shows how the photograph as an object, a thing that can be held and touched, something that has "volume, opacity,

11. Geoffrey Batchen, *Each Wild Idea: Writing, Photography, History.* Cambridge: MIT Press, 2001. 57. See also: Stacey McCarroll Cutshaw and Ross Barrett, "In the Vernacular: Photography of the Everyday." *In the Vernacular: Photography of the Everyday.* Ed. Stacey McCarroll Cutshaw and Ross Barrett. Boston: Boston University Art Gallery, 2008. 11-27.
12. Batchen 60.
13. The distance between the vernacular and the art world remains even in those projects that deliberately turn to the extensive historical archive. Okwui Enwezor, for instance, curating the exhibition *Archive Fever*, talks about the "degeneration of the photograph under the rapacious

tactility, and a physical presence in the world,"[12] seems invisible in so many academic discussions of photography. From the daguerreotypes and tintypes of the European 19th century to *fotoesculturas* made by 20th-century Mexican craftsmen to objects used in Nigerian funeral practices, the photograph has served as a key object in everyday rituals and practices. These, of course, seem utterly alien to the way a Wall or a Gursky are displayed in the monumental museum of our time, protected by maximum security systems, never to be touched.

It's not a very sound idea then to discuss such high-end art works as conceptually sound representations of the everyday.[13] Clearly, there's still a gap that needs to be closed between the elite rituals that often focus on the pure and singular image, anxious to isolate it from the quick exchanges of popular culture, and the practices generated by the popular culture, often narrative, often physical, sometimes superficial.[14]

Gerry Badger has described this problem by sorting photographers into two distinct groups. One he defines as "totally formalist, wholly exclusive, pandering to the relatively confined system of the museum." The other, Badger finds, is "more populist (in the best sense), searching for the interesting territory of potentially unlimited fertility," the photobook, defined as "a narrow, deep area between the novel and film."[15] Obviously, Eggleston belongs to the latter group. Intellectually rigorous and artistically ambitious, Jeff Wall has made it clear that he finds the borders of the "photo ghetto" much too narrow for his taste.[16] Ironically though, William Eggleston may have erased the barriers between that "ghetto" and the culture as a whole even as Wall was working his way toward the museum.

So in spite of the questions raised at the outset, we probably should consider *Eggleston's Guide* as a canonical text in photography's interactions with the everyday. And we should think about the tradition Eggleston shaped as photography's most powerful. In this man's work, the art form flourishes, "ground[ed] in the vernacular," as Vince Aletti observes.[17] The *Guide,* an awesome photobook, functions both in the image world and in the object world, a truly democratic cultural text. The lesson, thirty-three years later, is this: Eggleston and his peers paved the way – and photography is so strong and vibrant these days that the protocols of high art may have ceased to matter. The museum may need the energies photography has to offer more than the photography needs the museum. And none of the questions John Szarkowski was grappling with in his preface to *Eggleston's Guide* seem relevant anymore. Now, no curator must explain, as Szarkowski had to in Eggleston's case, "that such pictures often bear a clear resemblance to the Kodachrome slides of the ubiquitous amateur next door," though only in the way that "Jane Austen's sentences" were "presumably similar to those of her seven siblings."[18] More importantly even, a contemporary Szarkowski would have to point out that the photographic picture ranks as a "concrete kind of fiction" instead of "hard evidence" or "quantifiable data".[19] Luckily, we have long moved away from the tedious debates on photography's relationship to the real. Lev Manovich solved the whole issue by pointing out how "straight photography" had always functioned as just one branch of the medium, coexisting with many much more manipulative traditions.[20] Non-Western practices and collective theories of the photographic image (the Yoruba's, for instance) can teach Europeans and Americans that the effectiveness of the photographic image, in Olu Oguibe's words, depends on "faith", not "faithfulness".[21] As TJ Demos points out, "[p]hotographers have learned the lesson that 'reality' remains available only through the practices that represent it."[22] And that seems to answer this essay's initial question. In light of these findings, asking for the global reality in Eggleston's work may be beside the point.

machines of mass media, its banalization in popular culture, and its cult of sentimentality," pitting against this the artists represented in his show who – according to Enwezor – turn "archival materials into profound reflections on the historical condition" (Okwui Enwezor, "Archive Fever: Photography between History and the Monument." *Archive Fever: Uses of the Document in Contemporary Art* by Okwui Enwezor. New York: International Center of Photography, 2008. 46 [11-51]).
14. The hard question here, of course, is whether the book and thus the image as object will remain in this position in an increasingly virtual culture. Badger, quite the optimist, stresses that the computer, instead of killing the book,

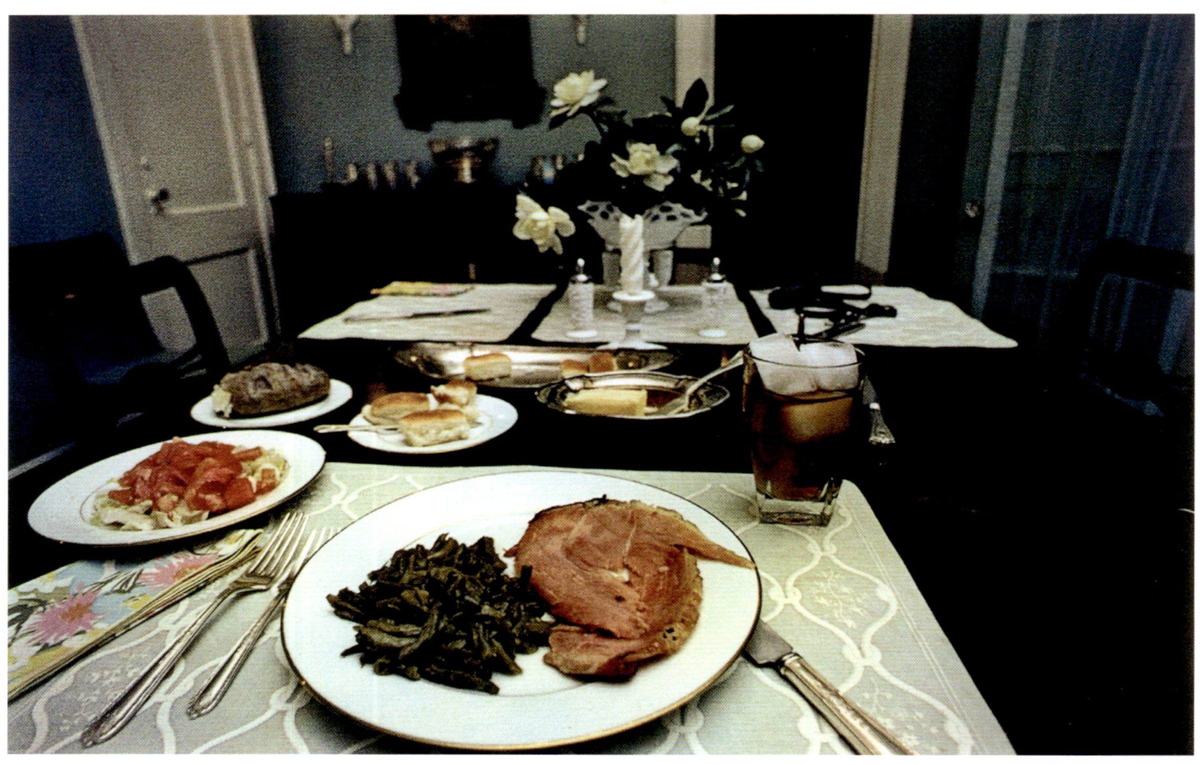

**William Eggleston** Untitled (Summer, Mississippi), c. 1969-71. Courtesy Cheim & Read, New York. © Eggleston Artistic Trust

However: The fact that all photographs are fiction doesn't mean that the real has ceased to exist and that these fictions don't relate to the real. The opposite is true. Following Batchen's groundbreaking work, our thinking about photography now includes thinking about the roles photo images and objects play in our day-to-day existence. So our perspective on the real, vernacular functions of these fictions is even more astute these days.

As Western observers, we find our own privilege and physical comfort in the pages of *Eggleston's Guide* and in the odd, charming works of the documentary photographers we may currently adore. And yet, as we seek and find pleasure in these scenes, we do risk being called utterly complacent if we didn't reflect on the hunger, violence, and atrocities that surround us on this planet. Knowing what we know, though, about the vernacular dimension of photography (and knowing that these may be the best years ever of this art form), this may be the time to consider ways in which to narrow the distance between what we consider excellent photography (Eggleston, Wall) and what we consider not-so-excellent photojournalism selling atrocity to slightly numbed audiences.[23] Even Judith Butler, a thinker famously "arguing with the real"[24] in the most sophisticated terms, now emphasizes the necessity of images reporting on global suffering, of photographs depicting lives previously thought "unnameable and ungrieveable," shown in their "precariousness and their destruction," moving "us", as Butler writes, to "a sense of ethical outrage that is, distinctively, for an Other, in the name of an Other."[25] This is more than a fuzzy idea. We need images that are both intellectually convincing and able to move us to outrage over the precariousness of other people's lives.[26] We need them, this writer assumes, like we need Eggleston's visions of people nobody knew and colors no one would forget. Let's see what happens.

has made it ever so much easier for photographers to produce their work in book form. This, he argues, takes the medium back to the time of the 19th century, the time of self-produced albums and calling cards. It is possible, then, to think of the photobook not as an elite coffee-table book, but as a key physical object of image exchange even in a world where most of our exchanges take place online (Martin Parr and Gerry Badger, *The Photobook: A History, Volume II*. London: Phaidon, 2006. 8; 16).

15. Parr/ Badger, *The Photobook:; A History, Volume I*. 11.

16. From an interview quoted in: Arthur Lubow, "The Luminist". *The New York Times Magazine*, 25 February 2007. www.nytimes.com/2007/02/25/magazine/25Wall.t.html. Accessed 20 February 2009.

17. Vince Aletti, "William Eggleston, *William Eggleston's Guide*". *The Book of 101 Books: Seminal Photographic Books of the Twentieth Century*. Ed. Andrew Roth. New York: PPP, 2001. 234.

18. Szarkowski 10.

19. Szarkowski 14.

20. Lev Manovich, "The Paradoxes of Digital Photography." *The Photography Reader*. Ed. Liz Wells. London: Routledge, 2003. 245 (240-249).

21. Olu Oguibe, "Photography and the Substance of the Image." *In/sight: African Photographers, 1940 to the Present*. Ed. Olu Oguibe and Okwui Enwezor. New York: Guggenheim Museum Publications, 1996. 246. (231-250).

22. TJ Demos, "Introduction: The Ends of Photography." *Vitamin PH: New Perspectives in Photography*. London: Phaidon, 2006. 7 (6-10).

23. See Sontag, *Regarding the Pain of Others*. New York: Farrar, Straus, and Giroux, 2003. Sontag refers to Jeff Wall's *Dead Troops Talk* as a conceptually sound example of sophisticated war photography.

24. A chapter in Butler's *Bodies that Matter: On the Discursive Limits of "Sex."* London: Routledge, 1993.

25. With reference to Emmanuel Levinas's theories of the face of the Other calling us "out of narcissism" (Butler 138), Butler argues that "under contemporary conditions of representation," we (the Western/American audience) "cannot [...] hear the agonized cry or be compelled or commanded by the face" (Judith Butler, *Precarious Life: The Powers of Mourning and Violence*. London: Verso, 2004. 150).

26. See, for instance, Demos's survey and his conviction that the most recent strategies in documentary photography manage to provide for a new kind of "ethical engagement," an opening up to "experimental ways of perceiving and responding to otherness." Demos concludes: "In today's climate of war and terror, these salutary developments are welcome" (10).

David Campany

# Yesterday's Everyday and the Depiction of Work

A few years ago I was invited to give a talk at Central Saint Martin's School of Art in London. I don't remember the theme of my talk that day but I do remember I arrived at the school a little early so I went to the student library. Browsing the shelves my eye was caught by a very worn copy of *Citizens of the Twentieth Century*, the grand opus of August Sander's inter-war portrait photographs of German "working types", published posthumously in 1986.[1] Saint Martin's has many art and design programmes but no specific photography course. It is a medium used by all the students in one form or another. The Sander book was obviously well used. It had been repaired twice at least and had dozens of date stamps on its record card indicating it had been borrowed many times over the years. It goes without saying that Sander is an important figure in the history of photography and the history of inter-war Germany, and of course his work looms large for many contemporary photographers. But who at this School was so interested in his work? I asked a librarian. The book had been borrowed most often by fashion students.

I was surprised, then slightly embarrassed at my surprise. Why should this be so unexpected? After all, Sander's work, like that of Eugène Atget and Walker Evans (who also photographed working types, incidentally) is endlessly discussed and theorised in "photography circles" because of its richness, its ambiguity, its *potential* for meaning. As such it is bound to lend itself to a great range of interests, far beyond the purview of Photography with a capital "P". The fashion students had as much of a claim on the work of Sander as anyone. Indeed they may have been alerted to Sander's work by Wim Wenders' film *Notebook on Cities and Clothes* (1989), in which the fashion designer Yohji Yamamoto talks of how Sander's photographs were a great influence on him. But could we ever know exactly what such a student is getting from the images? It may be information about how Germans dressed between the wars but it may be much else besides; perhaps things to do with the history of gesture and bodies, or the appearance of fabric when photographed in black and white, or something else.

In 1929 Sander published a sample of his portraits as the book *Antlitz der Zeit* [*The Face of Our Time*]. One can imagine German audiences of 1929 measuring the images against their own experiences, their own conception of themselves in that complex historical moment. Sander's work was a contribution, perhaps even an intervention into the conflicted idea of modern European or national identity. Of course, as time passes the images are not measured against experience so readily but can become a substitute for it. They no longer contribute to an understanding of a present and are instead slipped into the role of stand-in for the past. This historical and semantic shift is what Jean-François Lyotard had in mind when he spoke of the construction of the "reality" of the past: "Reality succumbs to this reversal: it was the given described by the phrase, it became the archive from which are drawn documents or examples that validate the description."[2]

If they live on, photographs have the potential to acquire far more authority in posterity than they ever had in their own lifetime and it is often difficult to recover the circumstances of their first appearance. But it can happen. Sander's *Citizens of the Twentieth Century* crops up in *Wings of Desire* (1987), the film Wim Wenders made just before his Yamamoto film. Two angels are wandering the divided city of Berlin. Unseen by the living they watch as the citizens try to go about their lives, caught as they are between the

1. Gunther Sander, ed., *August Sander. Citizens of the Twentieth Century* (MIT Press, 1986). It is the album Sander himself never managed to publish in his own lifetime, due to the intervention of the war and the confiscation of his work by the Nazis.
2. Jean-Francois Lyotard, *The Differend: Phrases in Dispute* (Minneapolis, 1988) p. 41

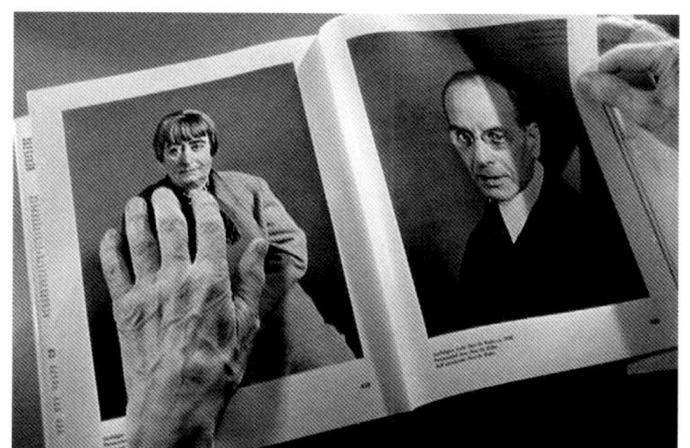

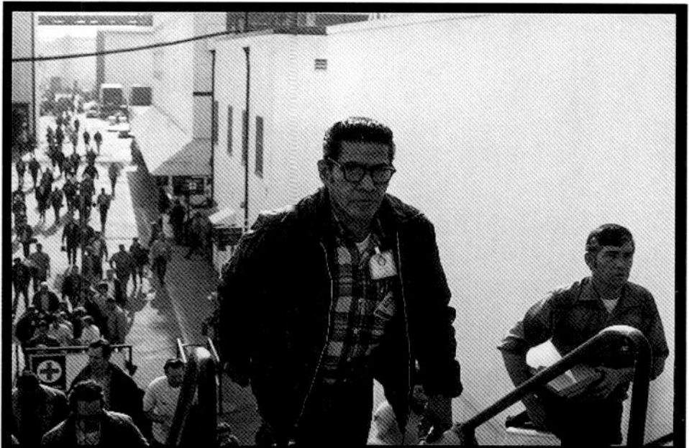

**Wim Wenders** Frame from the film *Wings of Desire*, 1987. © Wim Wenders
**Allan Sekula** *Untitled Slide Sequence*, 1972. 72 black and white transparencies projected at 13-second intervals. 17 minutes 20 seconds, looped. © Allan Sekula

upheavals of the past and the uncertainty of the future. In the grand Staatsbibliothek an old man is seated at a reading desk looking through the book, an angel at his side. The man is old enough to have been one of the three young farmers on their way to a dance in 1914 who can be seen in Sander's famous image reproduced on the book's cover. As he browses the pages he ruminates on the nature of history and his own life, and we are given to see Sander's project not as an uncomplicated historical record but as a set of images to be read in dialogue with their own time and their own people, to be measured against their experience. "What is wrong with peace that its inspiration doesn't endure and that its story is hardly told?" the man asks himself. Wenders cuts briefly to old newsreel footage of the human carnage left by a wartime bombing raid. Over time the generations caught up in the war are dying out and direct experience of the inter-war period has all but disappeared. For younger people who gaze upon them now they are perhaps a definitive record of the period and of "the way things were". But in this brief and simple scene of a man weighing the pictures against his own history, something of the provisional nature of Sander's project is permitted to resurface.

It is with this in mind that I would like to say a few things about a piece of work included in the present exhibition which has fascinated me for a number of years. It is Allan Sekula's *Untitled Slide Sequence* (1972). I saw it first in reproduction in the 1980s. The twenty-five black and white "slides" were printed on consecutive pages of *October*, the journal of art criticism and theory. It was only in 2001, almost thirty years after it was made that I saw it "properly", installed as part of Oxford's Museum of Modern Art show *Open City: Street Photographs Since 1950*. So I never saw it as a contemporary work "in its own moment", so to speak. I have not seen it since and this is how I remember it: in a dark space slides were shown sequentially at regular intervals on a single screen, interrupted by the black gaps so characteristic of slide carousel projection. They were monochrome 35mm reportage-looking "snapshots" of workers leaving a factory.[3]

Several slides showed the workers looking at the camera with a mixture of boredom, fatigue and sometimes suspicion. Sekula seemed to have been standing in their way so they had to negotiate his presence. I remember feeling how this "exchange of looks", for want of a better expression, seemed to foreground the camera and its operator. Each image was on the screen long enough to encourage the

3. Being a photographer myself, I noted how unusual it was to see black and white slides of that era, since there was at that time no monochrome transparency film. I presumed Sekula had made his transparencies from black and white prints.

viewer to begin to explore and reflect on what it offered. In fact I remember feeling the timing of the projection seemed calculated to frustrate both the comfortable "nowness" of an elapsing cinematic present and the "pastness" that defines all still photographs to some extent. It was neither fast enough nor slow enough. I cannot recall if that feeling was awkward or illuminating. It was probably both.

In 2001 I was watching a lot of early cinema, and Sekula's images seemed to me to allude to the very first film shown in public, the Lumière brothers *Workers Leaving a Factory* (1895).[4] In that film the workers are primarily women. They file out through the door of what is the Lumières' own photographic business and onto the sidewalk. Just a few of them look at the camera, which seems as if it is on the other side of the street. The subject matter and the means of representation are so intimately connected here. This group of workers, employed in the production of standard imaging equipment, is caught en masse in their everyday ritual by the mechanically repetitive rhythms of the filmic image. That cinema was inaugurated and set on its way by such a highly reflexive film seems bold and provocative even today.

The Lumières' film stops after forty-five seconds when the short reel of celluloid runs out. Sekula's slide sequence ends with a dissolute shot of feet, as if the photographer was either torn away from his task by force (perhaps he was trespassing) or had finished shooting and was simply firing the shutter to complete his roll of film. Sekula describes much of his work from the 1970s as "disassembled movies" and *Untitled Slide Sequence* certainly fits that description. He has talked of the influence of experimental documentary film on his work. Film has always had an experimental documentary tradition but by the 1970s photographic practices had become so entrenched and formulaic that the very idea of an experimental documentary photography seemed to many a contradiction in terms.[5] You could be an experimental photographer or a documentary photographer but not both. Sekula's whole oeuvre strikes me as exemplary in its refusal to accept that simplistic reduction. *Untitled Slide Sequence* both documents workers leaving a factory while also documenting the act of making such documents. Its strategy is up-front and anti-illusionistic. There is no pretence to neutrality here, and no pretence to totality either. For example when the workers look into Sekula's camera, we cannot tell if they are quick glances or longer stares because still photographs have few ways of indicating whether the human expressions they capture last longer than the length of the shutter speed. These are "fragmentary and incomplete utterances" to use one of Sekula's own descriptions of the photographic image, and he has the good sense to make no more or less of them than that.

Walker Evans was an experimental documentary photographer but to really grasp what that means one would have to look at how he used the printed page. In November 1946, he published *Labor Anonymous* in *Fortune* magazine. It was a double spread of eleven photographs. At first glance it looks like a set of serial portraits taken surreptitiously of anonymous workers leaving a factory. That is how the images are usually presented when recycled in exhibitions and monographic books. But in this spread there are telling details with which Evans deliberately complicates such a reading. His accompanying paragraph of text makes no reference to the end of a working shift. It is in fact subtitled "On a Saturday Afternoon in downtown Detroit" suggesting this might not be a day of work at all, even if this is one of America's foremost industrial cities. In addition Evans' words remind the reader that there is no physical consistency here: laborers cannot be visually stereotyped, neither in appearance nor disposition, nor dress: "His features tend now toward the peasant and now the patrician. His hat is

4. Given the potential interest of Sander's photography to fashion, I note that on the website of the International Movie Database, the synopsis for the Lumières' *Workers Leaving a Factory* remarks that "the film would be of virtually no interest (except to students of late 19th century clothing) were it not for the fact that it was the first film ever to be projected to a paying audience."
5. Sekula was looking to the experimental documentary films of Chris Marker, Fernando Solanas, Jean-Luc Godard and Jean Rouch. See Benjamin Buchloh's conversation with the artist in Sabine Breitwieser (ed), *Allan Sekula: Performance Under Working Conditions*, Generali Foundation, (Vienna, 2003) pp. 20-55.

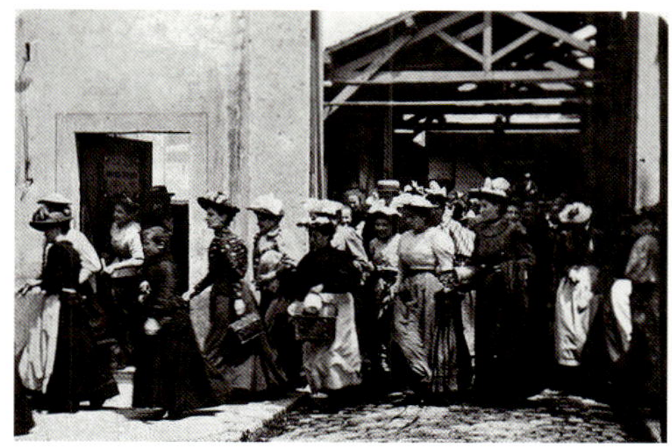

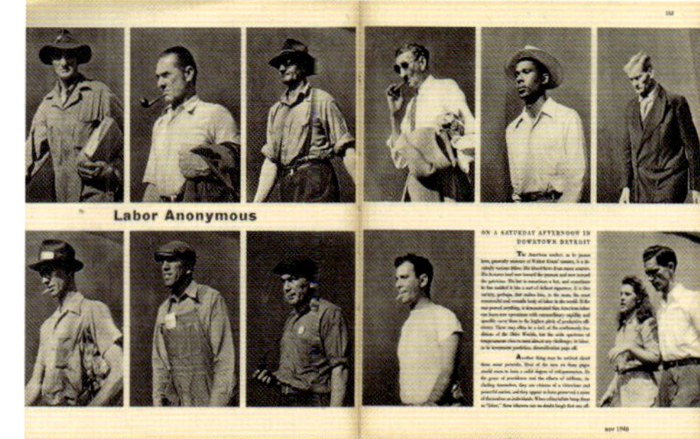

Labor Anonymous

**Louis Lumière** *Workers Leaving a Factory*, France, 1895. 35mm print, black and white, silent, 45 seconds. © Louis Lumière
**Walker Evans** "Labor Anonymous", *Fortune* magazine, November 1946. © Walker Evans

sometimes a hat, and sometimes he has molded it into a sort of defiant gesture." He concludes: "When editorialists lump them as 'labor' these laborers can no doubt laugh that one off." It is an obvious point but it is easily forgotten: a person cannot be anonymous in and of themselves. They are only anonymous to, or in the eyes of an other. The title *Labor Anonymous* is thus revealed to be at least partly ironic and even critical of the assumptions of the magazine's readership. Looking again at the photos we see they are not entirely serial (even though this was about as serial as Evans' work got). In the first, a man in overalls seems to look directly at the photographer. The brim of his hat casts a heavy shadow over his eyes, giving the impression that he sees the photographer without revealing himself. It undercuts the illusion of the unseen observer and I sense Evans placed this image first in order to suggest that the shots that follow should not be taken "at face value". The final photo shows a man and a woman together as a couple, complicating any simple distinction between "labor relations" and "sexual relations". All this in a single spread!

The Lumières' workers leaving their factory; Sander's catalogue of social types; Evans's sequence of laborers; Sekula's sequence of laborers. In all these projects connections are made between the seriality of manual work, the seriality of the means of representation and that particular experience of everyday that characterizes modern life. It seems clear enough that what has come to be called "the everyday" in current critical parlance is intimately bound up with notions of alienation and repetition both in work and leisure; with over-familiarity and an often fatalistic sense that life as it has come to be organised is inevitable (and that only its beautiful estrangement by art or literature can make it endurable). But grouping these works together we may be reminded that nothing will last forever, not even the everyday.

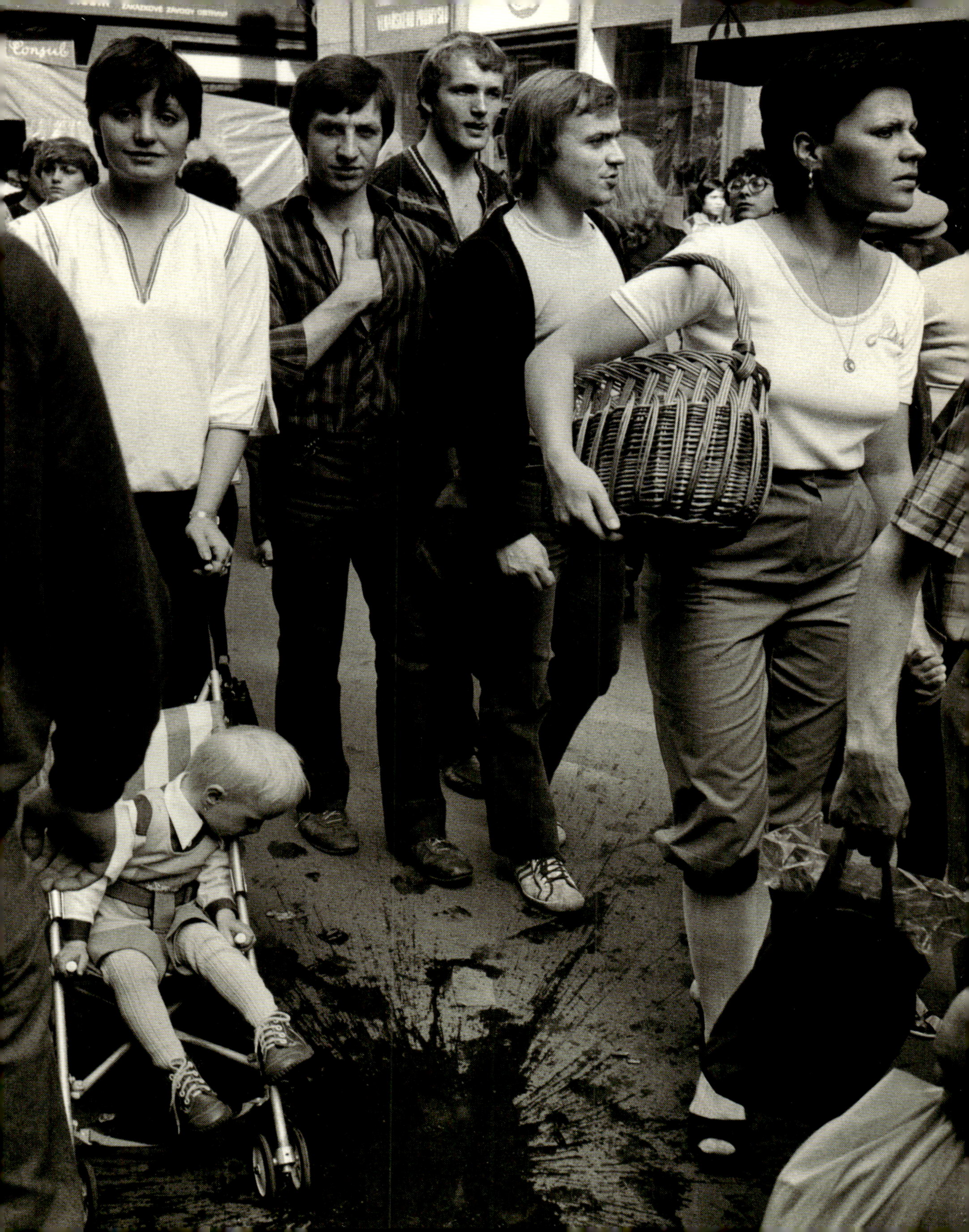
Consul
ZAKÁZKOVÉ ZÁVODY OSTRAVA

# Larry Sultan & Mike Mandel. Evidence

## Conceptual Reformulations of the Documentary Image: the *Evidence* Project

The *Evidence* project by American artists Larry Sultan (Brooklyn, New York, 1946) and Mike Mandel (Los Angeles, California, 1950) is more than an ordinary photography book with artistic aspirations, among other reasons because the authors conceived of it as a conceptual project rather than a catalogue of subjective images to justify their photographic skill or personal style.

Published and exhibited in 1977, the *Evidence* project works as a diffuse narrative that revolves around the same common theme: photography as a cultural artefact of representation. Through the exhibition's recontextualisation of over fifty anonymous images taken from various archives and presented as signs of a methodically thought-out plan, they all seem to allude to the same subject to which the book's authors try to direct our attention.

The photographs chosen were found by exploring the archives of various institutions, the police department and government agencies as well as those of other research departments – technical, medical or aeronautical – where scientific experimentation and its effects were the main objective of photographic records.

The images published in this project act as *objets trouvés*, or in other words, authentic ready-mades purposefully sought and found among documentary photographs of a scientific nature. Coming from sources that were hard to access, these shots show to the general public fairly uncommon, if not totally unusual, settings and experiments.

Precisely because of this, more than informing us about the technical and aesthetic qualities of these two creators, the group of images selected conveys a visual discourse that speaks to us of their own inherent political, ideological and cultural nature (as vestiges, in Althusser's terminology, of "state ideological apparatuses"). The way in which the motifs have been photographed is perhaps more important than the subjects themselves. The visual conventions used when taking these photographs allude clearly to a "directed" way of representing events that try to pass – without success – as something apparently ordinary and natural.

Sultan and Mandel's selection of these photographs undoubtedly also obeys aesthetic motivations, but what really inspired these authors to self-publish such a strange and innovative book for the era in which it was conceived was specifically their desire to endow the recorded image with a new logic of meaning using photographs of a scientific, documentary nature from such different and disparate archives. Both the publishing and the exhibition projects superimpose the internal logic of the complete series on any attempt to explain each isolated image. Just as any other conceptual work of the era, only the group, gathered in a visual narrative whose code of interpretation has not been completely deciphered, is capable of transmitting to us the true dimension and meaning of *Evidence*.

The series begins with a photographic record of simple hand and foot prints and traces of various human actions shown in different settings. Logic would have us believe that the protagonist missing from the spaces captured in the introductory photos of *Evidence* has left the "crime scene" only a few moments before. The "archaeological" evidence of these first shots leads us to reflect anew on photography as the inevitable record of a past time. According to this argument, we can only access the meaning of an event that has been photographed through the visual representation of signs or clues that are recorded and frozen on the photosensitive support.

Nevertheless, and as the project advances, the direct presence of human intervention in the recorded processes plays an increasingly important role and the temporalisation of the shots is projected toward a present time.

The presence of what is human next to technological artefacts or in scientific tests and the appearance of slanted compositions showing various body parts (particularly arms and legs) lead us to think that the half-photographed individuals appearing in these photos (almost always recorded outside the field of view) are both active and passive subjects in the experiments presented here. As viewers, we frequently ask ourselves about the enigmatic presence of these characters and the role they play in the event described. But we almost never obtain a clear reply.

The project and sequential arrangement of the images acquire their own logic enabling decontextualisation of the photos selected, uprooted from their original files and from the documentary functions for which they were created. In this way, the *Evidence* project proposes a new recontextualisation process that has more to do with the political and critical discourse with which the authors convey the way we currently perceive and understand the world. Actually, they speak to us of this kind of "pseudo environment" that we build socially on top of "the real" through the symbols produced by the camera lens and disseminated by the mass media. Therefore, in *Evidence* we should look for a critical and aesthetic undercurrent. We should consider the reasons behind this – evocative, enigmatic and poetical – juxtaposition of images, apparently so distant and made with intentions that are so far from being artistic, instead of trying to find a logical meaning to each individual image.

There is no doubt that *Evidence* constitutes a profound reflection on the photographic medium itself, on its perverse use as a tool to bear witness to the world and its greater or lesser capacity as a linguistic and artistic medium. The book also invites us to question ourselves about the concept of "artistic authorship" through the conceptual appropriationism made by its authors.

In this series, the "evidence" of the documents as well as our own ability to visually interpret their hidden meanings as neutral, transparent and objective records of the world, is not going to be as simple to figure out, above all if we do not know the reasons, specific contexts and circumstances in which these images were made.

[José Gómez Isla]

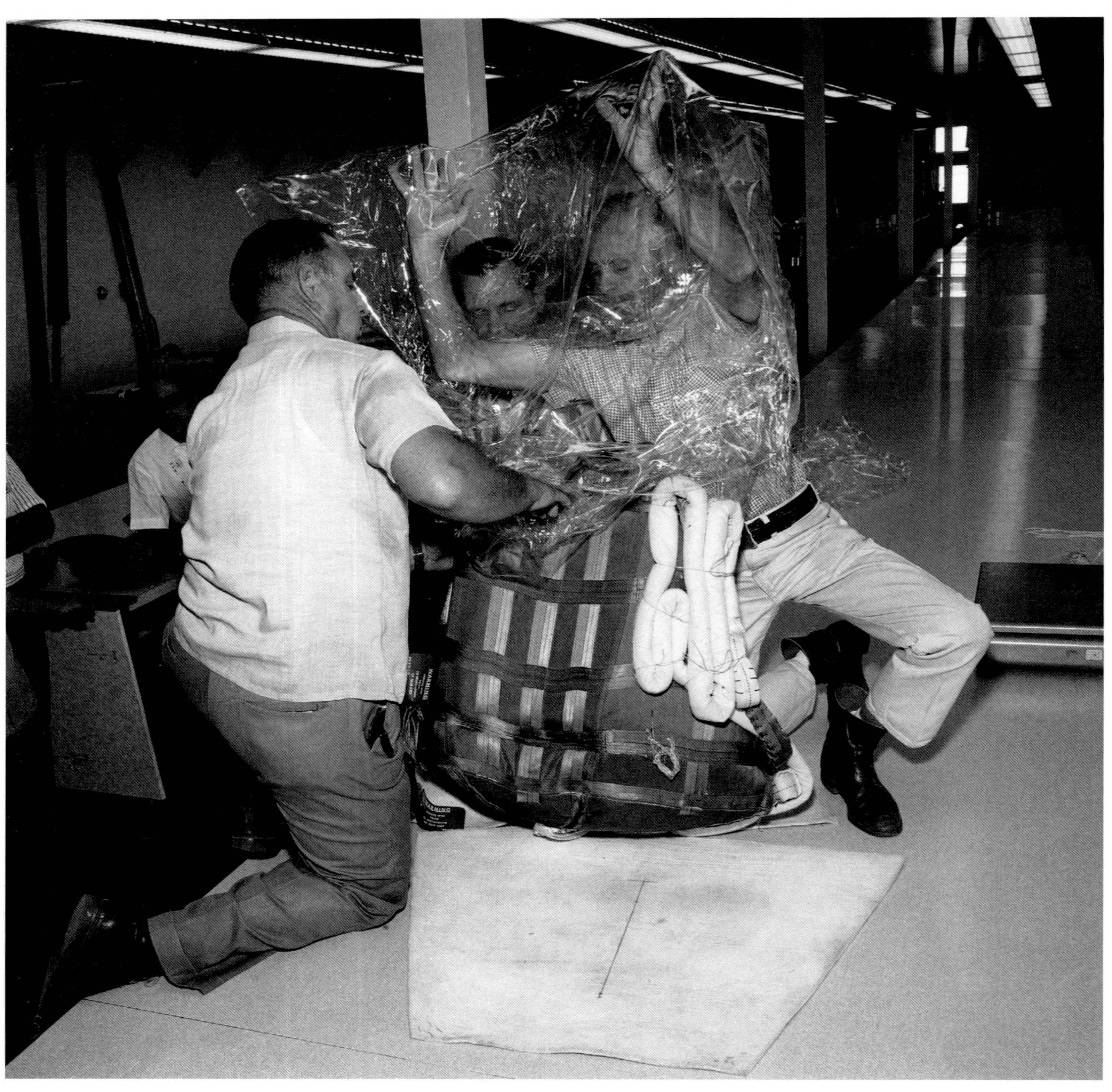

Untitled. From the series *Evidence*, 1977
Courtesy Galerie Thomas Zander, Cologne

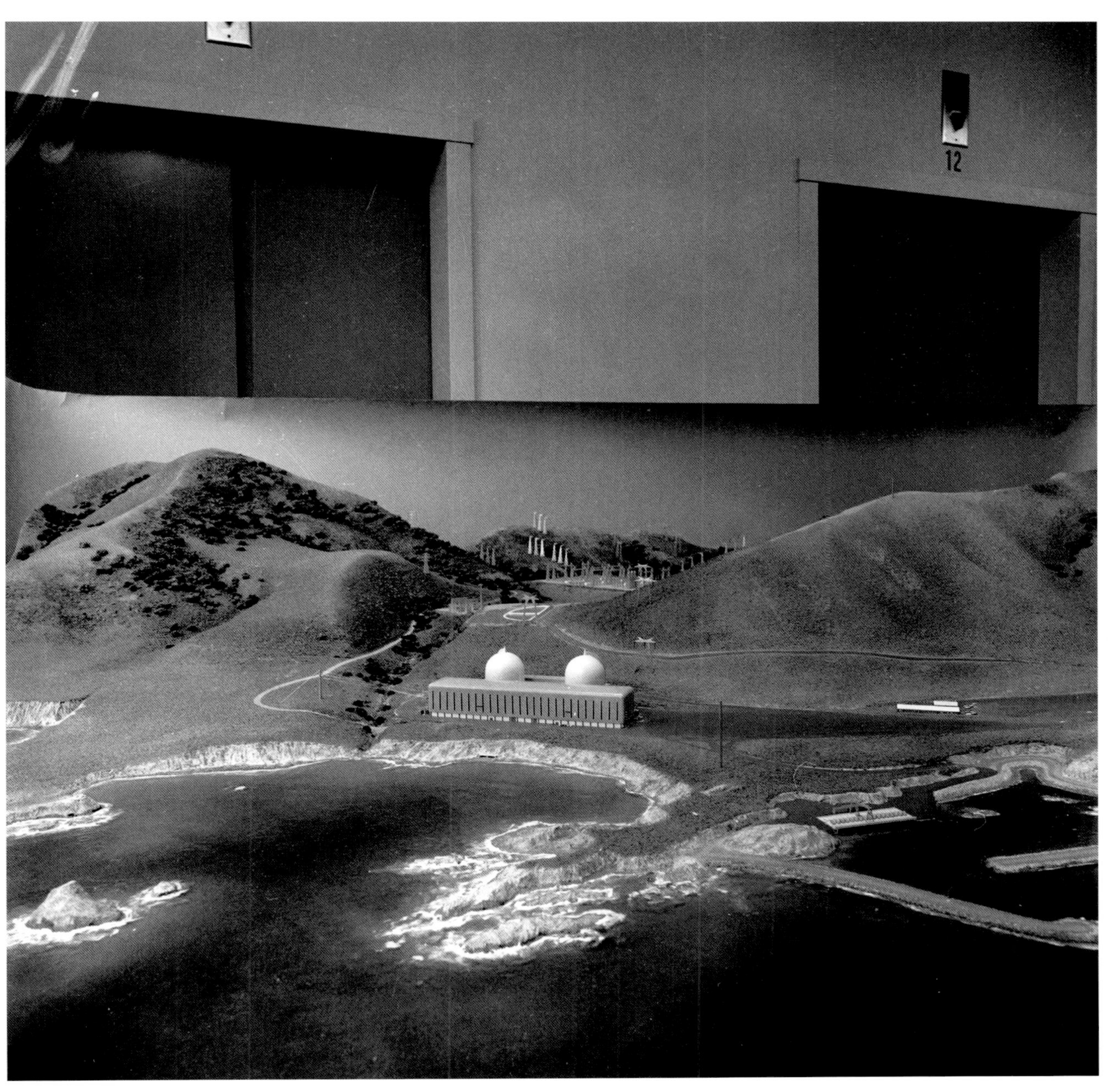
12

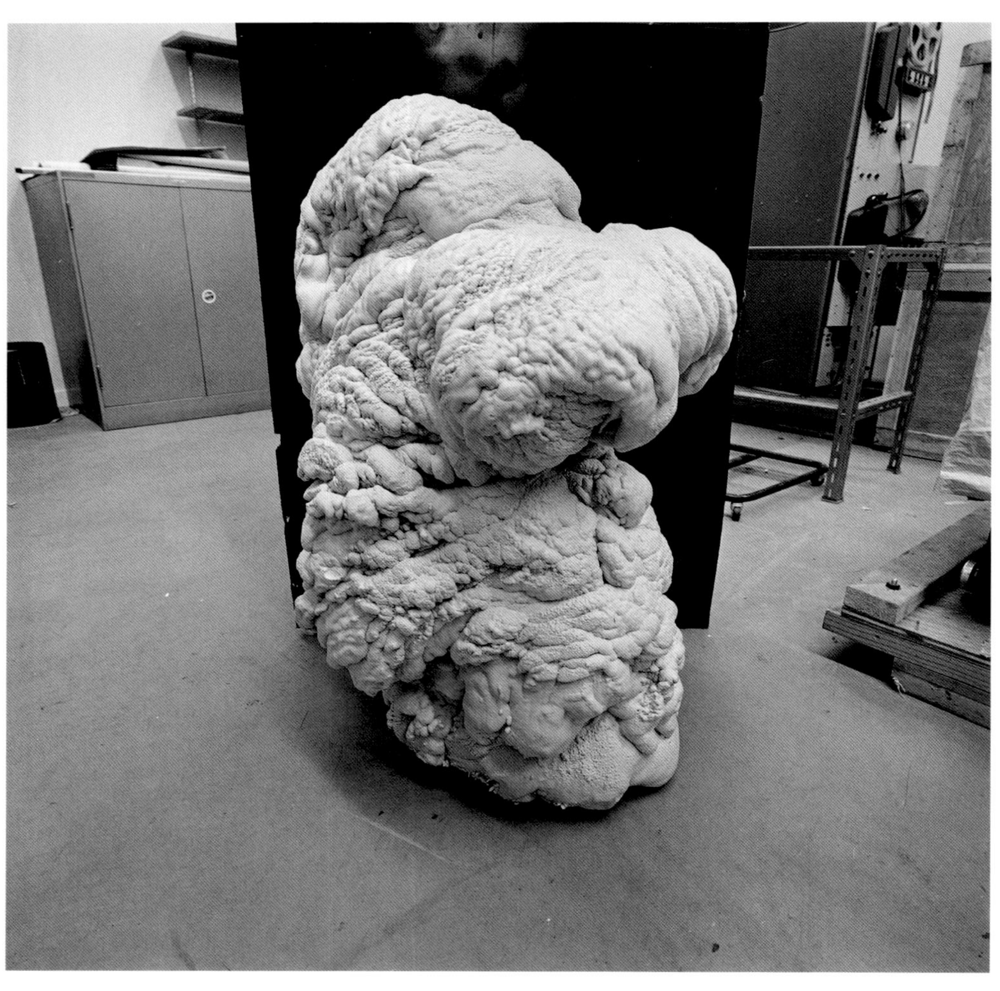

Untitled. From the series *Evidence*, 1977
Courtesy Galerie Thomas Zander, Cologne

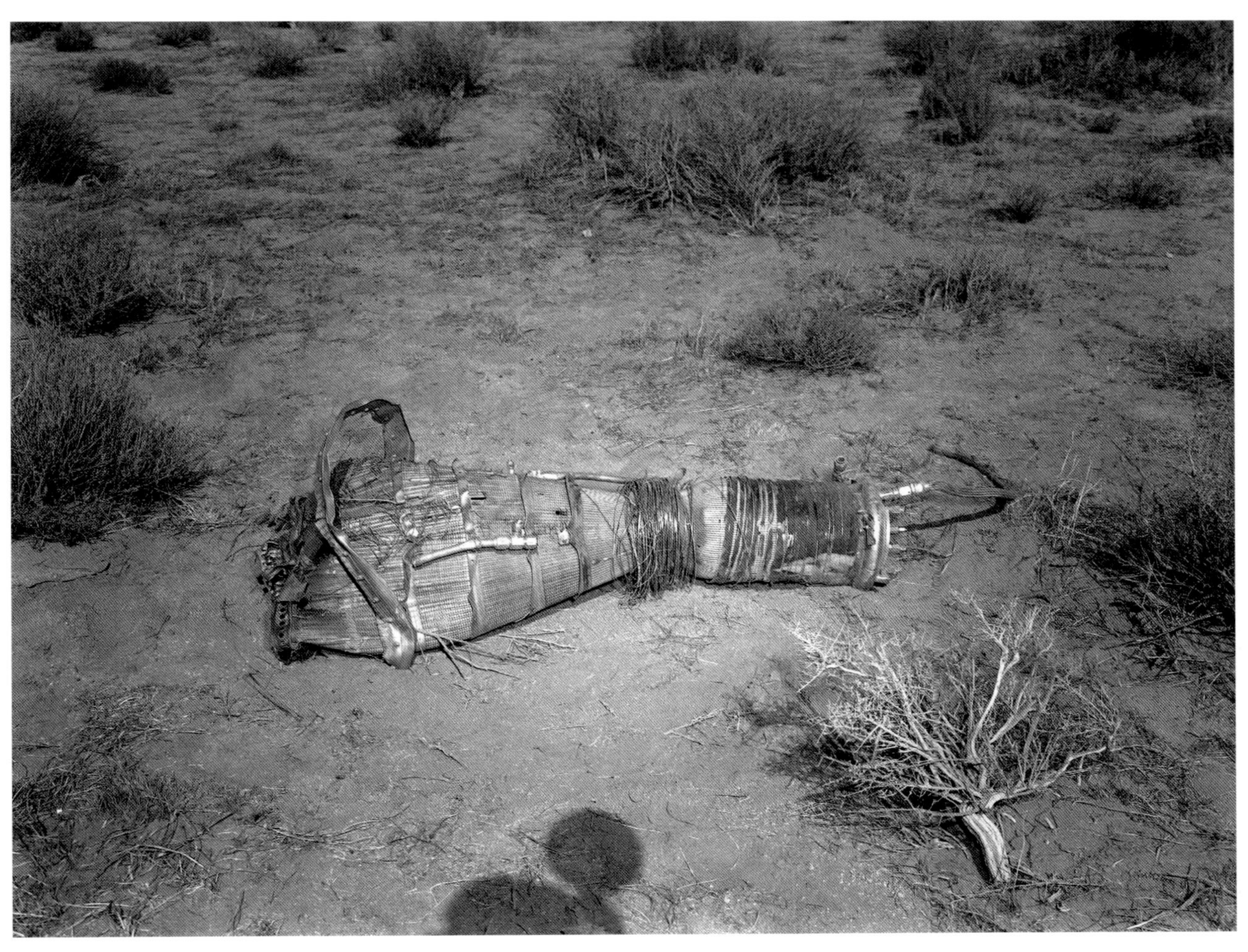

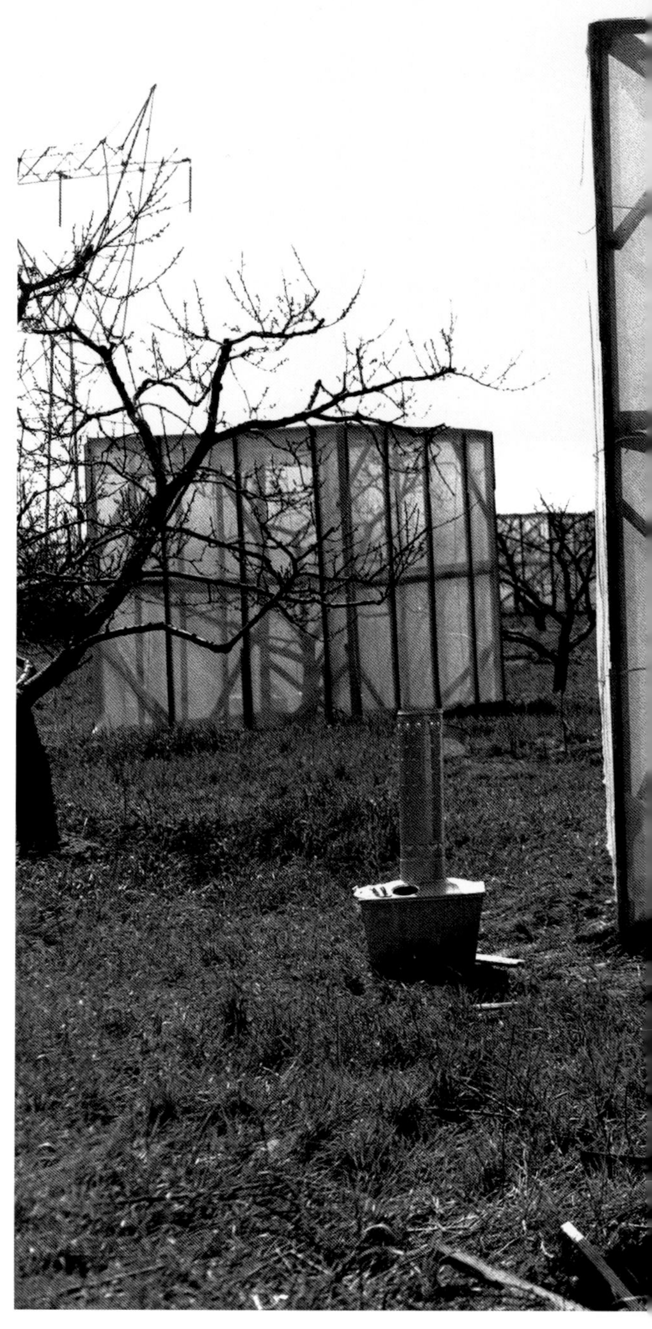

Untitled. From the series *Evidence*, 1977
Courtesy Galerie Thomas Zander, Cologne

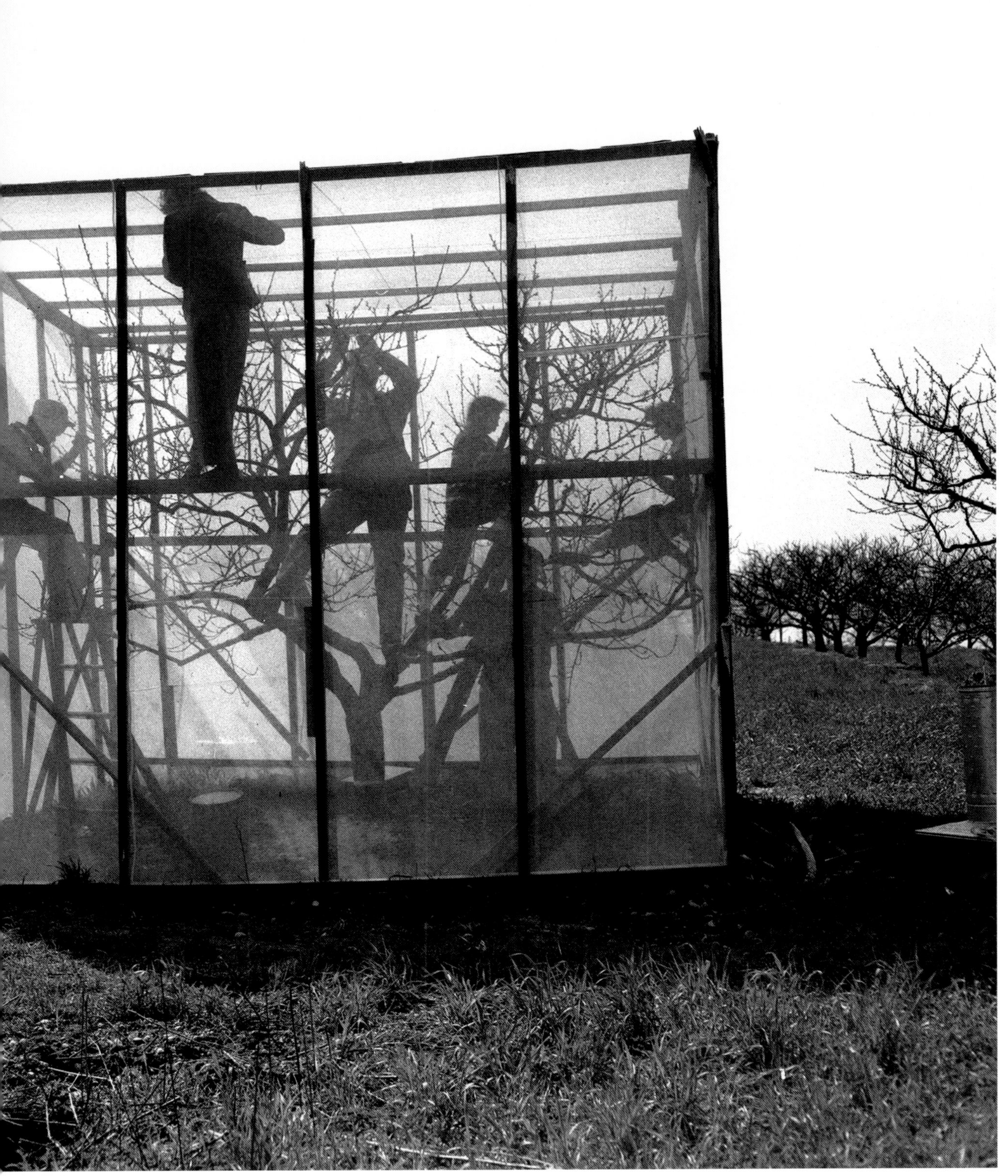

### The Silence of the Everyday

The term *quotidian,* a substantified adjective, refers, it would seem, to a field, a type, a mode of *experience*: the domain of commonplace day-to-day life, governed by habit, where human experience presents itself at a level before any qualification as history or event can come into play. This anthropological dimension has always existed but it has not always been recognised for what it is, nor, a fortiori, has it attracted critical attention. For that, it was necessary to separate experience from legend, from history, and even from the calendar, which institutes and perpetuates a cyclical notion of time[1]. The identification and promotion of the quotidian as an idea, a value (or anti-value) therefore has a history: the history of a present time emancipated from cyclical time. An emancipation that reflects a victory of chronological time, but also a negation insofar as the quotidian silently perpetuates the reign of cyclical time by resisting the grasp of historical events.

Maurice Blanchot talks of a *present without particularities*. He might just as well have said "*without qualities"* in reference to the English title of the great novel by Musil, "A Man Without Qualities", in German *Der Mann ohne Eigenschaften*[2]. For that present without events (in which nothing happens) *escapes* and, as Blanchot observes, escapes even the *fait divers* —journalistic exaggeration. Omnipresent, ungraspable, it develops in the domain of modern living, it springs up in the deserts of statistical thinking. After having been pinned down in innumerable realist and naturalist descriptions, it has become the great mirage of rational modernity. Musil had already put in the mouth of Ulrich (the man without qualities) the following troubling supposition: "Perhaps it is precisely the petit-bourgeois who has an intuitive, prophetic glimpse of the beginning of an immense, new, collective ant-like heroism? It will be called 'rationalised heroism' and it will be regarded as very beautiful[3]."

In communities organised around a collective belief, day-to-day living, is subject to the ambivalence of the sacred when not sacrificed to work[4]. Tasks and ritual share between them a quotidian never identified in words. But the fact that the quotidian had not been named did not mean that it did not exist. One might even see in the quotidian the persistence, or even the permanency, of that which resists the chronological ordering of historical discourse, despite the fact that the concept of the quotidian came to be against the backdrop of secularised thinking about history, compliant with a productive, or even productivist, idea of culture. In the silence of the autistic body, resistant to language, Fernand Deligny recognised the domain of the *customary* (*le coutûmier*), that is to say, for him, in his own idiom, that which creates *custom* when the quotidian can be a *work of art* in itself: *acting* freed of the obligation of *doing*, an activity without ultimate productive purpose or value, dissociated even from habit[5].

*To overcome the everyday in the everyday*: Vsevolod Meyerhold's marvellous formula[6] is perhaps the last *watchword* for avant-garde movements which continues to be topically relevant, given that it corresponds even to Deligny's attempt at communal living with autistic children, at the furthest point from any project, if not from any ideology.

* * *

Faigenbaum has also taken his œuvre into that strange domain of silence where few artists dare to go without having equipped themselves beforehand with a project, a method, the backing of a discourse, a

1. The calendar is generally confused with historical segmentation. Calendar time does not necessarily lead to the idea of chronological *era*: the year as a cyclical unit is sufficient to it. On this point, see Daniel S. Milo, *Trahir le temps*, Paris, Les Belles Lettres (1991), Hachette/Pluriel, 1997, p. 111. The author criticises here the chronological conception of calendar time developed by Paul Ricœur in his three-volume *Time and Narrative* (*Temps et récit*, 1983-1985), trans. Kathleen Blamey and David Pellauer, Chicago: University of Chicago Press, 1984-1988.
2. Maurice Blanchot, "La parole quotidienne", *La Nouvelle Revue Française*, June 1962; trans. Susan Hanson in *The Infinite Conversation* (*L'Entretien infini*, 1969), Minneapolis: University of Minnesota Press, 1992. Blanchot bases his thinking on the trilogy by Henri Lefebvre, *Critique of*

model, a protocol ... or without a blind confidence in the magic of recording an image. None of this – except perhaps the blind confidence – is bad in itself, but the problem is that the image usually loses more than it gains.

Here, the image is positioned, as is ordinarily the case for photography, between the fine arts and the media, but also between experience and archive – and somewhat nearer experience.

The media provide the vehicle for an extensive popular culture in which the image functions as *attraction* (following a logic of entertainment) or *shock* (masquerading as information). The cash flows circulating between these two repertoires are vehicles for metaphors of "consumption": an idealised naturalism applied to the image of the body and to the product is perpetuated thanks to a few minor and deliberate transgressions (or intensities). Once beyond an initial stage of research and on the pretext of breaking with an aristocratic culture, the production of *Cultural Studies* has reinforced and validated an effective system of differentiation between audiences. But the quotidian escapes and withdraws into the silence of the body.

The quotidian passes, leaving behind traces, a vague sediment (occasionally deposited in some archive). The photographer is assumed to record the present in the same manner as a historian catalogues the traces of the past. One might think that the promotion of the quotidian in western culture since the nineteenth century has *realised itself* simultaneously in the idea of "long duration" put forward by historians and the pop cult of "banality". But these two polarities, which frame the "rationalised heroism" to which Musil was referring, lack the intensity of ordinary experience captured and transformed by the narrative in images. The photographs of Faigenbaum show that it is in the narrative – or in poetry when it sides with things – that the quotidian finds its substance, when sediment is transfigured by style.

At the risk of seeming to confirm a reputation as proponent of intimism – which is meaningless other than in terms of reference to a neo-pop norm – Faigenbaum has never ceased to look at what moves or becomes immobile in the repetition of daily acts and in the postures inherited from pictorial culture. These two dimensions trace out for him the domain – psychological and social – of the portraitist. He contemplates a face in which the lips of time are opening. Caught up in the silences of the narrative, by the enigma of genealogical relationships, he has never ceased to accept the gaze of that which in the image renews the fascination of childhood.

The quality of his images, which can be experienced only by looking at them in some venue or, second-best, in a folded volume (a book), stems from just that. Photography is rediscovered as a high form of popular art related as much to film as to painting and which contributes to the quality of the everyday overcome in the everyday.

[Jean-François Chevrier]

*Everyday Life* (*Critique de la vie quotidienne*, 1947, 1961, 1981), trans. John Moore and Gregory Elliott, Verso Books, 1992, 2002 and 2006.
3. Robert Musil, *The Man Without Qualities*, part one, chapter II.
4. It is also possible to say that life is *dedicated, devoted to* work. Such religious terminology corresponds to the Christian idea of work as punishment or penitence.
5. Cf. most notably Fernand Deligny, "Quand le bonhomme n'y est pas" (1978), in *L'Arachnéen et autres textes*, ed. Sandra Alvarez de Toledo, Paris, L'Arachnéen, 2008, p. 210.
6. Vsevolod Meyerhold, "Balagan" (1912), in *Meyerhold on Theater*, ed. and trans. Edward Braun, New York: Hill and Wang, 1969.

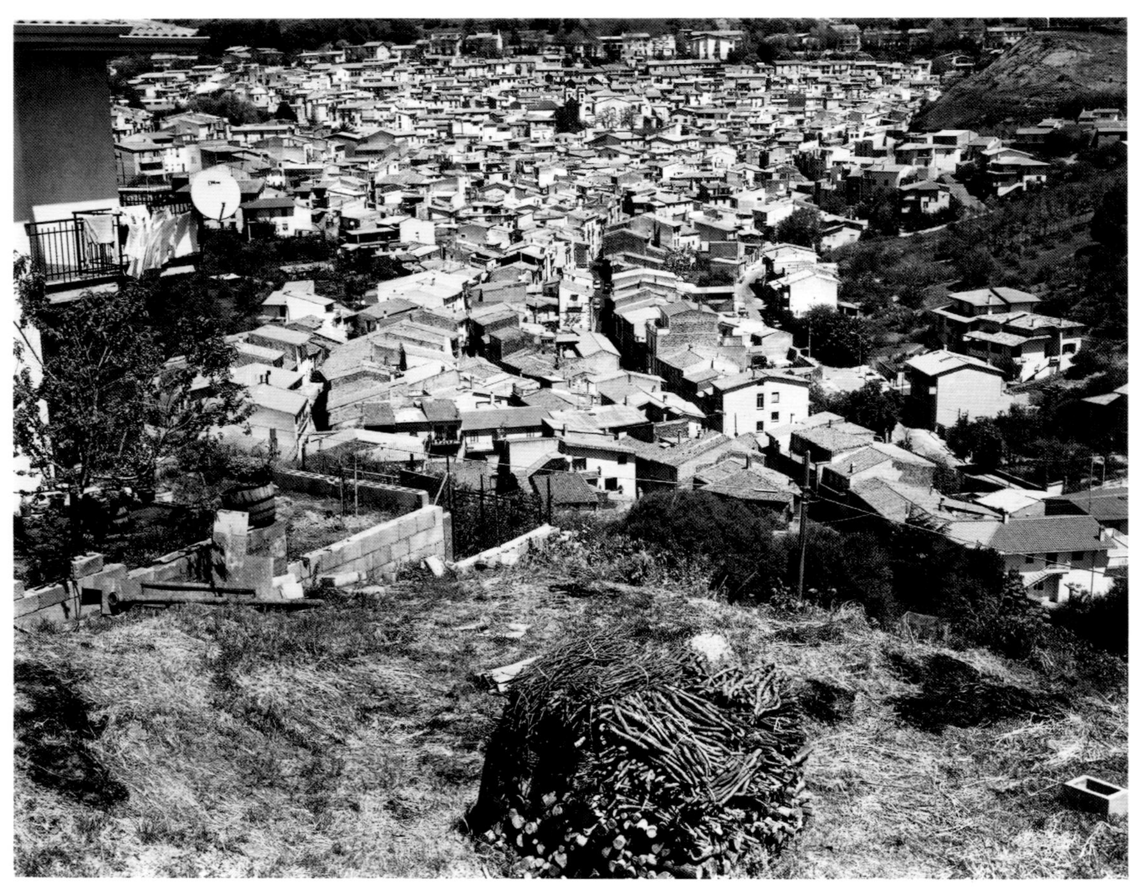

*Santulussurgiu from Su Tancadu, Sardinia*, 2008
© Patrick Faigenbaum

*Salvatorica, Santulussurgiu, Sardinia*, 2005
© Patrick Faigenbaum

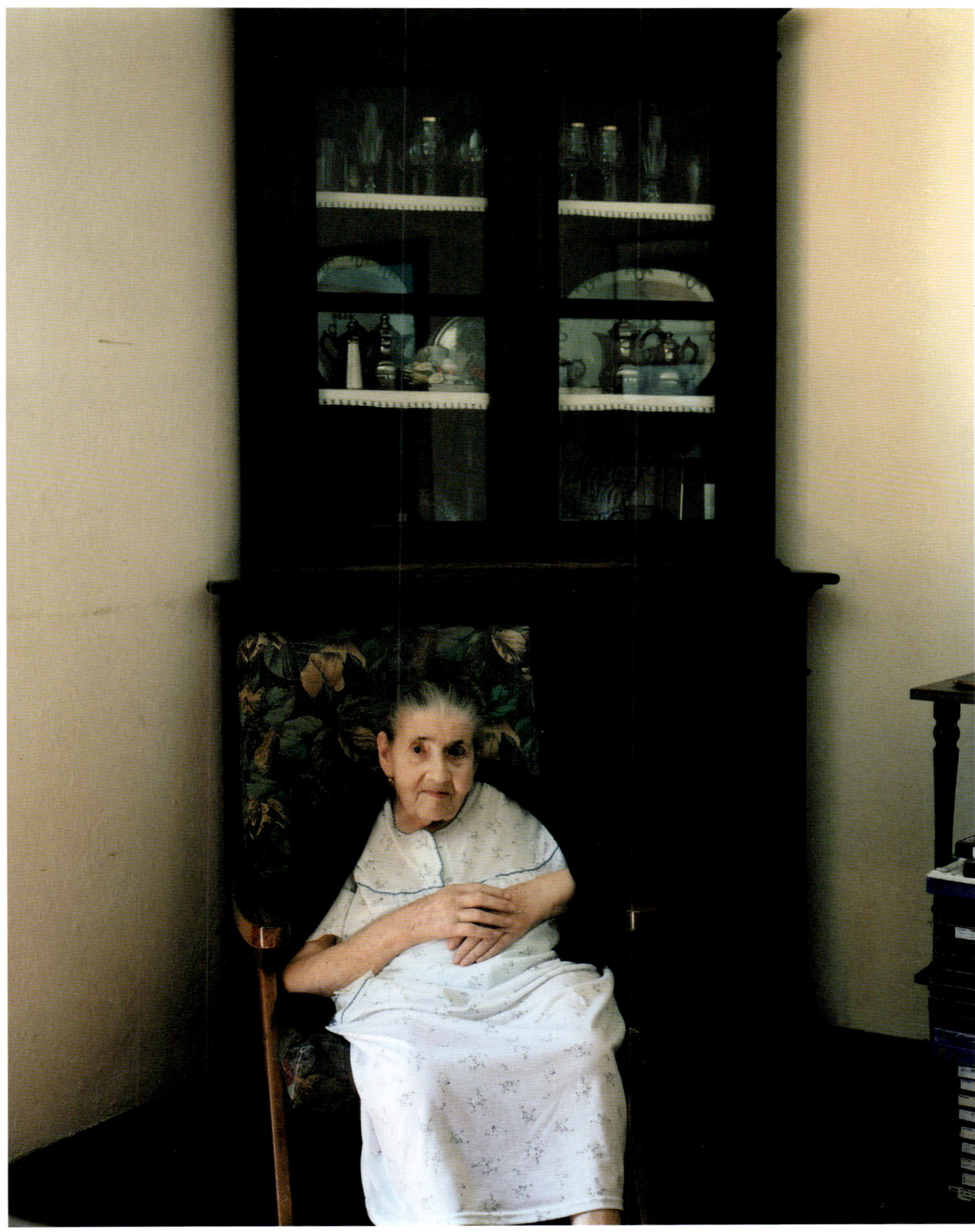

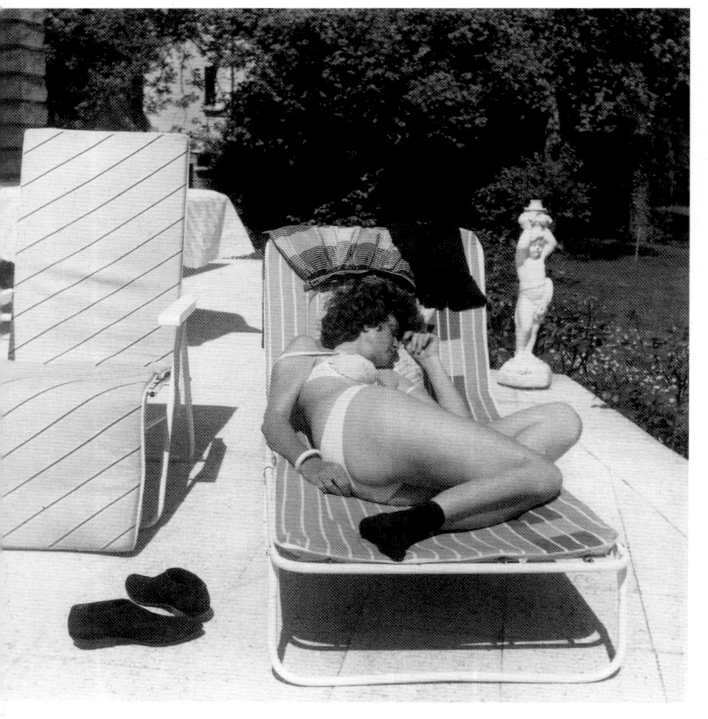

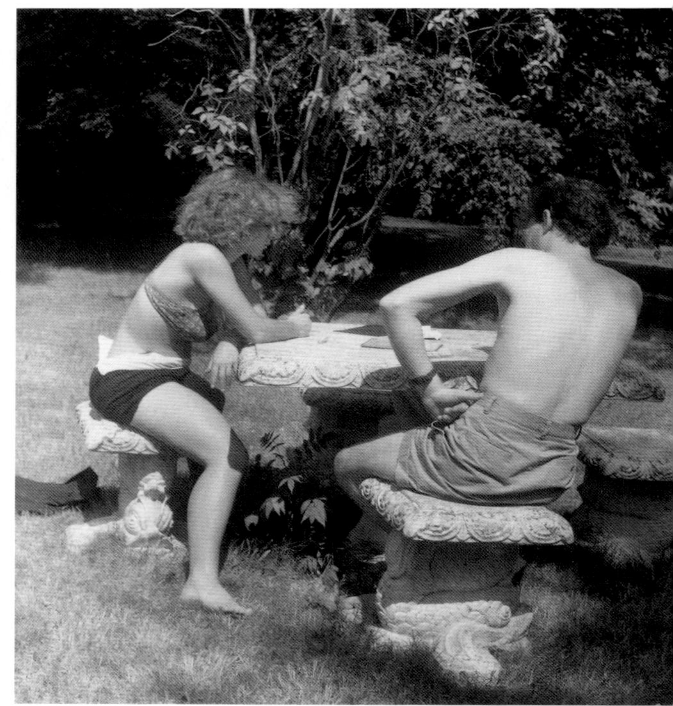

*Lys Chantilly*, 1989

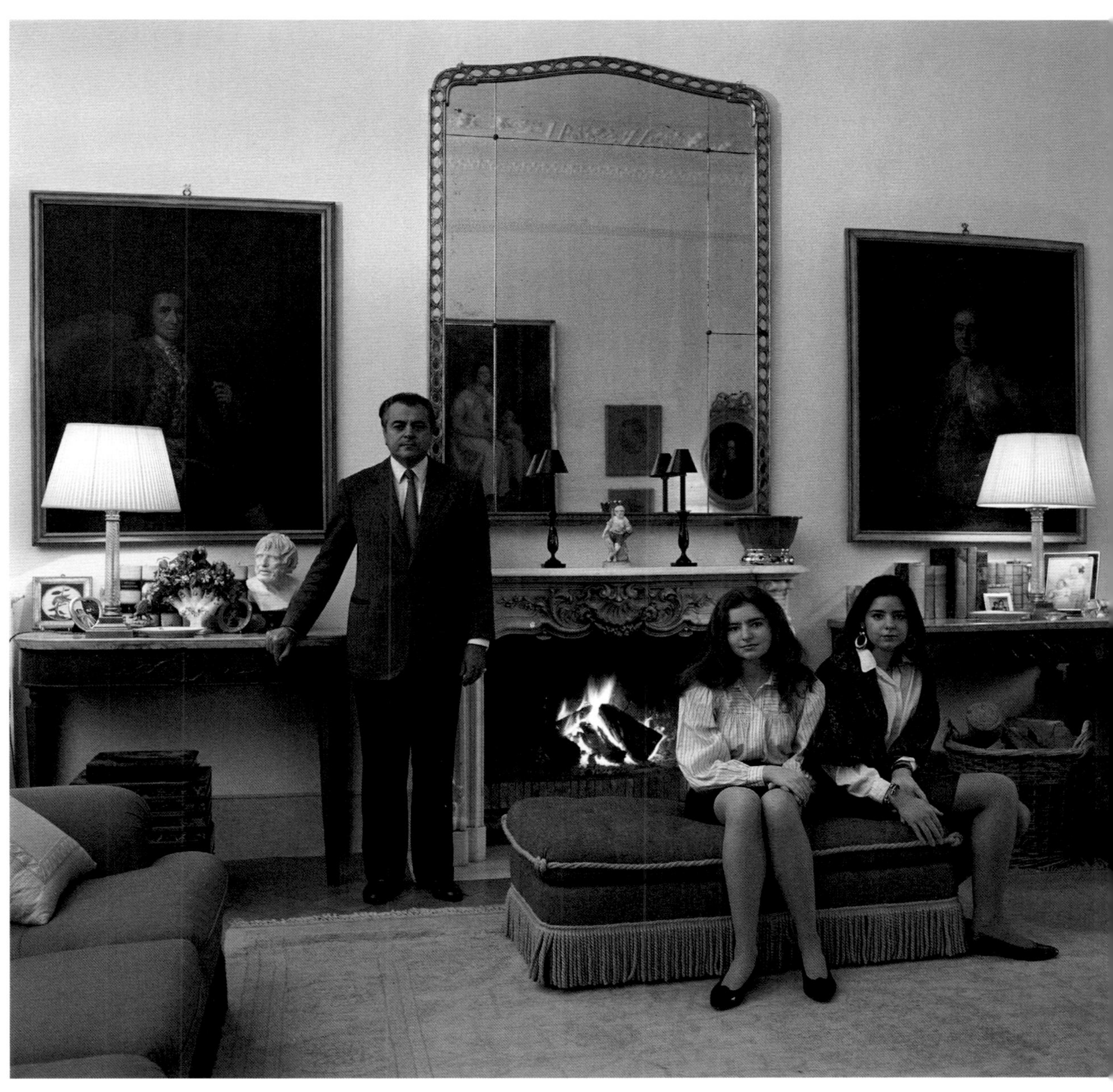

*Granito Pignatelli Family from Belmonte, Naples*, 1990

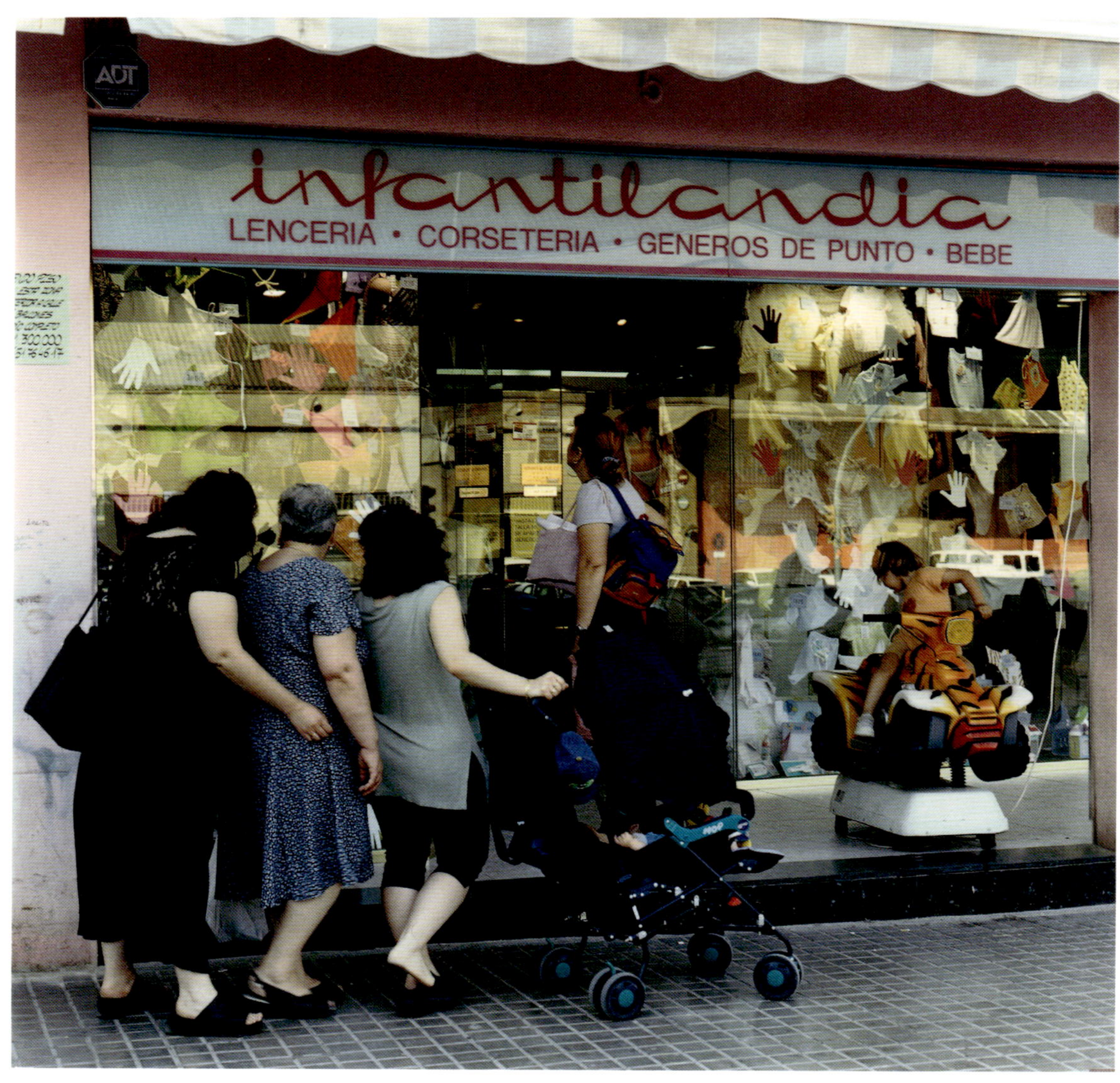


*Carrer Llull, Besós Neighbourhood, Barcelona*, 2001
© Patrick Faigenbaum

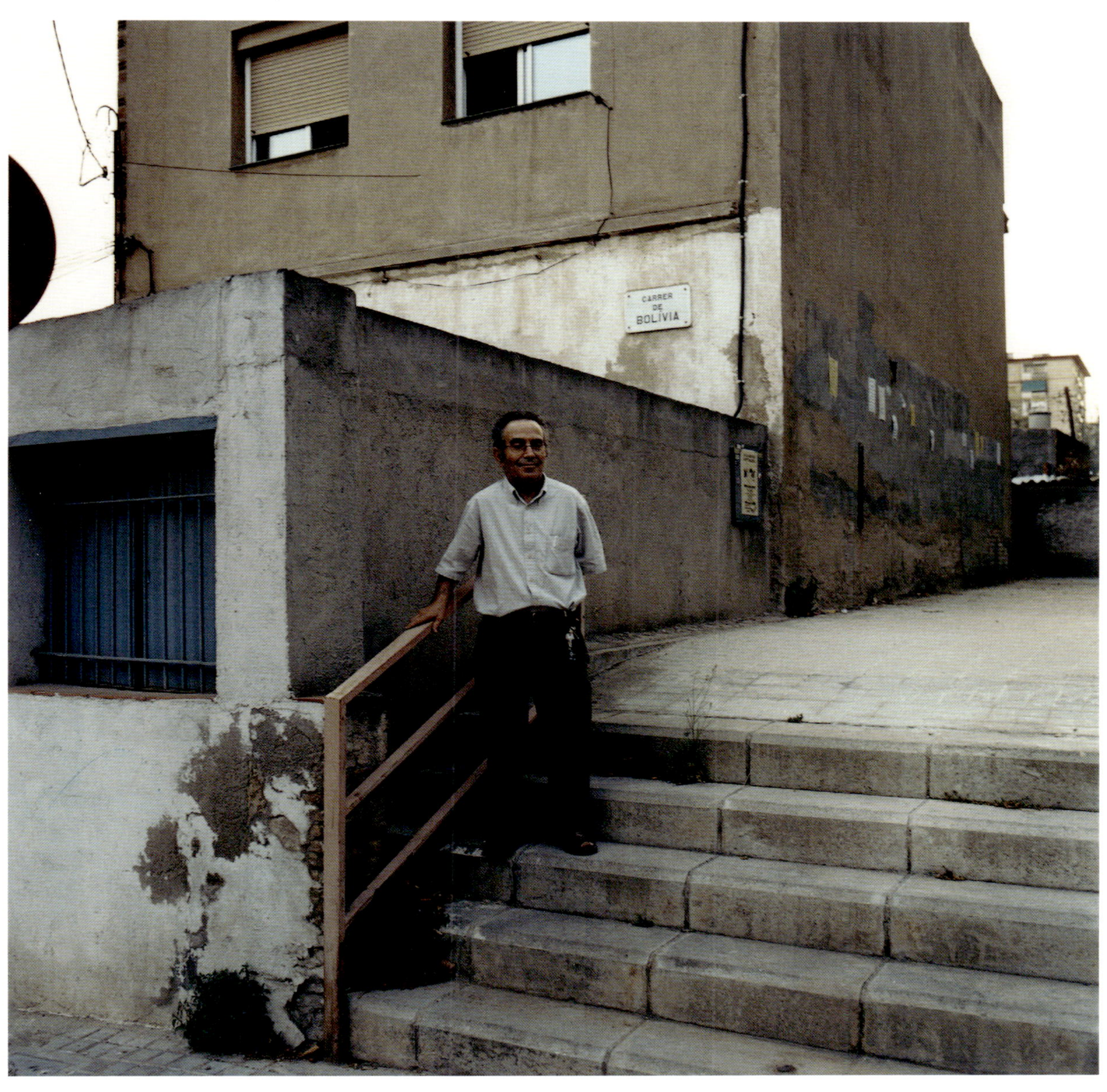


*Mr. Gil, South West of Besós, Barcelona*, 2001

## The Atlas Group (1989-2004). A project by Walid Raad

### An Archive of Words and Images

The relation between life and art has always been a complex one, and has motivated multiple discussions. It's impossible to pinpoint what art does to life, and vice-versa. One knows of the multiple aspects of this relation, and life remains (even in the radical cases of Nietzsche and Wilde, in which nature imitates and competes with art) the eternal motif of artistic efforts. And in here, motif is different from theme.

The work of Walid Raad — or should one say of the Atlas Group collective — is not about the contaminations between art and life, but about the way in which fiction has the power of turning into historical, social, political, and aesthetical fact, i.e., about the extension of fictional facts into everyday reality. The categories used to construct his universe (impossible to distinguish between a careful and elaborated metaphor, or a detailed depiction of an historical period) are so prolific that one can't even be sure whether to speak of the work of Raad or not. We know that the identity of this apparent collective, which is also an archive, an institute, etc. has changed over the years because, as Raad mentioned in as interview, "the designation — whether a foundation or an artistic project or some other thing — also changes because my way of thinking the Atlas Group also changes."[1] This continuous mutation in the designation of Raad's project is representative of the extreme flexibility that is needed to achieve the various requirements of the project.

Whatever its designation might be, that which motivates and impels this artistic project are the tensions of Lebanon's contemporary history. Very generically, the Atlas Group, seated in New York and Beirut, is dedicated to the collection and/or production of documents on the recent history of Lebanon. These documents are photographs, notebooks, films, videos, etc. Consequently, the group appears fundamentally as a sort of archive compiling a series of documents and historical objects. In one of the archive's notebooks, one finds a possible classification system for the numerous documents it contains, based on their origin: authored documents, found documents, and finally, documents that were produced by the Atlas Group itself. This classification system, that one believes to be horizontal, has the advantage of demonstrating the absence of hierarchy, making it clear that there is no preoccupation in distinguishing between factual documents and fabricated or fictional ones. To this one should add the fact that every time these documents are shown, in exhibitions or publications, only their copies are presented: the group "never shows the original documents that are at the base of its archives. I show photographs, but not the original ones; I show what has been written in diaries, but not the diaries; I show images of images,"[2] said Raad in the same interview. It is not about "fetishizing" the objects in some way (and one can feel here a sort of criticism to the way in which the art market is organized around the valorization of the original object), but rather a preoccupation with the models that allow thinking about reality in its multiple levels. The objects that they construct are a kind of synthesis of the social, political, epistemological, military, etc. dimensions of the civil war in Lebanon. And this is the feature one needs to retain. Or as the artist declares in regard to the explosion of car bombs, so frequent during this war, and the theme of one of his works: "the detonation of a car bomb is not only an act of violence, but also produces a discourse that directly and indirectly affects individuals, families and communities."[3]

1-2. Walid Raad interviewed by Vanessa Rato, *Jornal Público*, 28.09.2008
3. Walid Raad, *Scratching on things I could disavow*, Culturgest and Verlag der Bunchhandlung Walther König, Lisbon and Köln, 2007, p. 91

The artist states that the need to classify, sort and archive information derives from the amount of information generated by a particular occurrence: "the translation of the world into information allows for the emergence of the archive, because once you have the information, you need to think about its classification."[4] And every time, you rehearse the most effective modes and schemes for storing information that is not merely material (inventories or detailed descriptions of the damages produced by a bomb, of the people that were killed, of the buildings that disappeared, etc.), but also psychological: how do you document the pain and the trauma that a war can inflict on a person, on a family, or on a community? The paradox of the archive and of the historical document is, precisely, that it is completely ineffective to preserve what is most important.

That the visible feature of the Atlas Group is the documentation of documentation, the archive of archives, photography of photographs, etc., does not affect its artistic and political pertinence. Because this ambiguity shows that in order to have an effect, repercussions and echoes over reality, it is not necessary to create a detailed archive that registers, as is, everything that happens, but that sometimes that which is more important can only be discussed through non factual, poetical devices. And the devices created by Raad in order to show history (not as a dominant discourse set in manuals and official records, but in the form of an individual and sentimental discourse) are this type of constructions. What one is confronted with in each of Raad's exhibitions is a vast and elaborated allegory that does not copy reality, but which has a scope that embraces the whole reality and exerts an influence over it. The character Dr. Fakhouri, an eminent specialist in the contemporary history of Lebanon, who died in 1993, is one of the keys for this archive under construction. His documents witness not only that historical facts are not positive, meaning that they are not clear in relation to what they portray, but that, as Nietzsche said, there are not facts, only interpretations. And this is why, in a set of the only known photographs of this character, the historian appears as a tourist. In his only trip, to Paris and Rome, the historian photographed himself, and this series of self-portraits introduces another type of paradox that is related to the illusion created by documental photograph. These images aim at representing, and even substituting, an absence, but when that which they portray has ceased to exist (for example, during a war) what is left is the photograph that becomes independent and autonomous: the disappearance of its referent makes the image independent of any entity that is external to itself. And the work of the Atlas Group progresses with this type of paradoxes. It is as if it were always saying: we only have words and images, it's not much and we know it, but it's all we've got.

[Nuno Crespo]

4. Walid Raad, *Scratching on things I could disavow*, Culturgest and Verlag der Bunchhandlung Walther König, Lisbon and Köln, 2007, p. 91

Document title
***Civilizationally, We Do Not Dig Holes to Bury Ourselves***

Category_File_Type_Plates
**[cat. A]_Fakhouri_Photographs_962-986**

Date
**1958-1959**

Attributed to
**Dr. Fadl Fakhouri**

Summary
**The only available photographs of Dr. Fakhouri consist of 24 black and white self-portraits that were found in a small brown envelope titled, *Civilizationally, we do not dig holes to bury ourselves*. The historian produced the photographs in 1958 and 1959 during his one and only trip outside of Lebanon, to Paris and Rome.**

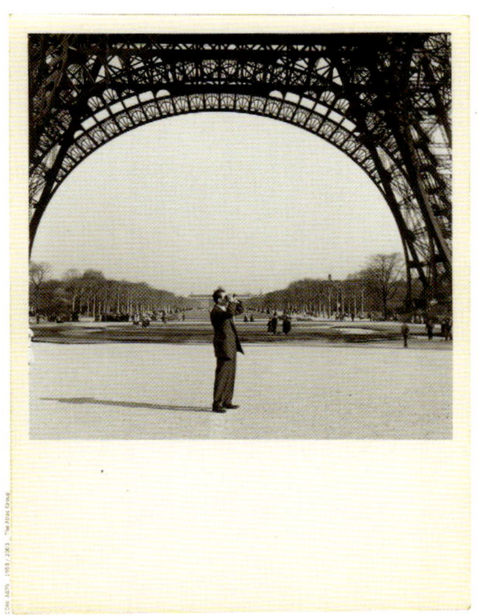

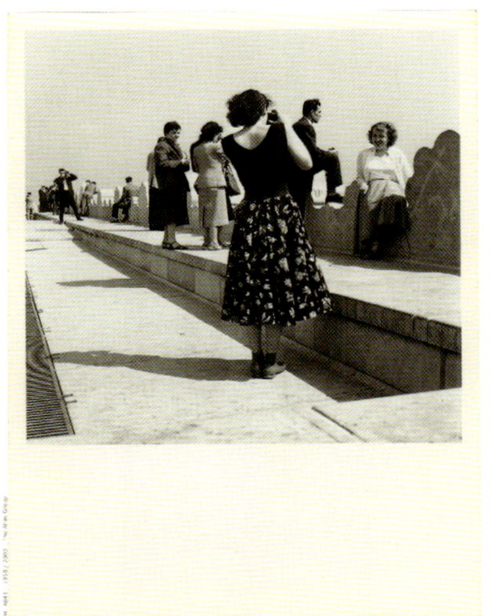

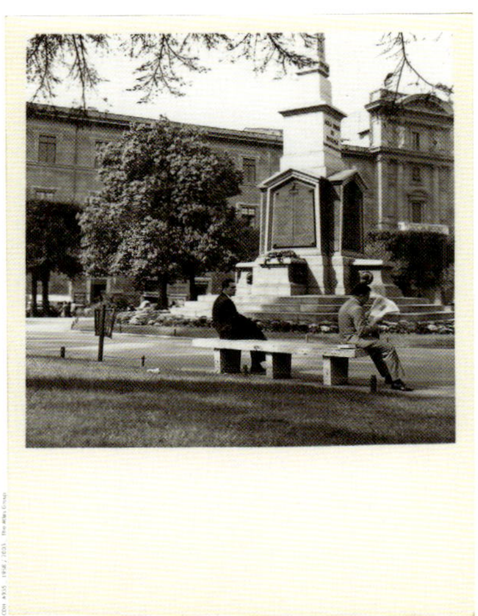

Document title
***Notebook Volume 72: Missing Lebanese Wars***

Category_File_Type_Plates
**[cat. A]_Fakhouri_Notebooks_72_131-149**

Date
**1989**

Attributed to
**Dr. Fadl Fakhouri**

Summary
**It is a little known fact that the major historians of the Lebanese wars were avid gamblers. It is said that they met every Sunday at the race track — Marxists and Islamists bet on races one through seven; Maronite nationalists and socialists on races eight through fifteen.**

**Race after race, the historians stood behind the track photographer, whose job was to image the winning horse as it crossed the finish line, to record the photo-finish. It is also said that they convinced (some say bribed) the photographer to snap only one picture as the winning horse arrived. Each historian wagered on precisely when — how many fractions of a second before or after the horse crossed the finish line — the photographer would expose his frame.**

**Each of the following notebook pages includes a photograph clipped from the post-race-day issue of the newspaper, *Annahar.* They include Dr. Fakhouri's notations on the race's distance and duration, the winning time of the winning horse, calculations of averages, the historians' initials with their respective bets, the time discrepancy predicted by the winning historian. Written on each page is also a brief paragraph in English. Dr. Fakhouri's widow, Zainab Fakhouri, has attributed these to her husband's habit of including short descriptions of the winning historians in his notebooks.**

MLW_v72_p133
1976-1983 / 2001
The Atlas Group

*Date:*
18 April 1989

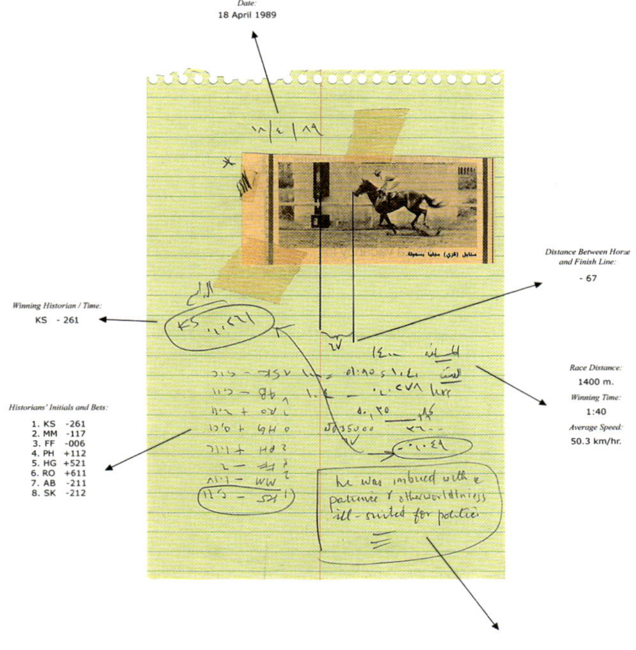


*Distance Between Horse and Finish Line:*
- 67

*Winning Historian / Time:*
KS - 261

*Race Distance:*
1400 m.

*Winning Time:*
1:40

*Average Speed:*
50.3 km/hr.

*Historians' Initials and Bets:*

1. KS -261
2. MM -117
3. FF -006
4. PH +112
5. HG +521
6. RO +611
7. AB -211
8. SK -212

*Description of the Winning Historian:*

He was imbued with a patience and otherworldliness ill-suited for politics

MLW_v72_p134
1976-1983 / 2001
The Atlas Group

*Description of the Winning Historian:*

What mattered to her most was to avoid anything that might be reminiscent of empathy

*Distance Between Horse and Finish Line:*
- 17

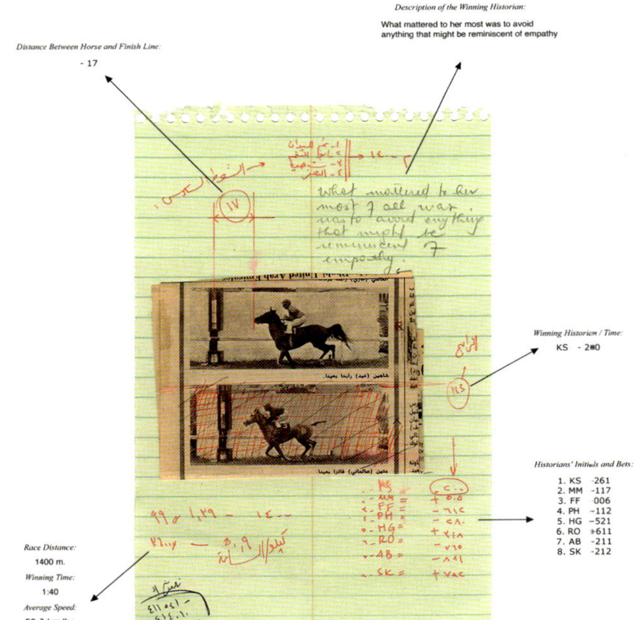


*Winning Historian / Time:*
KS - 2[illegible]0

*Historians' Initials and Bets:*

1. KS -261
2. MM -117
3. FF -006
4. PH -112
5. HG -521
6. RO +611
7. AB -211
8. SK -212

*Race Distance:*
1400 m.

*Winning Time:*
1:40

*Average Speed:*
50.3 km/hr.

Document title
***We Decided to Let Them Say, "We Are Convenced", Twice***

Category_File_Type_Plates
**[cat. A]_Raad_Photographs_001-015**

Date
**2002**

Attributed to
**Walid Raad**

Summary
**The following photographs are attributed to Walid Raad who donated them to The Atlas Group in 2002. In the statement accompanying the donation, Raad noted:**

**In the summer of 1982, I stood along with others in a parking lot across from my mother's apartment in East Beirut, and watched the Israeli land, air, and sea assault on West Beirut. The PLO along with their Lebanese and Syrian allies retaliated, as best they could.**
**East Beirut welcomed the invasion, or so it seemed and that much is certain.**
**West Beirut resisted it, or so it seemed, and that much is certain.**
**One day, my mother even accompanied me to the hills around Beirut to photograph the invading Israeli army stationed there. Soldiers rested their bodies and their weapons as they waited for their next orders to attack or retreat.**
**I was 15 in 1982, and wanted to get as close as possible to the events, or as close as my newly acquired camera and lens permitted me. Clearly not close enough.**
**This past year, I came upon the carefully preserved negatives from that time.**
**I decided to look again.**

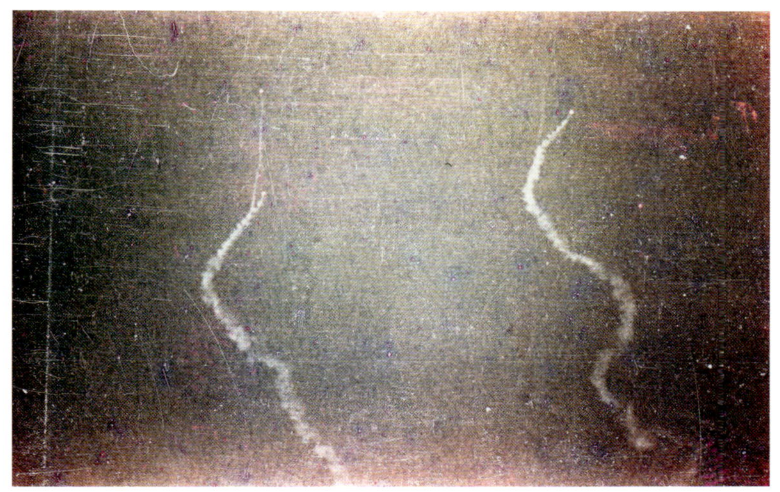

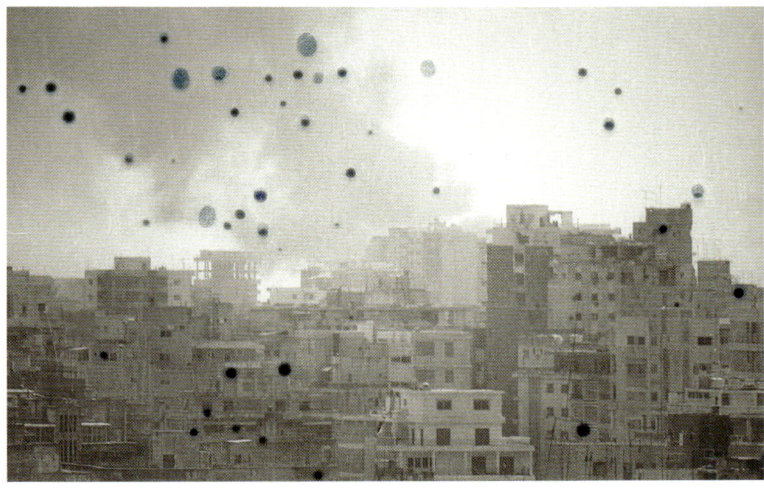

Document title
***Let's Be Honest, the Weather Helped***

Category_File_Type_Plates
**[cat. A]_Raad_Photographs_001-007**

Date
**1998**

Attributed to
**Walid Raad**

Summary
**The following plates are attributed to Walid Raad who donated them to The Atlas Group in 1998. In the statement accompanying the donation, Raad noted:**

**Like many around me in Beirut in the late 1970's, I collected bullets and shrapnel. I would run out to the streets after a night or day of shelling to remove them from walls, cars, and trees. I kept detailed notes of where I found every bullet and photographed the sites of my findings, covering the holes with dots that corresponded to the bullet's diameter and the mesmerizing hues I found on bullets' tips. It took me 10 years to realize that ammunition manufacturers follow distinct color codes to mark and identify their cartridges and shells. It also took me another 10 years to realize that my notebooks in part catalogue 17 countries and organizations that continue to supply the various militias and armies fighting in Lebanon: Belgium, China, Egypt, Finland, Germany, Greece, Iraq. Israel, Italy, Libya, NATO, Romania, Saudi Arabia, Switzerland, U.S.A., U.K., and Venezuela.**

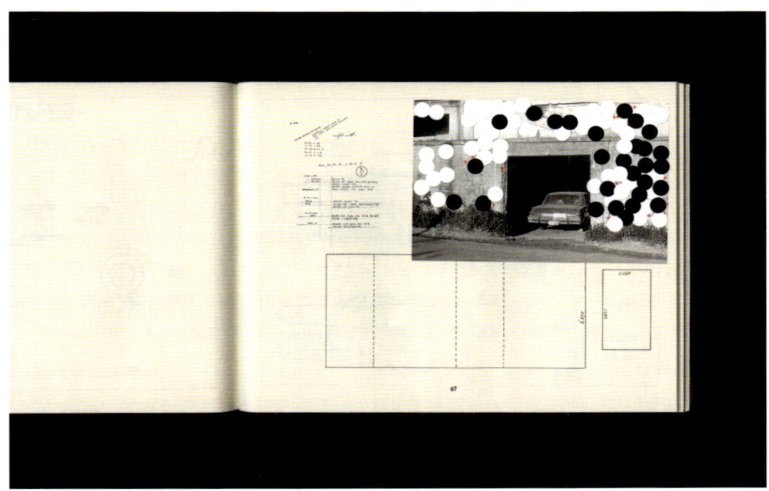

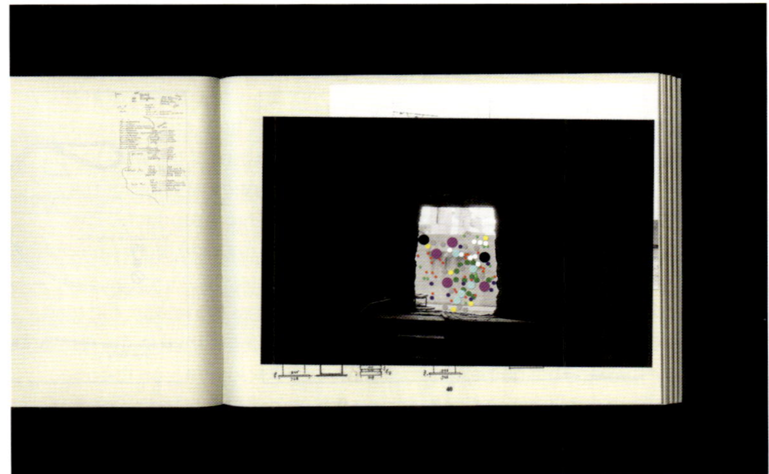

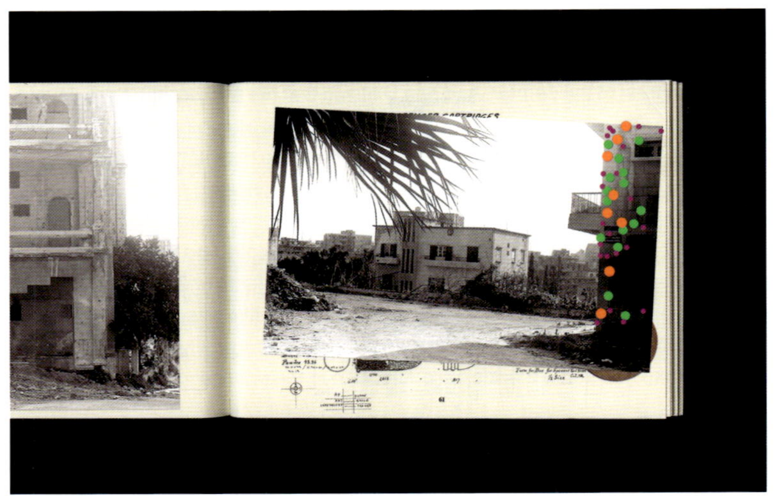

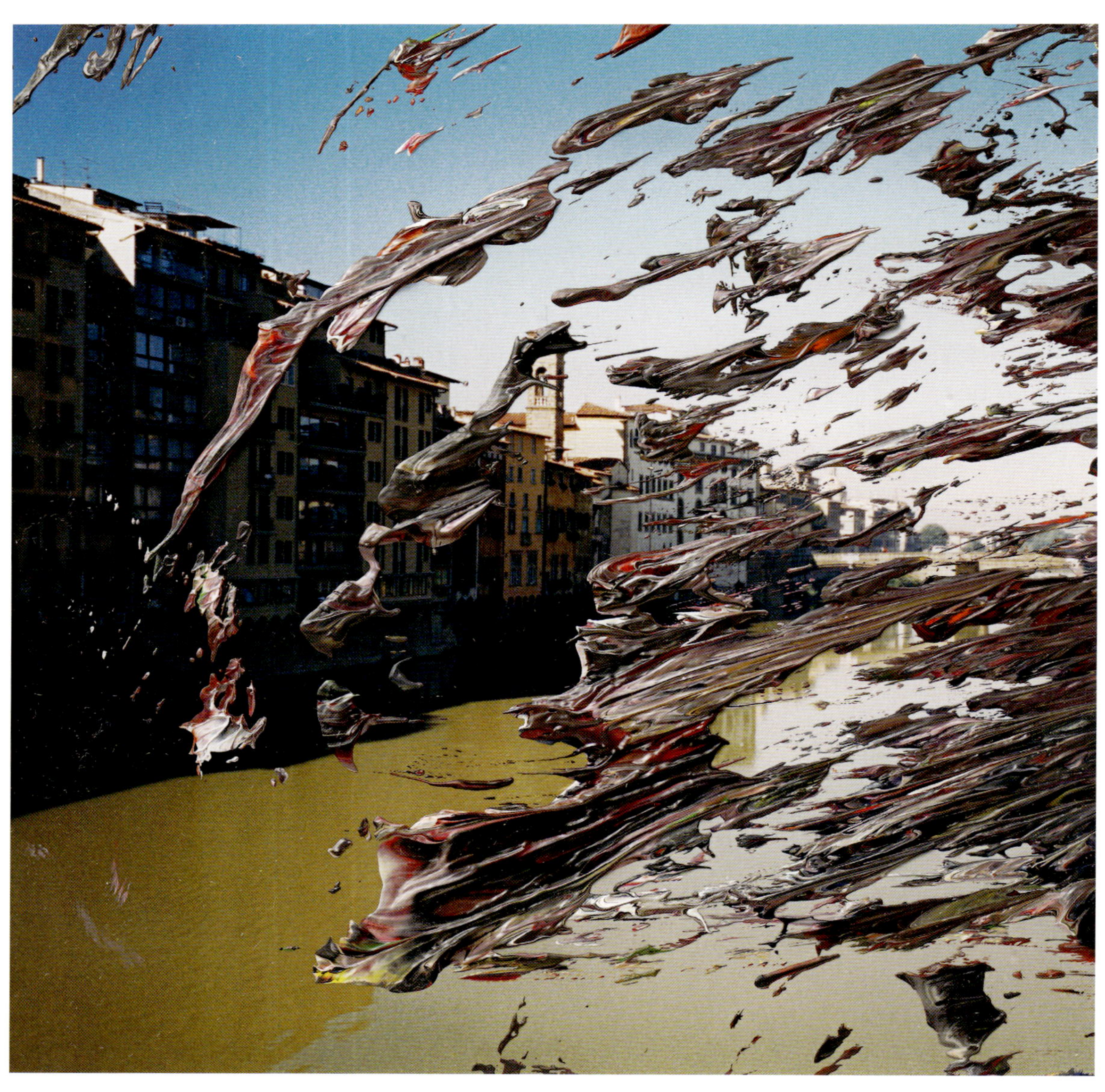

*Firenze 11/99, 2000*
Courtesy private collection
Published in *Gerhard Richter. Overpainted Photographs*,
Hatje Cantz Verlag, Ostfildern, 2008

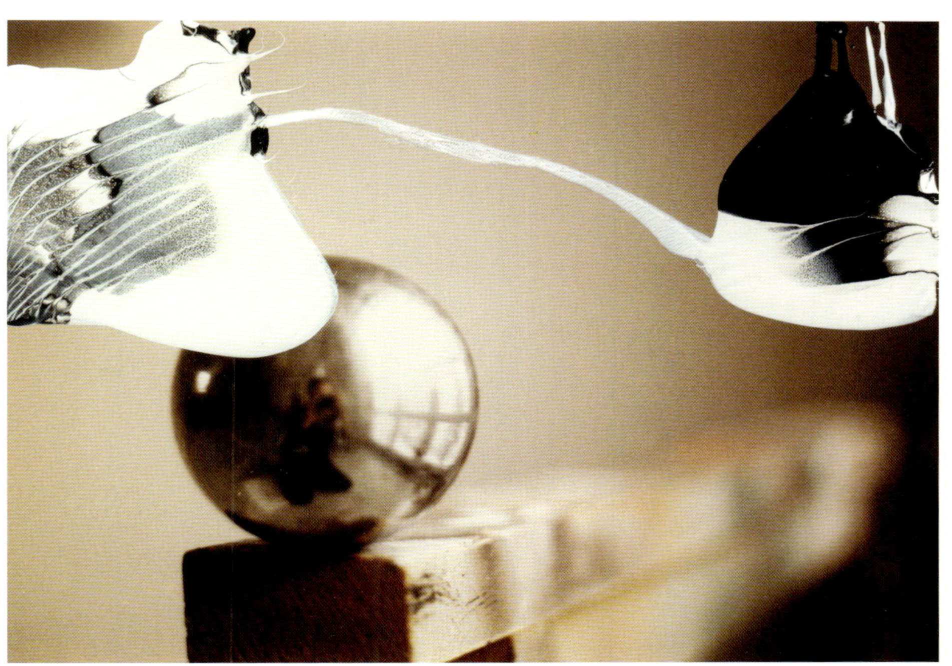

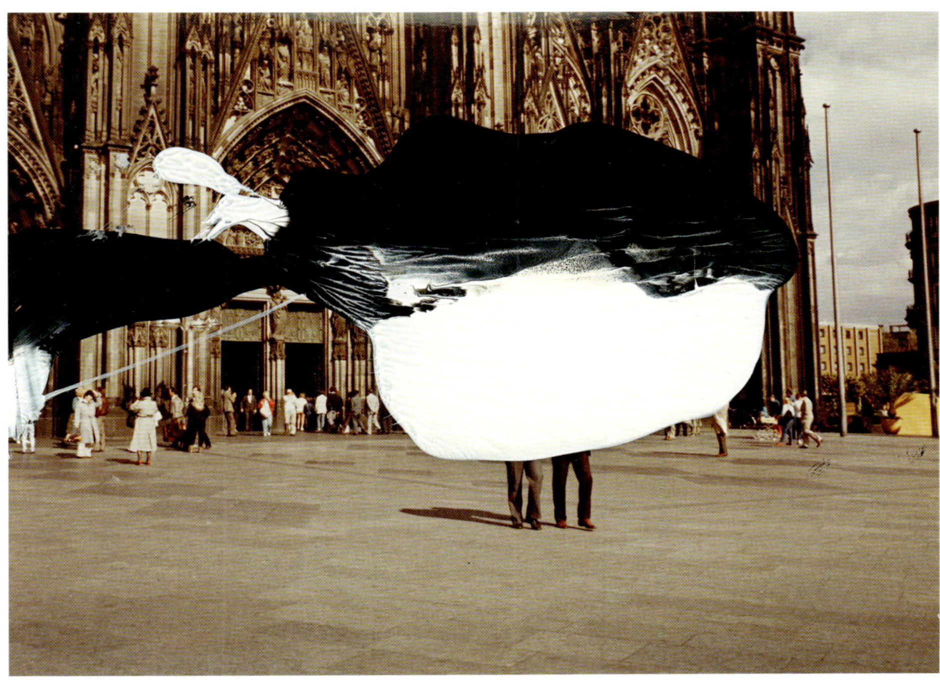

*8.2.1992*
Courtesy private collection
Published in *Gerhard Richter. Overpainted Photographs*,
Hatje Cantz Verlag, Ostfildern, 2008


*8.2.1992*
Courtesy private collection
Published in *Gerhard Richter. Overpainted Photographs*,
Hatje Cantz Verlag, Ostfildern, 2008

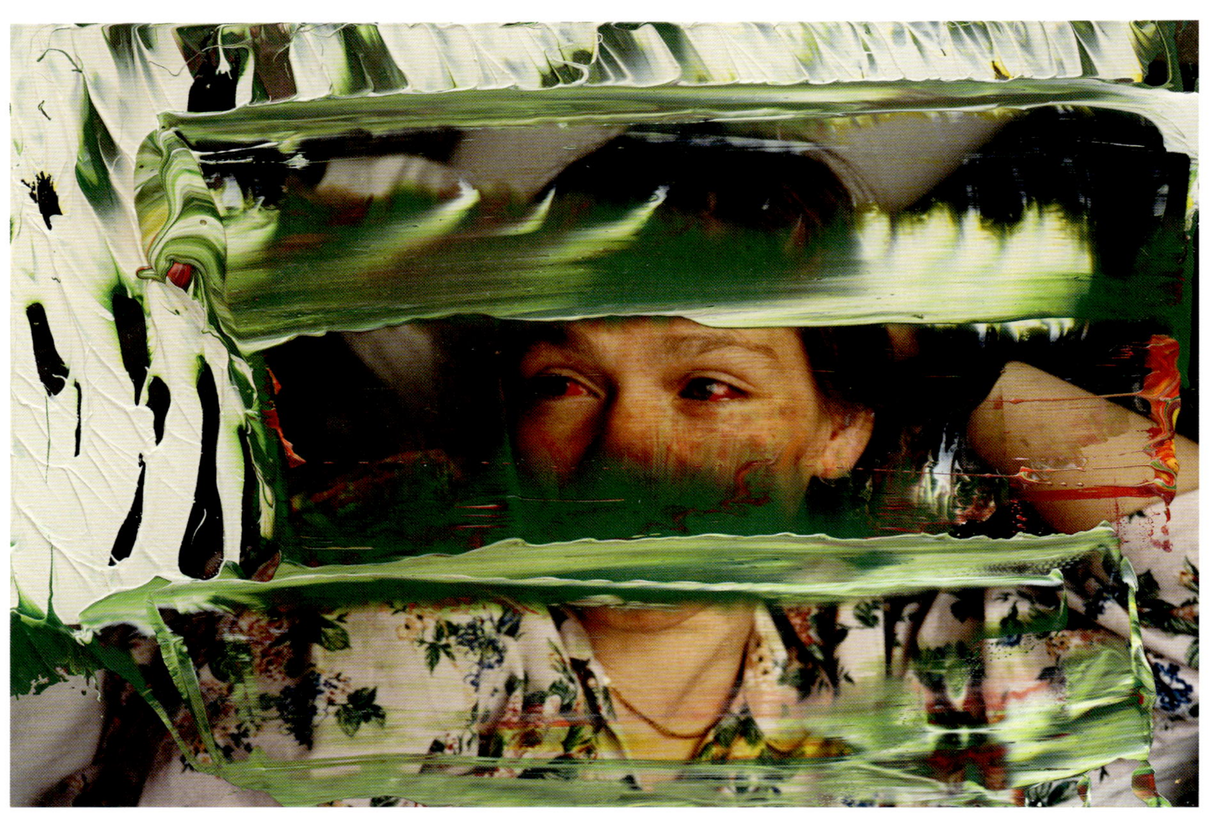

*11.2.98*
Courtesy private collection, Germany
Published in *Gerhard Richter. Overpainted Photographs*,
Hatje Cantz Verlag, Ostfildern, 2008

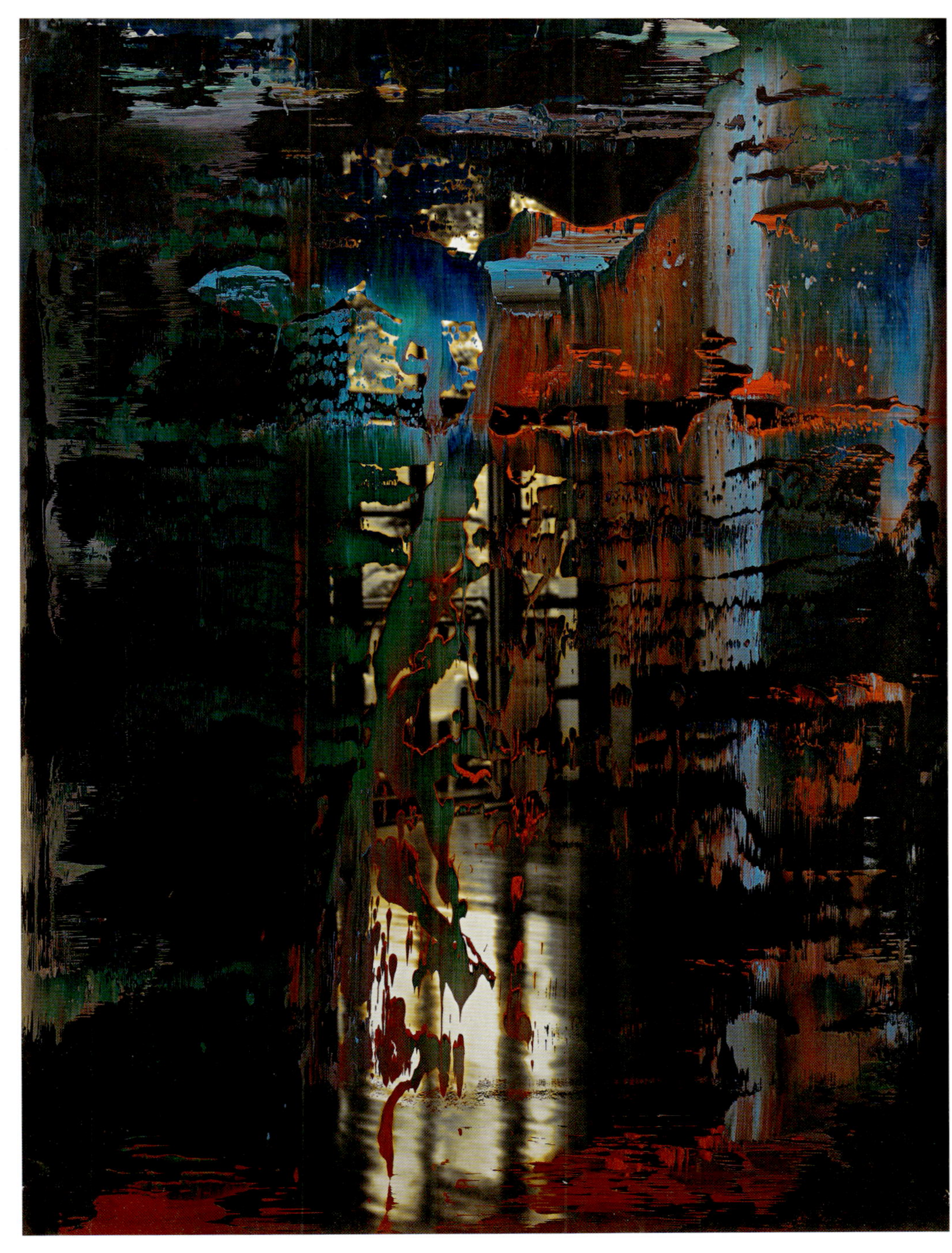

*10. Jan. 1990*
Courtesy private collection, Munich
Published in *Gerhard Richter. Overpainted Photographs*,
Hatje Cantz Verlag, Ostfildern, 2008

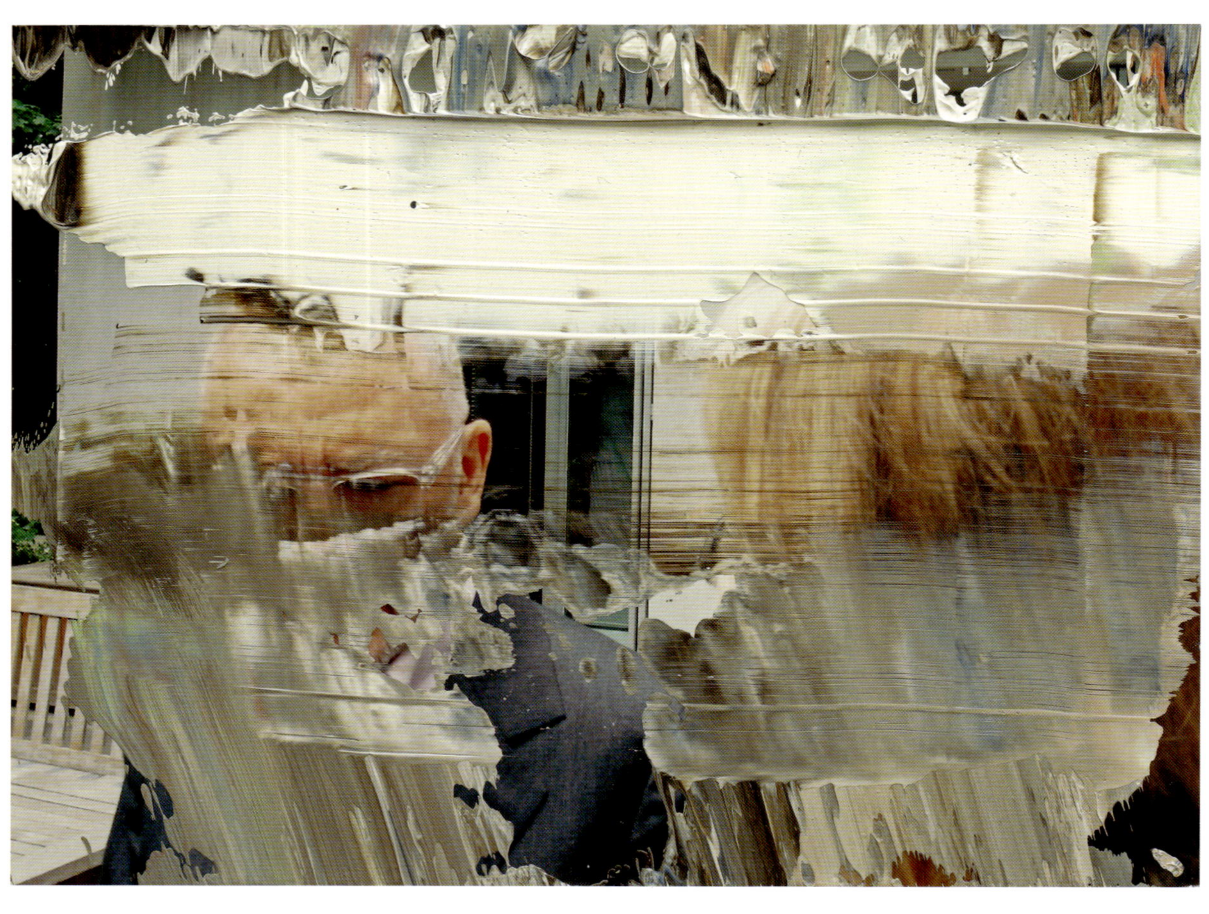

*4.12.06*
Courtesy private collection, Germany
Published in *Gerhard Richter. Overpainted Photographs*,
Hatje Cantz Verlag, Ostfildern, 2008

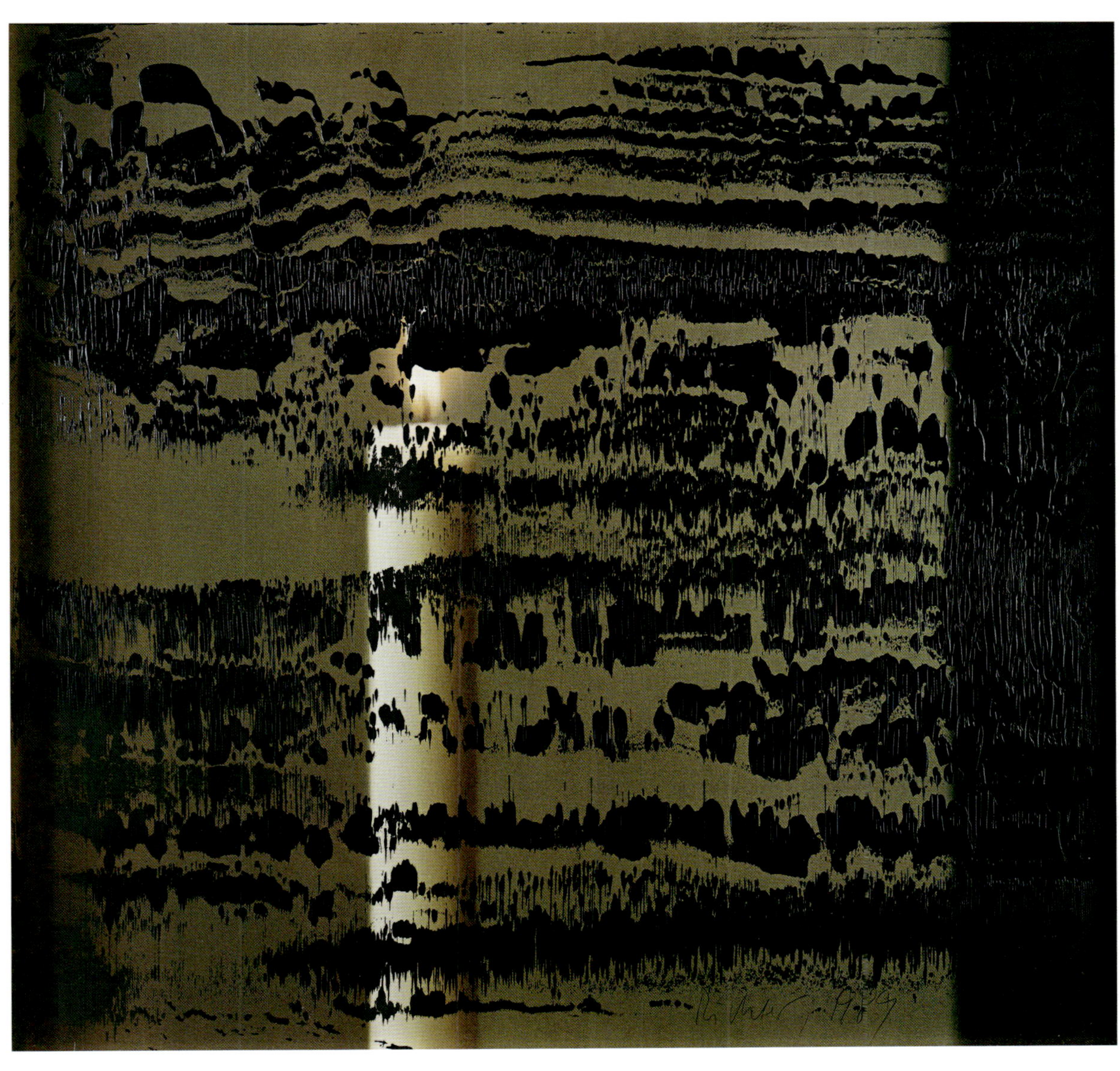

*Kerze III, 13/30, 1989*
Courtesy Springer & Winckler Kunsthandel, Berlin
Published in *Gerhard Richter. Overpainted Photographs*,
Hatje Cantz Verlag, Ostfildern, 2008

# Sara Ramo

## Breathless (Almost Full, Almost Empty). Notes on the Work of Sara Ramo

You wake up in the middle of the night, and find out that all your toys that usually stay in the closets and on the higher shelves of the cupboards are now scattered all over the room, corridor and living room, covering the parquet floor of the house. You think you're going to get yelled at from your parents, because the toys should be put away, but you don't know whether you're dreaming or not, and believe everything is right. Although apparently in chaos and all mixed up, the toys are actually quite organized; they are arranged in a new order that has nothing to do with the controlled order of the high and inaccessible shelves of the cupboard. This is an organization that transforms the toys into living things. It is not like in a horror movie, where the toy train whistles during the night and the doll speaks without moving her lips. These are flowerbeds, flowers, and brooks created with areas made up of your toys, scattered on the ground. You think it is poetry; fear mixes with admiration. You stop to think for a minute, not knowing whether you're a child or a grown up, but aware of the relation between dream, cupboard and attic.

You take a closer look at the toys, and notice that these are different toys, that their appearance can change according to the context in which the fantasy takes place. When you're a child and you're home sleeping, they are the toys that gain life and climb down from the closets at night. But if you're successful, young, artistic, and slightly bourgeois, you know that the epicenter of your vanity, euphemistically called self-image, is the bathroom, where some fragments of your recent existence are dispersed in the closets and on the toilet table: perfumes, soaps, hotel gifts, an odd sex toy, underwear, ointments, and pharmacy drugs. Displayed indifferently, they "say" something about you. Reorganized by this other person, using the same toilet facilities, its furniture, exhibiting the entrails of your intimacy, they propose a new way of "looking" at you. A portrait, a new organization, filled with something else. It "sees" you in a way that you did not know (*Como aprender o que acontece na normalidade das coisas*, 2002-2005 [How to Learn What is Happening within the Normality of Things]).

Now, if you are a curator, just starting your career in a small institution, and this institution is located in a building filled with stories, with an attic full of things and ghosts, the best that could happen to you would be if the things and ghosts came out of the attic, leaving the limbo, neither dead nor alive, to transform into a beautiful garden, a garden made out of inanimate things, but more alive than that other garden full of plants that surrounds the museum building (Cassino da Pampulha, Belo Horizonte, 1943, architecture by Oscar Niemeyer, landscaping by Roberto Burle Marx). You know this building used to be a casino, and you start imagining the amount of pleasure, acceleration, and ecstasy that those gambling chips, now scattered over the floor emulating innocent vegetation, have once afforded. You also imagine all of the courtships, engagements and marriages ruined by the gambling, and the fortunes depleted by those chips. And, one day, all of this was turned into a Museum, which in the strict view of the municipal administration, shows little or no difference from any other public division that makes up the public service. Then, things are bought — chairs, tables, fans, typewriters, rulers, frames, waxing machines, lamps, curtains – and, as they stop being used, or wear out, they pile up in this attic. One day, a truck arrives and takes everything to central storage – the attic of attics. And these

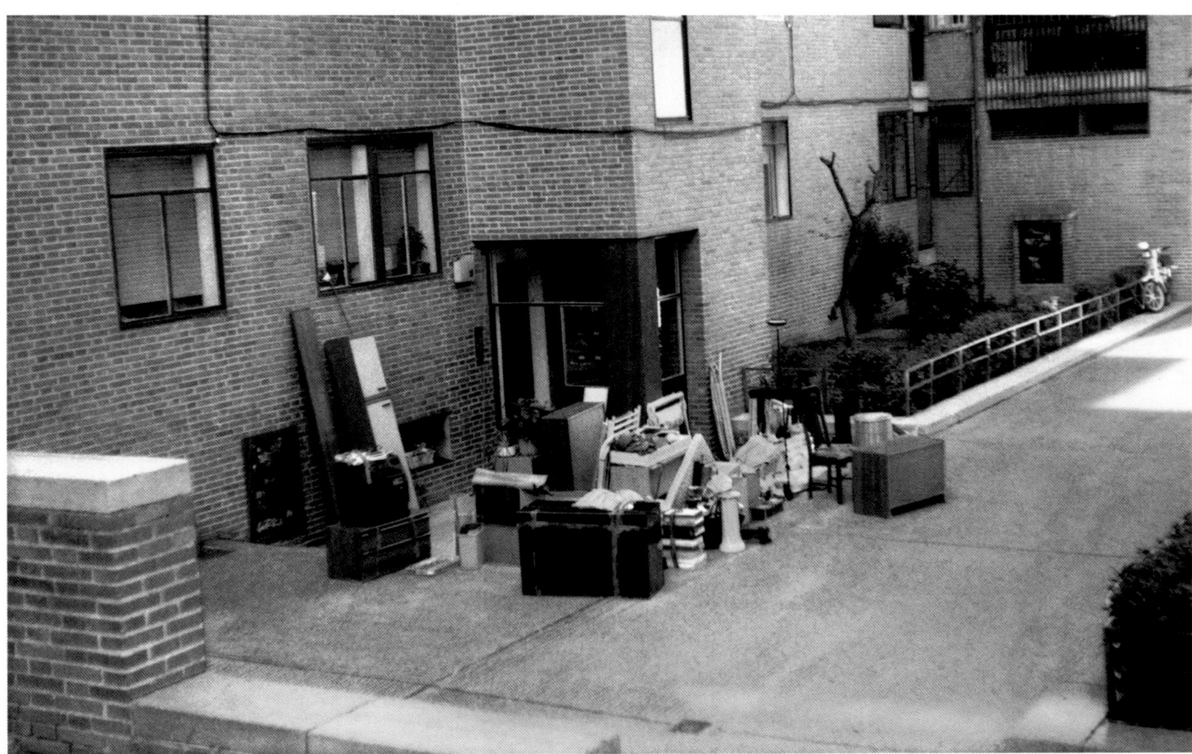

things that belong to the city cannot be thrown away, because they belong to everyone. And you think, oh, this is it, this is what a public thing means. It cannot be discarded because it really does not have an owner. And then, if you think again, these things have no more usage, those who are authorized to use them have already determined the end of their useful lifespan. But things resist beyond people. And then she arrives and transforms it all. Maybe it "is" not art, but it "is in a state of" art. And, when the exhibition ends, the things go away, they lose their semantic tension, losing their state as art (*Jardim das coisas do sótão*, 2004 [Garden of Things from the Attic]).

You know that if you want to travel, you have to pack your bags. But there is a kind of trip in which you empty the suitcase, and only after it is empty you can climb in and start your voyage (*Translado*, 2008 [Move]). And, if you suffer from asthma, you know that the trick is not to lose your patience and breathe really slowly. Because if you try to fill your lungs in one breath, there is no way they will fill up (*Quase cheio, Quase vazio*, 2008 [Almost Full, Almost Empty]).

[Rodrigo Moura]

*Added*, 1993-2008
Courtesy Fortes Vilaça Gallery, São Paulo

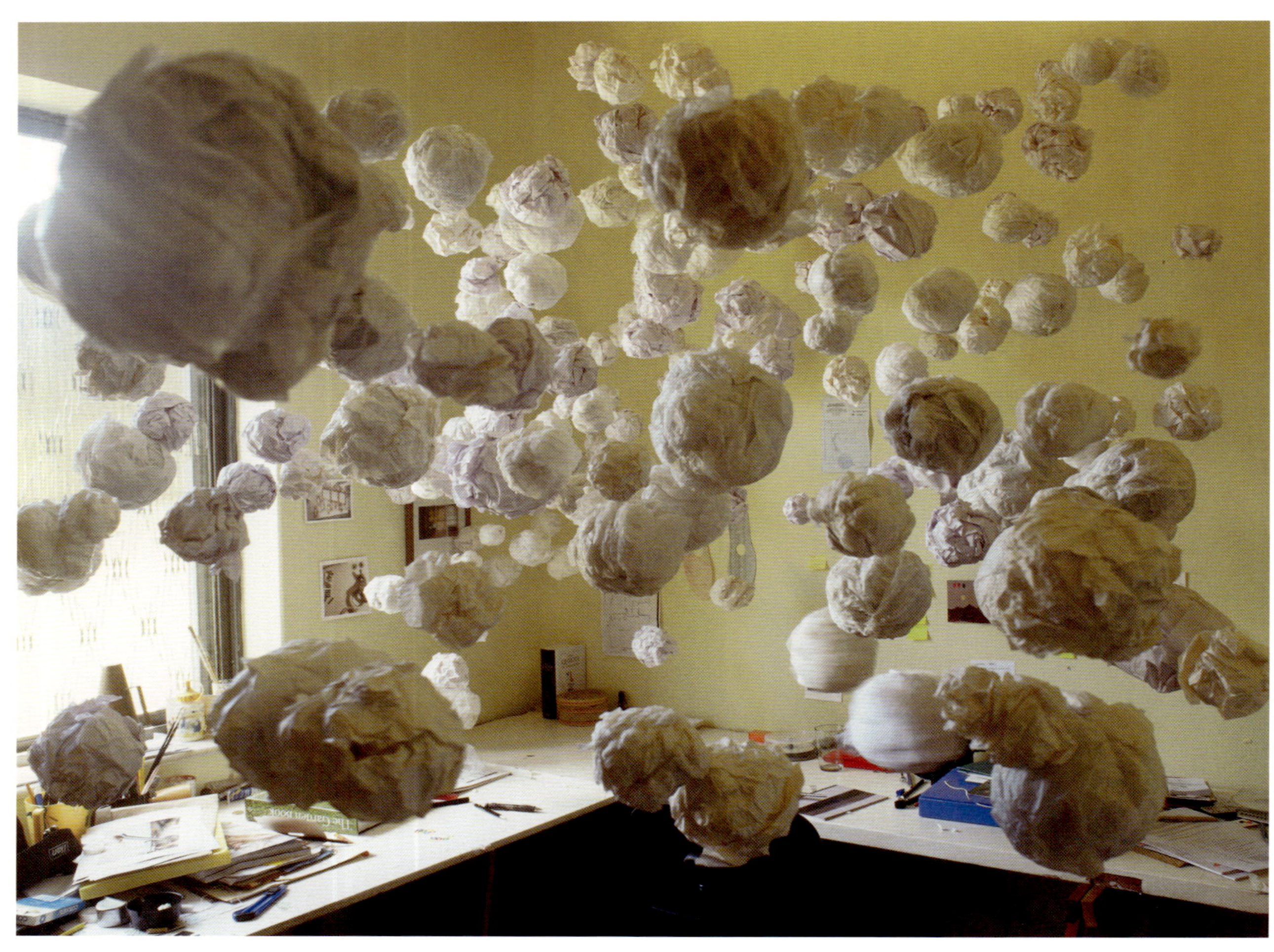

*Invasion of Everything Which Was Contained*, 2005
Courtesy Fortes Vilaça Gallery, São Paulo
© Sara Ramo

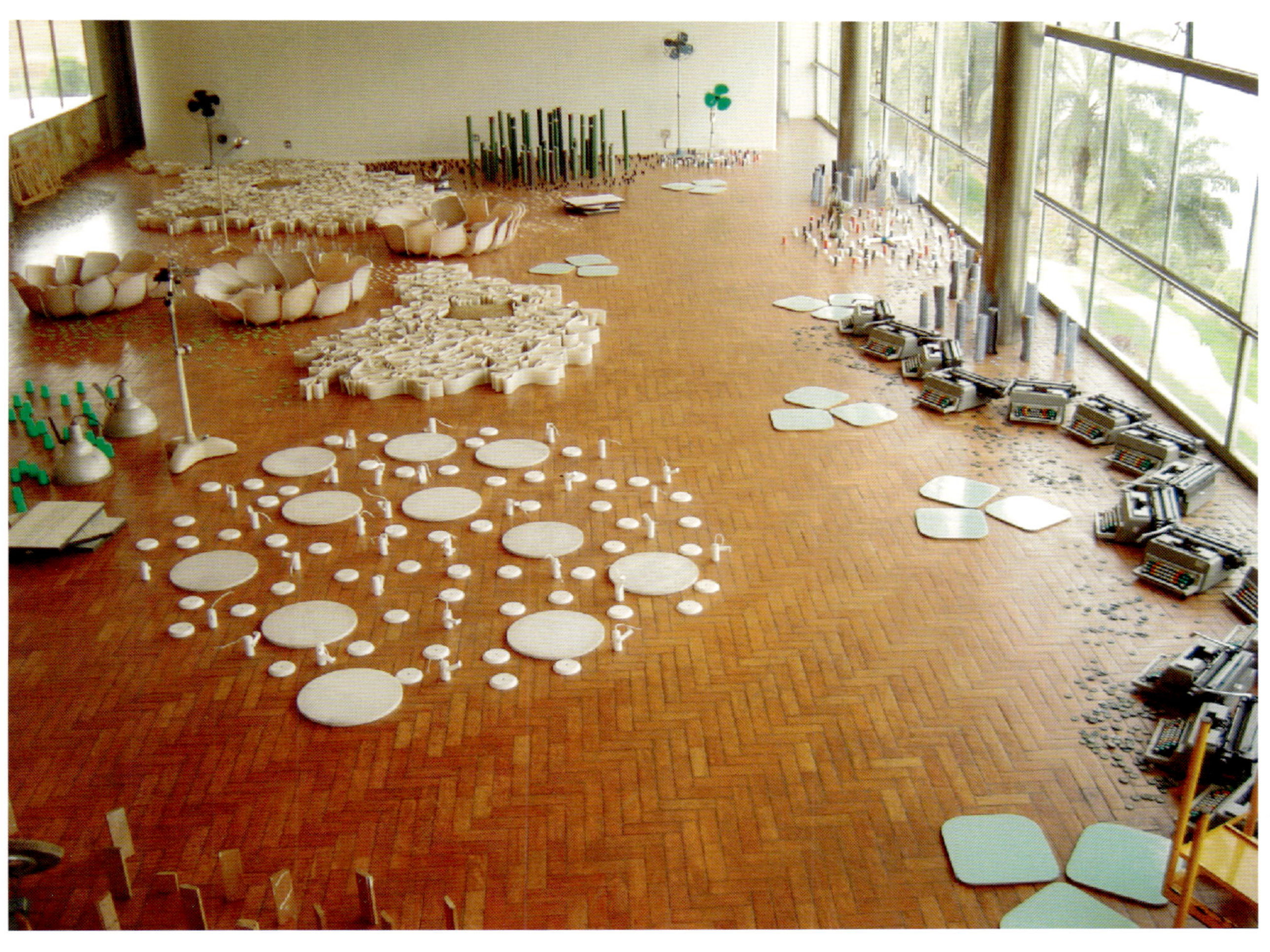

*The Garden of Things from the Attic. Installation,* 2004
Courtesy Fortes Vilaça Gallery, São Paulo
© Sara Ramo

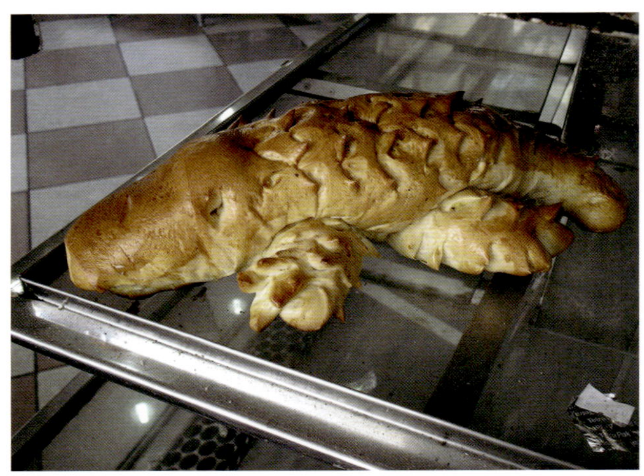

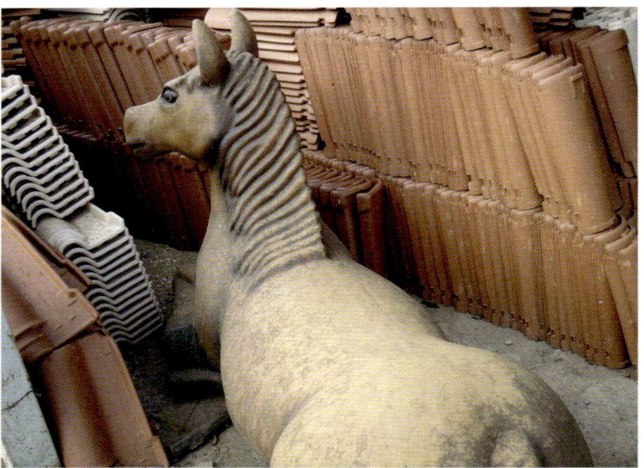

*Zoo (Group F)*, 2008
Courtesy Fortes Vilaça Gallery, São Paulo

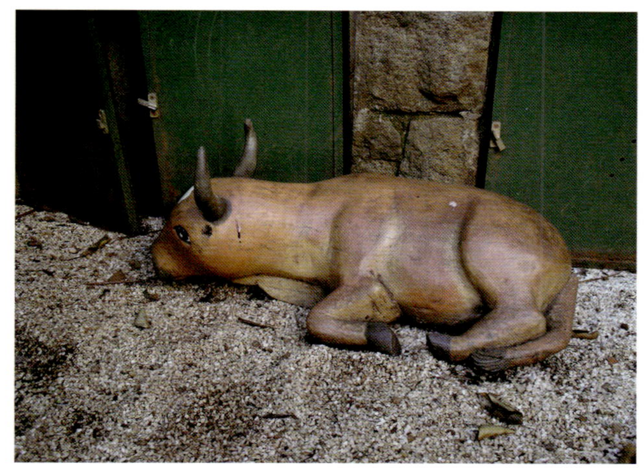

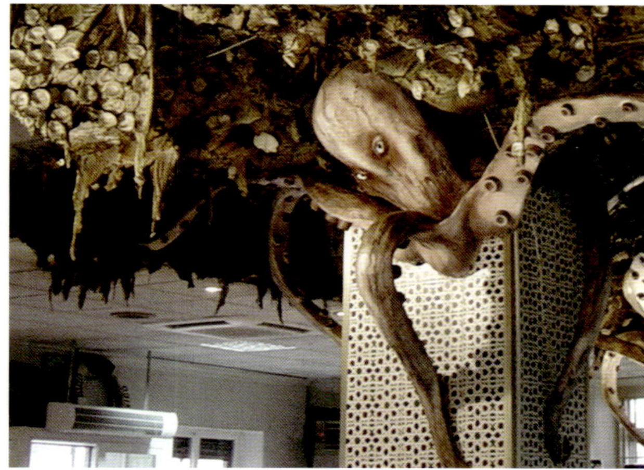

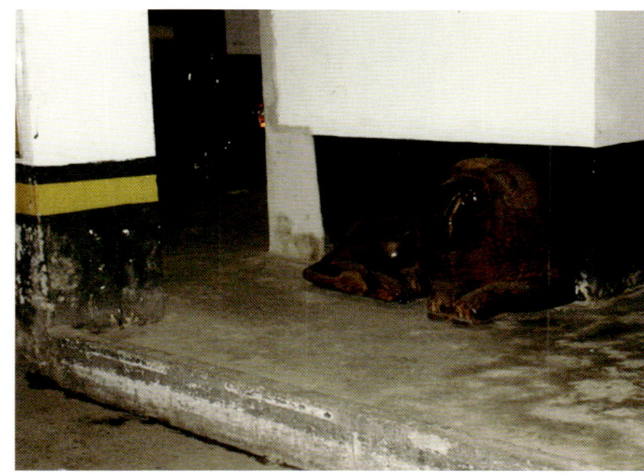

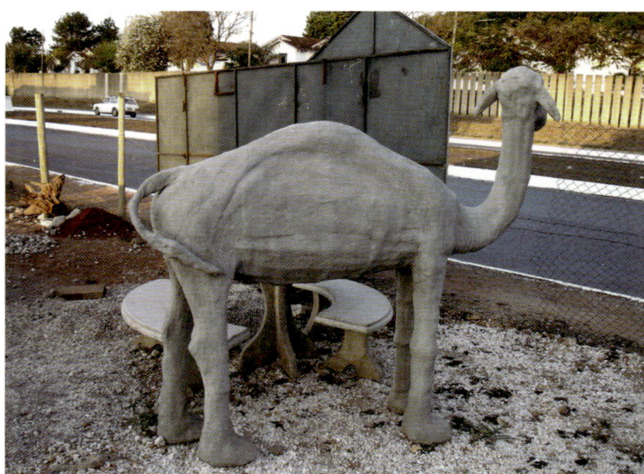

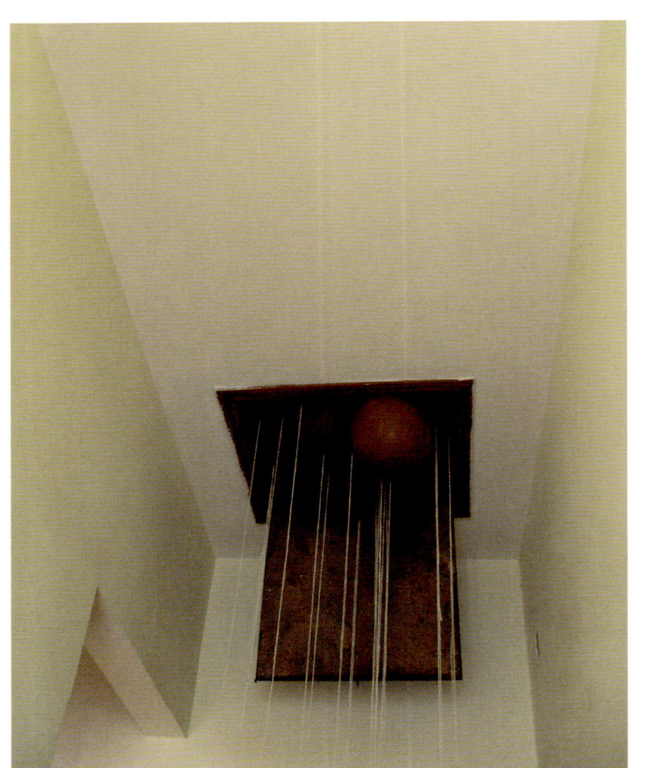

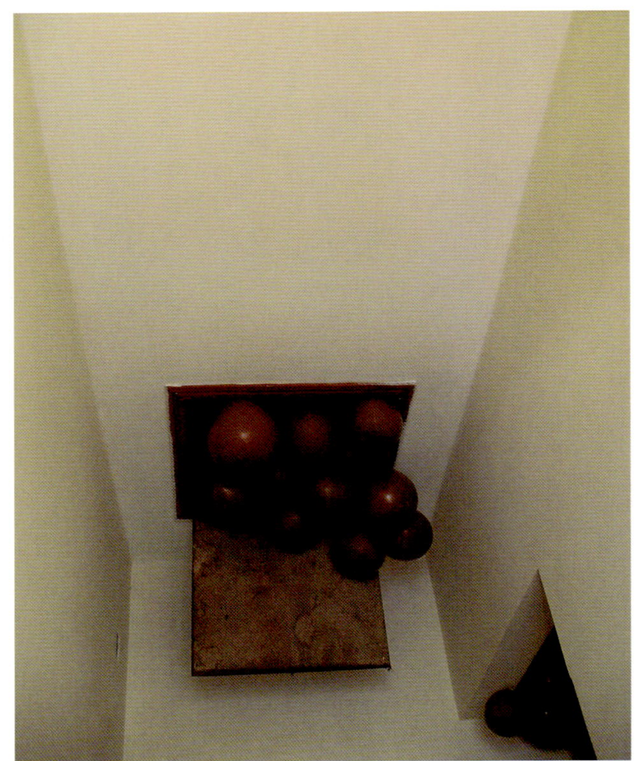

*Symmetries*, 2008
Courtesy Fortes Vilaça Gallery, São Paulo

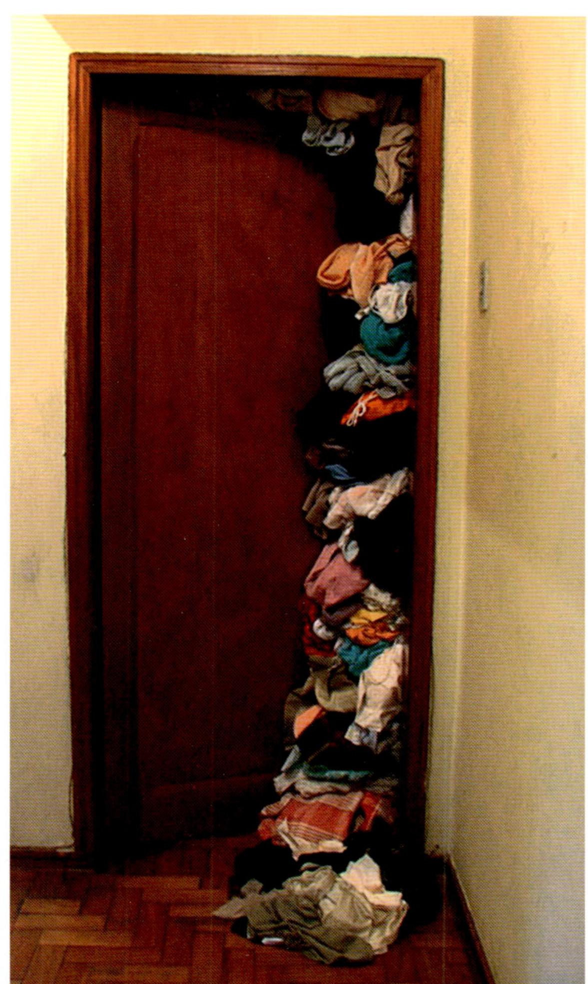

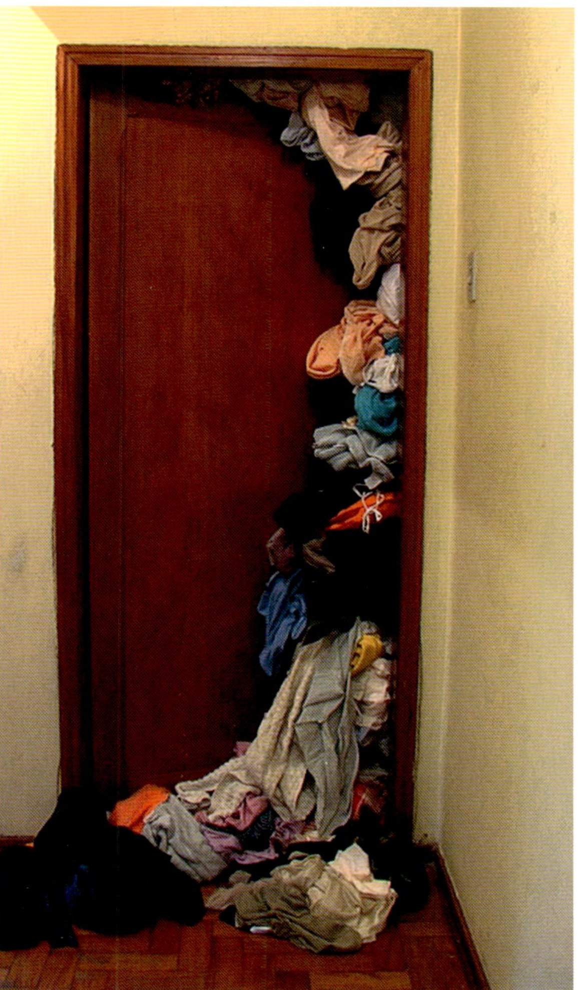

*Welcome*, 2008. HD Digital video
Courtesy Fortes Vilaça Gallery, São Paulo

# Jindřich Štyrský

## On the Needles of These Days. Photographs from 1934 to 1935

Jindřich Štyrský was born on August 11, 1899 in the Czech village of Dolní Čermná. He graduated from the School of Education at Hradec Králové. He briefly worked as a teacher and then studied at the Academy of Fine Arts in Prague. Since 1923, Štyrský was one of the most distinctive members of the avant-garde Devětsil Artistic Union, which joined young artists across all fields. At that time, he was creating the so-called "picture poems", a synthesis of text and collage, which were used on poetry and prose book covers. He lived with Toyen, the Czech Surrealist painter, in Paris for several years (1925 - 1928). In France he researched, among other things, material for the biography of Arthur Rimbaud as well as of Marquis de Sade later on. In the late 1920s, he illustrated the anthology of Comte de Lautréamont's *The Songs of Maldoror* (its first edition was confiscated). During this time he also created covers for the ten-part edition of *Fantomas*. After returning to Prague, Štyrský worked in the avant-garde Free Theatre (*Osvobozené divadlo*), among other activities, and issued the *Erotic Review*. His bibliophilistic *Edition 69*, published only for subscribers, included his own text titled *Emily Comes to Me in a Dream* (1933), accompanied by reproductions of erotic collages. In this work, he returned to his childhood, the tragic death of his step-sister Marie and other family tragedies, depicting them with radical directness.

In 1934, the artist – together with Toyen, the poets Vítězslav Nezval and Konstantin Biebl, the composer Jaroslav Ježek, the theater director Jindřich Honzl and several other friends – participated in the founding of the Surrealist Group of Czechoslovakia, which was in close touch with the French circle of André Breton.

Štyrský's first attempts in photography date back to as early as 1932. In the following years, he created the cycles *The Man with Blinkers* and *The Frog Man* (both in 1934) as well as *Afternoon in Paris* (1935). The photographs seemingly captured trivial everyday-life topics. They included views into shop windows with a variety of bizarre objects (prosthetic aids, hairdresser's requisites), details of fairgrounds or pictures from cemeteries in Paris or other places. The objects were often old, damaged, rotten, after the zenith of their planned useful life. The things themselves or their awkward clusters expressed certain monstrosity or obsession. Together with Nezval, Štyrský also published an enquiry called *An Attempt to Recognize the Irrationality in Photography*. The photographer's balancing on the edge of a knife was described by his friend Karel Teige of the same artistic generation: "...reality is becoming a torturing and cruel ghost to him, which scares, recognizes, and fascinates desire at the same time...". The author's works were a reaction to Eugène Atget's work, published not long before that, which fascinated several generations of European photographers.

With the painter Toyen "and the psychoanalyst" Bohuslav Brouk, Štyrský was an exception to the Czech scene due to his interest in pornography, kitsch and other peripheral cultural and social phenomena.

One year before the photographer died, his book *On the Needles of These Days* was illegally published in the Surrealism Edition. This cross-section of his photographic cycles from the 1930s was complemented by texts of a young poet named Jindřich Heisler. Jindřich Štyrský died on March 21, 1942 in Prague at the age of 43 as the consequence of an inherited heart disease. His book, whose title we have used for this exhibition, was legally published only after the Second World War. The extensive artistic legacy of the author includes, in addition to the photographic cycles mentioned above, paintings, book and free graphics, collages, poems, theoretical and sharply controversial texts. After the Communist coup in 1948, surrealism as well as Štyrský's book were again prohibited in Czechoslovakia for decades.

[Jan Mlčoch, Lucie Vlčková]

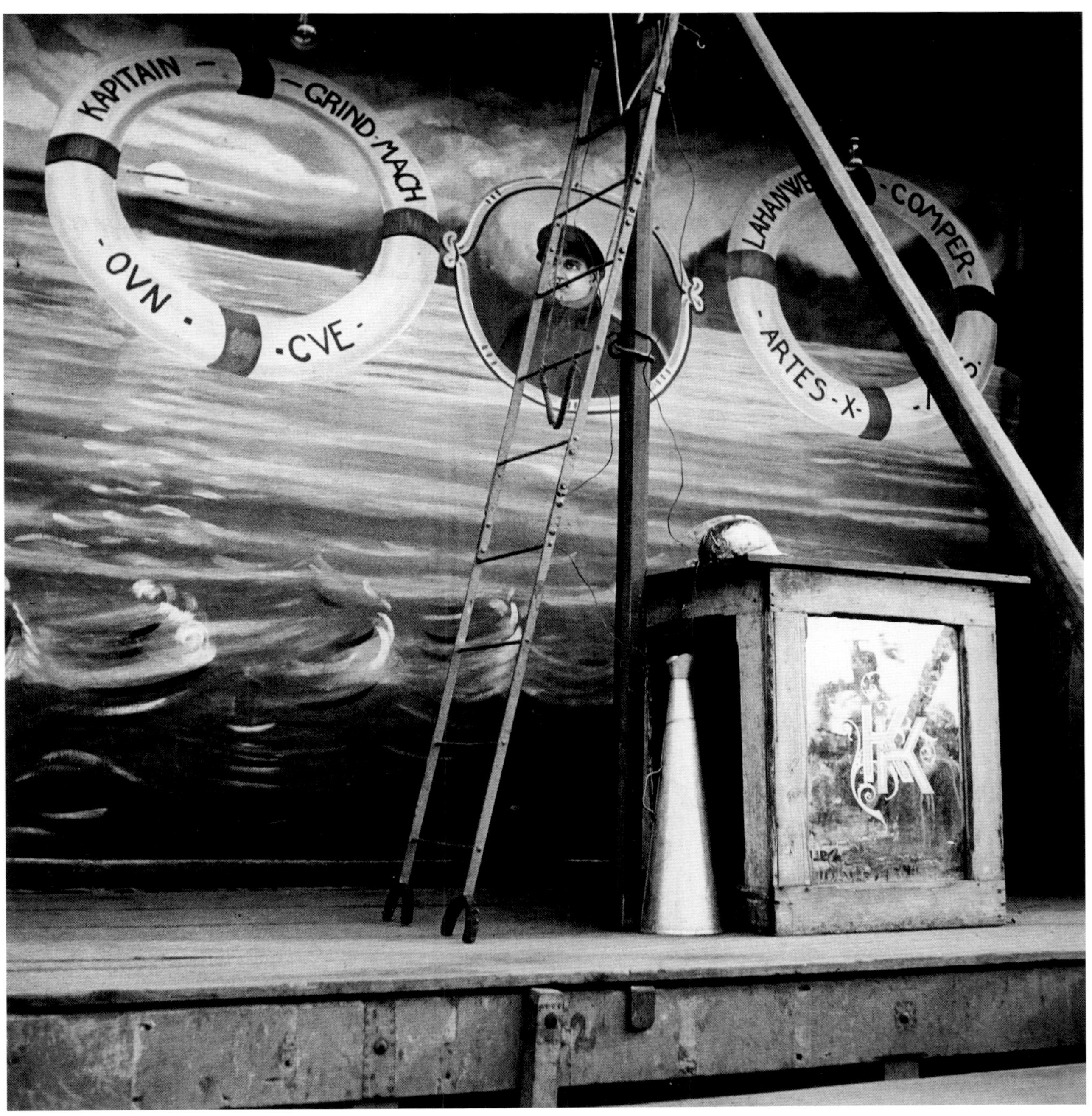


From the series *Man with Blinkers*, 1934-35
Courtesy Museum of Decorative Arts in Prague

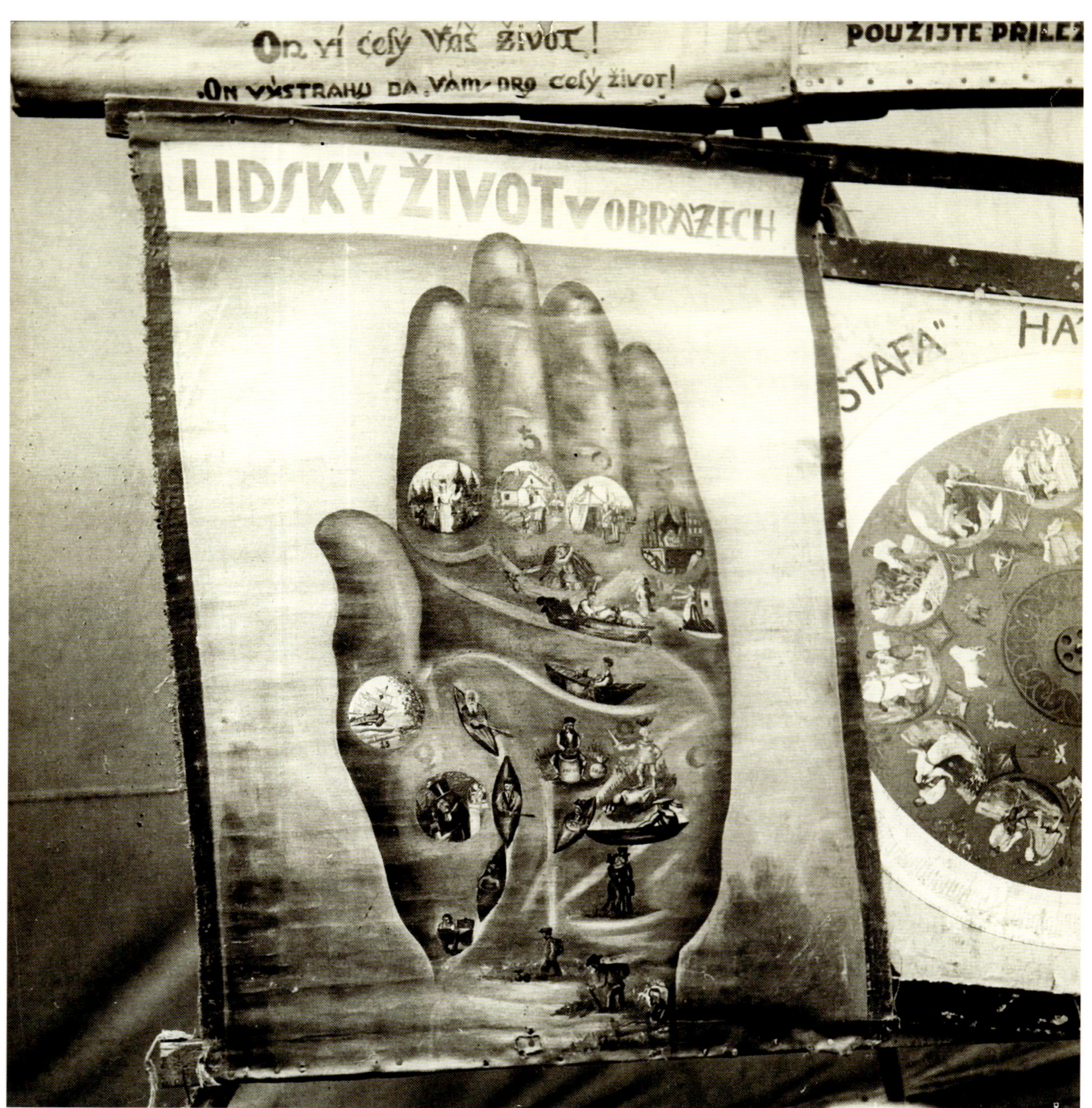


From the series *Man with Blinkers*, 1934-35
Courtesy Museum of Decorative Arts in Prague

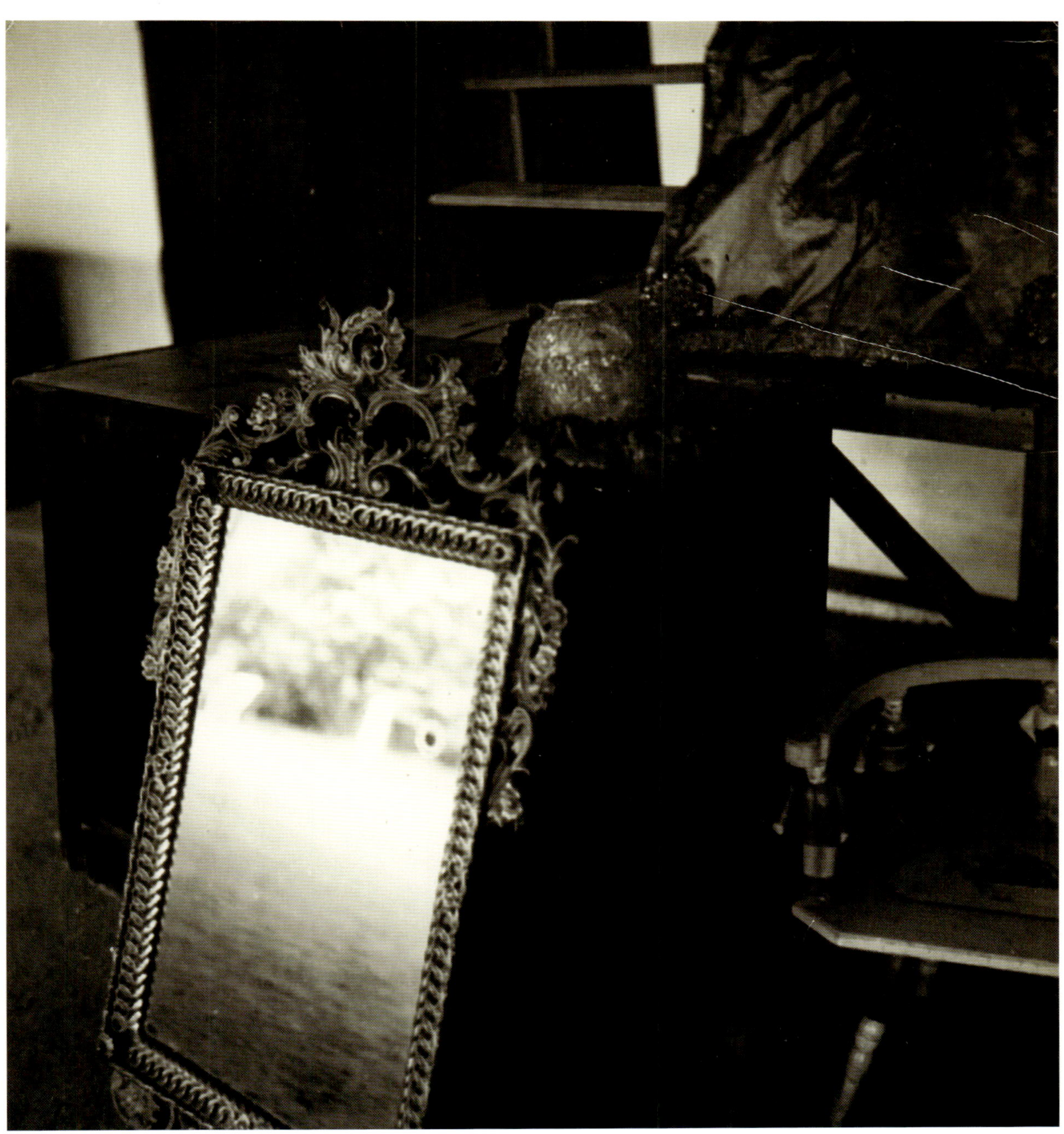

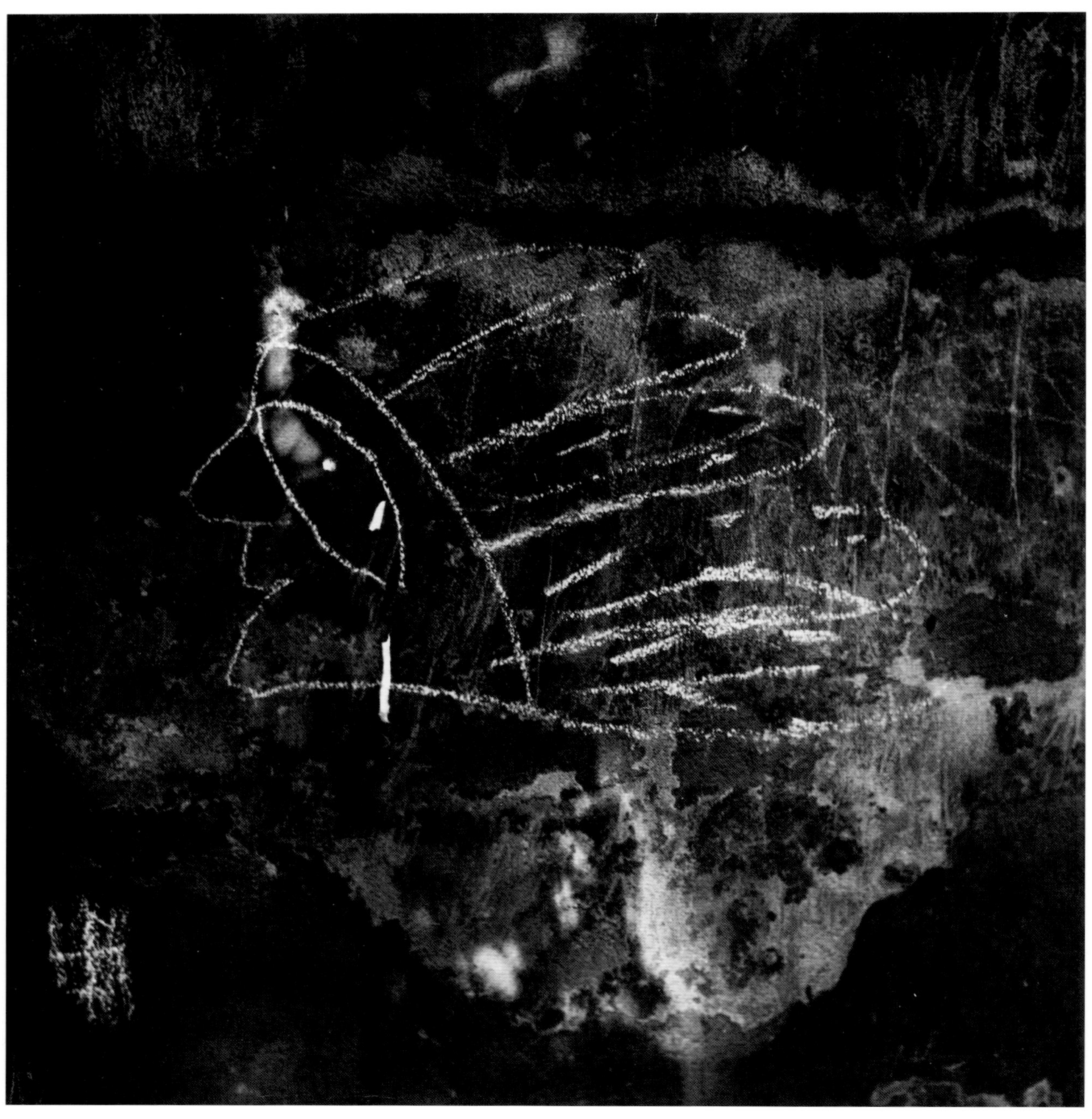

From the series *Man with Blinkers*, 1934-35
Courtesy Museum of Decorative Arts in Prague

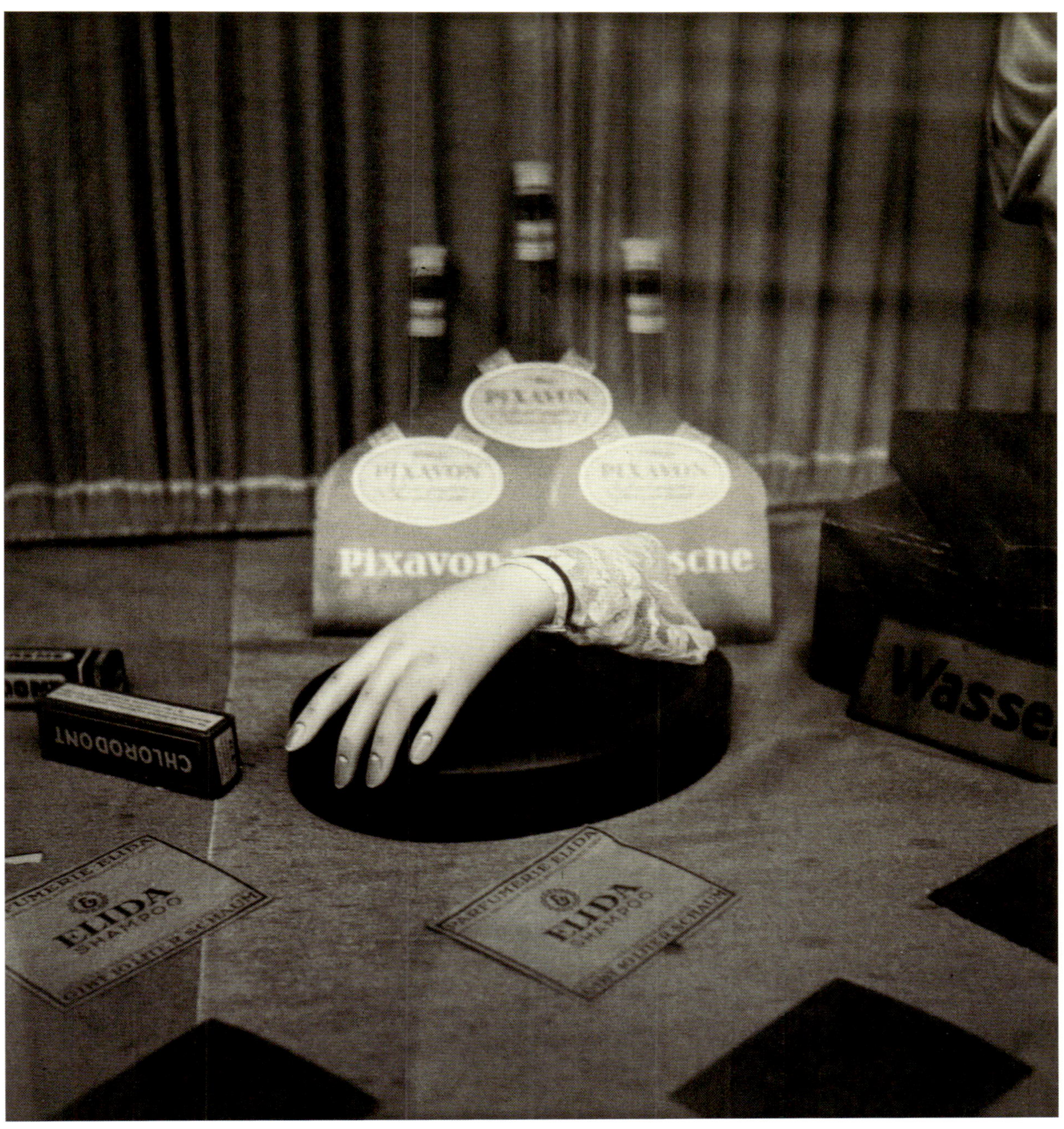


From the series *Frog man*, 1934-35
Courtesy Museum of Decorative Arts in Prague
© Jindřich Štyrský

## Ventura's Letter

"A change in scale", might be a way of summing up what is new in *Colossal Youth*, the third and most beautiful film in the Pedro Costa's trilogy about the inhabitants of the shantytown of Fontainhas, since demolished. At the beginning, we see high, metallic grey walls dimly lit in the half-darkness. Through a window we see objects falling to hit the ground below.

In the next shot, a woman stands before us, the embodiment of the furies of ancient times, holding a knife that also seems to be serving as a torch to light the darkness. She is speaking, as if delivering a monologue, explaining how as a young girl in Cape Verde she would plunge into the sea without fear of sharks, ignoring the boys who spoke to her of love, prudently from the shore. These two sequences will later be given an "explanation": the woman, Clotilde, has just thrown her husband out, a former bricklayer called Ventura, and has also thrown his furniture out of the window. But the real point is not this. What matters here is the space that has been constructed by this opening, the tone it sets for the story. We seem to be a very long way from the space and the characters of *In Vanda's Room*.

Then, the camera wended its way through the labyrinth of streets, crept into the corners of tiny bedrooms and stood eye to eye with half-asphyxiated characters fighting for their lives between two fixes. Here, space has opened out, and the camera has moved to the top of this apartment block that resembles the fortifications of some medieval or more ancient castle, from which springs a woman, wild in appearance, noble in language and with a theatrical diction reminiscent of Clytemnestra or Medea. *Bones* and *In Vanda's Room* introduced us to young people living on the margins of society and coping with life one day at a time. *Colossal Youth* revolves around two mythological figures whose origins are far away in time and space: the first is Clotilde, whom we do not see again, but who continues to inhabit the words of her rejected husband, asking for suitable housing for his large family and later telling "daughter" Bete how he tamed his shrew on independence day when she sang a hymn to liberty (off key). The second is Ventura, a nobleman fallen on hard times, exiled from his African kingdom, incapacitated for work by an injury and for society by a broken spirit, a sort of sublime wanderer somewhere between Oedipus and Lear, but also between Ford's heroes Tom Joad and Ethan Edwards. Thus does tragedy enter the domain of the chronicle. *In Vanda's Room* struggled, shot by shot, to bring out the poetic potential of a squalid setting and the suffocated expression of atrophied lives, with the aim of bringing together, beyond any attempt to make poverty aesthetic, the artistic potentialities of a space and the capacity of the most disadvantaged individuals to get a grip on their own destinies. An image which sums this up is given us in the episode in which one of the three squatters insists – out of a concern for aesthetics – on using his knife to scrape away stains on a table doomed to disappear between the jaws of the demolition equipment. The very character of Ventura resolves the problem. Here there is no abject poverty that the camera is charged with transcending. Between the camera and Vanda, a mother currently coming off drugs, and Nurro, now a respectable employee, comes Ventura, the incarnation of tragic destiny, whom nothing can reconcile with the white walls of new housing and the images of television soap operas. This is no disabled jobseeker whose difficult return to society's mainstream we are following, but an exiled prince who rightly rejects all forms of "social" rehabilitation. Two episodes in the film, Ventura's two incursions into places where he is out of place, two confrontations with his brothers in colour who have themselves played along with the integration process, provide a striking illustration of this. The first is the

Jacques Rancière, "La lettre de Ventura", *Trafic*, No. 61, Spring 2007.

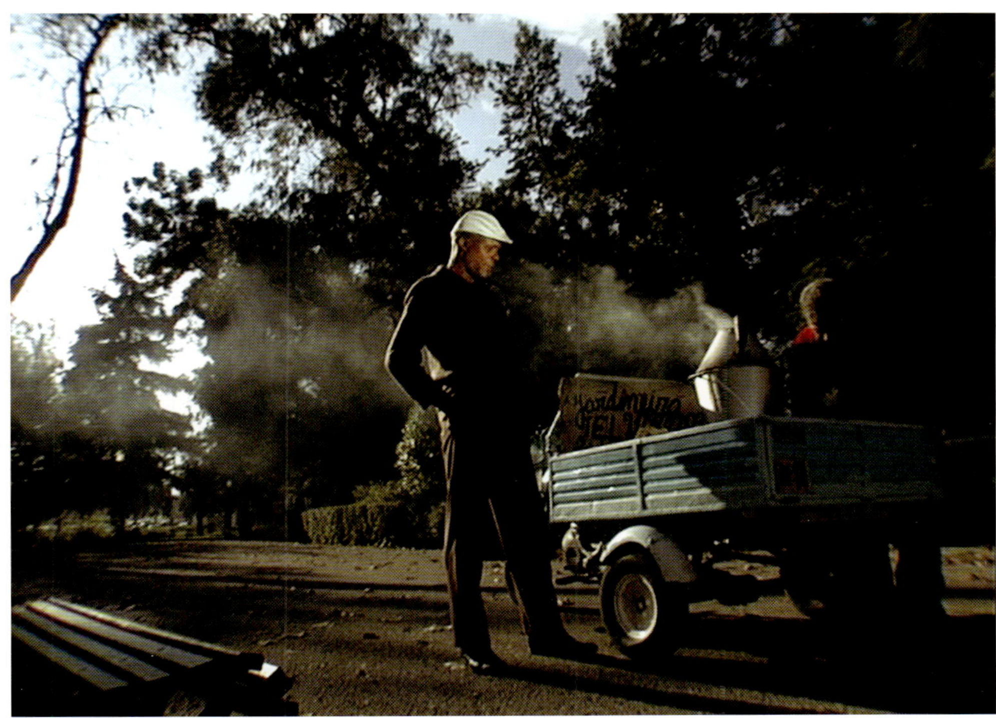

visit to the brand new apartment where the municipal employee, standing at the window, lists the benefits the sports and cultural facilities in the area will offer Ventura's "wife" and "children". Ventura, a black silhouette in the foreground, seen from the back, slowly and majestically raises one arm towards the ceiling: "It's full of spiders," he simply says. With this one gesture the tables are turned between the social housing manager and the beneficiary of his bounty. In his attitude, the former bricklayer has brought together two arts that tradition keeps apart: the art of the means, the mechanical arts of the builder of buildings, and the art of the ends, of those who know how to live in buildings. The unliveable-in white walls of a space filled with a continuous murmur of sound by Vanda's television are the opposite of the grey walls of the slum where Bete – yet to be rehoused – and Ventura, head resting on the lap of his "daughter", interpret the fantastic designs drawn randomly by life and the very mould of the building: we see that the art of living in a building mastered by the poor is a close relative of the reading of random patterns celebrated by that greatest of painters, Leonardo da Vinci.

This link between high art and the art of living of the disadvantaged is the real subject of the film. It is dramatically illustrated in another episode, the visit to the museum, if it can in fact be described as a visit. This is because the film takes us, with no narrative transition, to a room in the Gulbenkian Foundation where we find Ventura has preceded us and is leaning against a wall between the portrait of Hélène Fourment by Rubens and *Portrait of a Man* by Van Dyck. Silently, a museum employee, black like

*Colossal Youth*, 2006. Film still
© Pedro Costa

the municipal employee, comes up to Ventura and indicates that he must leave, before producing a handkerchief and wiping away any trace left on the floor by the intruder, just as the housing department official had done for the marks left by Ventura's head on the white wall of the new apartment. Later he comes to get Ventura, who is sitting in meditative silence on a Regency sofa, making him leave, still without a word, by the service entrance. The museum employee is satisfied with the job he has done: nothing to do with the cosmopolitan, light-fingered fauna frequenting the hypermarkets. Here, he says seriously to Ventura, we enjoy tranquillity, except when people like us come in, which is not often. Ventura does not respond to these comments. Sitting above him, without looking in his direction, the garden's trees in the background, he talks of the country from whence he came, of the marshes that were there before and the hundreds of frogs on the land he dug and drained, where he laid flagstones and lawn, until, with an imperial raising of his hand, he points out the place where one day he fell from scaffolding. What is important here is not the contrast between the sweat and pain of the builders of museums and the aesthetic joys of the rich. What is important is the confrontation of story with story, space with space and discourse with discourse. And indeed, this film breaks with its two predecessors in its treatment of the spoken word. The fictional story in *Bones* is characterised by a certain incapacity for verbal expression, that of Tina, the young mother unable to cope with the life to which she herself has given birth. *In Vanda's Room* adopted, along the lines of a documentary, the tone of a private conversation. *Colossal Youth* places periods of silence between two distinct types of speech. On the one hand, there is the conversation which continues in Vanda's new room, the bedroom of the mother who, a little thicker in the waist, has "settled down", a room overfilled by the marital bed with its supermarket aesthetic and continuously occupied by the noise of the television set whose screen we cannot see. Here, Vanda tells us in the same intimate tones of her difficult return to normal life. As for Ventura, he is not a conversationalist. He frequently falls silent, making felt the full weight of the dark mass of his body or the force of a gaze that may be judging what it sees, or may perhaps be lost in reverie, but which in any event resists all interpretation. The words that emerge from this silence, and which seem to be nourished by it, vary between pithy comments reminiscent of an epitaph or a hemistich from a classical tragedy, and lyricism. It is in this latter mode that he describes for us, behind an interlocutor towards whom his eyes never turn, his departure from Cape Verde in a big aircraft on 19 August 1972, which reminds us of another departure, that of a poet and his two friends in a tiny car on the thirty-first day of August 1914.

Listening to these heartfelt words that seem to issue directly from the inner depths of a whole being and its history, rather than simply from the lips of a speaker, it is difficult not to think of the art of filmmakers Danièle Huillet and Jean Marie Straub, to whom Pedro Costa has devoted a film. They transformed Vittorini's narratives into an oratorio score which they put in the mouths of proud men of the people who, reciting the text without a glance at any of their interlocutors, testify to the fact that the poor have just the same capacity to work with clever hands, to speak with nobility and to build a new world for all. We can feel here, more than in any other film by Pedro Costa, the resonance with what Huillet and Straub taught us in film. In terms of Straubian poetry and politics, the components of this film are nevertheless disparate. The nobility of commonplace lives is expressed in two distinct modes: the first is the conversational mode of *In Vanda's Room*, the other the "literary" mode suited to that mythical space defined by Ventura's wanderings between slums and new housing, between past and present, Africa and Portugal. But the grand discourse of which Ventura is the sole source here – occasionally somewhat upstaging Vanda and her conversation – shows the same patchwork composition. This is illustrated by the superb letter episode with variations which gives the film its refrain: a letter sent by the émigré to the woman left behind in the home country, a letter expressing both the daily reality of work and suffering and a love that promises the beloved a hundred thousand cigarettes, a car, a dozen dresses and a cheap bouquet. This is the letter whose recitation Ventura variously modulates in order to teach it to Lento, who is illiterate. He sometimes recites it as if lost in a daydream, and sometimes, on the contrary, with the authority of a teacher hammering every word into an unwilling brain. This is in a way the only wealth Ventura possesses, the literary grandeur of the self-taught man who "each day learns new words, beautiful words, just for the two of us, just the right size for us, like pyjamas in fine silk". But Pedro Costa composed the letter from two different sources: from real migrants' letters – like those for which he once took on the role of postman and which gave him access to Fontainhas – and from a letter by a poet, one of the last sent by Robert Desnos to Youki from Flöha camp. The words of the French poet who died at Terezin merge with those of literate migrants to form a musical score of the kind hewn by Danièle Huillet and Jean Marie Straub from the texts of Vittorini. Lento will never learn the letter - and indeed no longer needs it - but, in a dwelling ravaged by fire, Ventura the madman, the nobleman, will always stretch out a hand and place it hand in his, his eyes turned away, and confer upon him a tragic dignity, the right to shed tears over the misfortunes of his friend, as his friend sheds tears over his own.

The difference in poetic stance is also a difference in politics. In order to assert for men of the people a political dignity identical to their aesthetic dignity, the Straubs dismissed day-to-day misery from both concerns and language. Their manual workers and peasants stand only before the powers of nature and myth to give us several hours of communism directly, several hours of tangible equality. But Ventura, despite the letter that gives the film its momentum, offers no form of communism, past, present or future. To the end he continues to be the Outsider, the one who comes from far away to testify to the possibility for every human being to possess a destiny and to be equal to that destiny. In the Vittorini films of the Straubs, dialectic dispute and lyrical capacity are ultimately fused together in the collective epic of an eternal communism. With Pedro Costa there is no epic unity: political concerns cannot, in order to glorify common humanity, be ripped away from the painful birth of the lives of ordinary folk. The capacity of the poor continues to be painfully split between Vanda's intimate conversation and Ventura's tragic soliloquy. There are no far horizons of common adventure, no clenched fist of the irreconcilable rebel to conclude *Colossal Youth*. The film ends, as if elegantly bowing out, in Vanda's room, where Ventura, the man who invents children for himself, is charged with the task of babysitting, although we cannot be sure whether it is indeed he who is looking after Vanda's little girl or the child who is watching over the repose of a broken man. The faith in art as testimony to the greatness of the poor – to the greatness of all human beings – shines through here more than ever. But it is no longer the faith that sees in that greatness the affirmation of salvation. This is perhaps the new locus for the irreconcilability of which Pedro Costa is today's leading poet.

[Jacques Rancière]

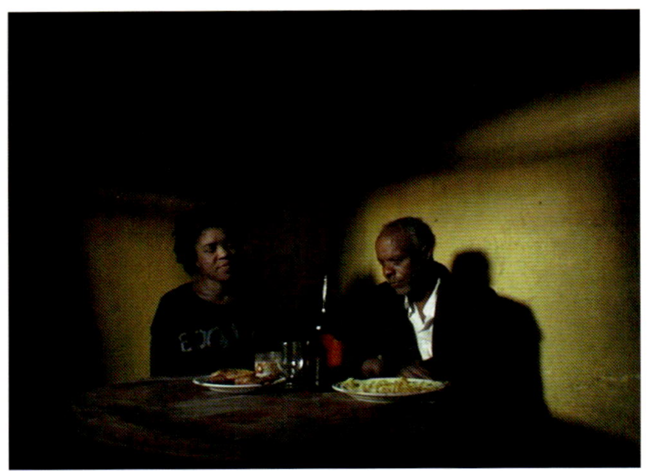

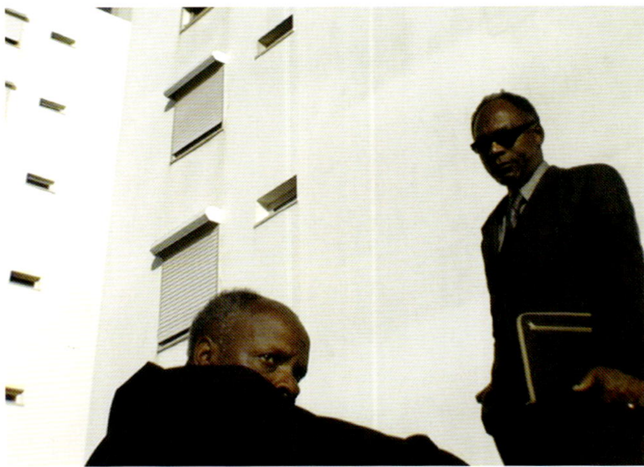

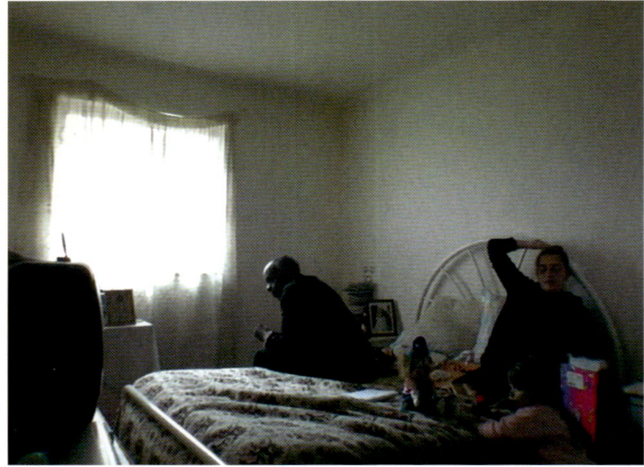

*Colossal Youth*, 2006. Film stills

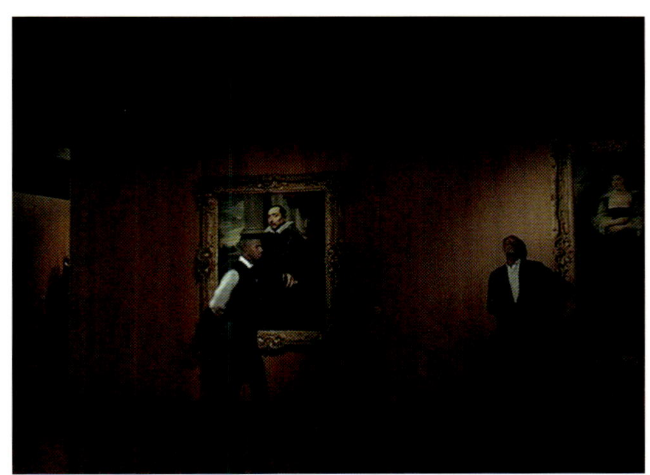

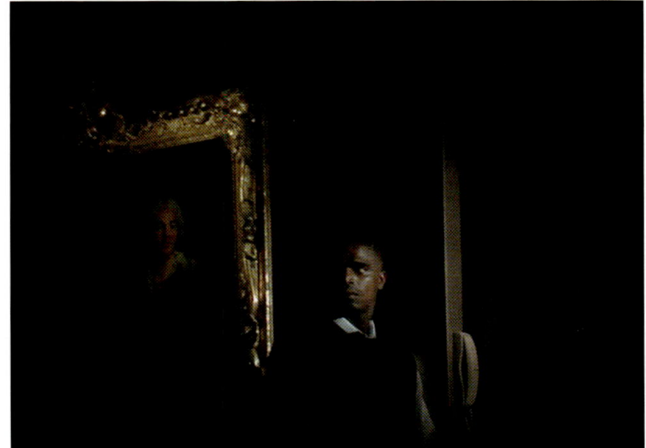

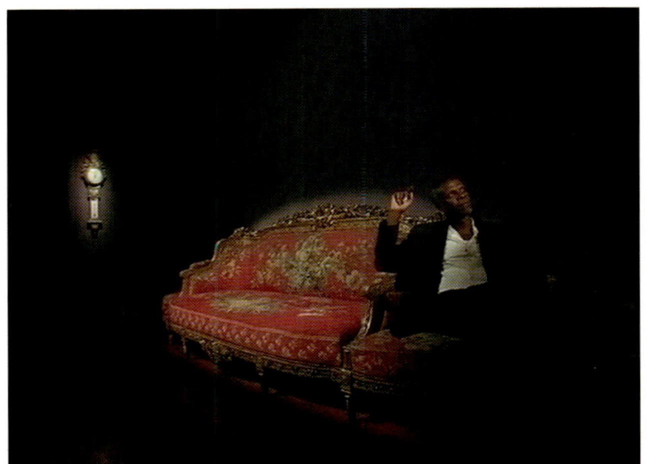

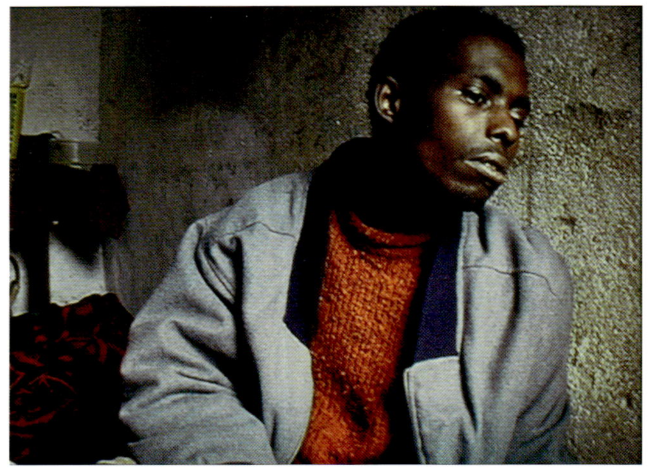

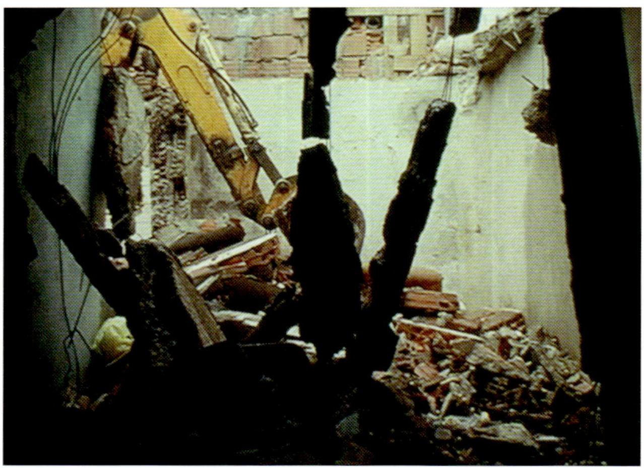

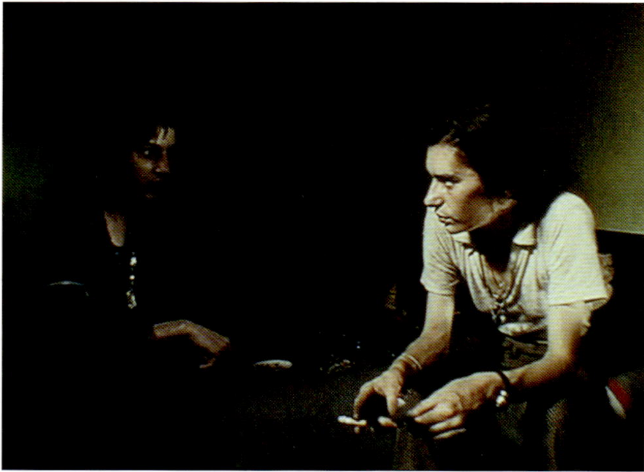

*In Vanda's room*, 2000. Film stills

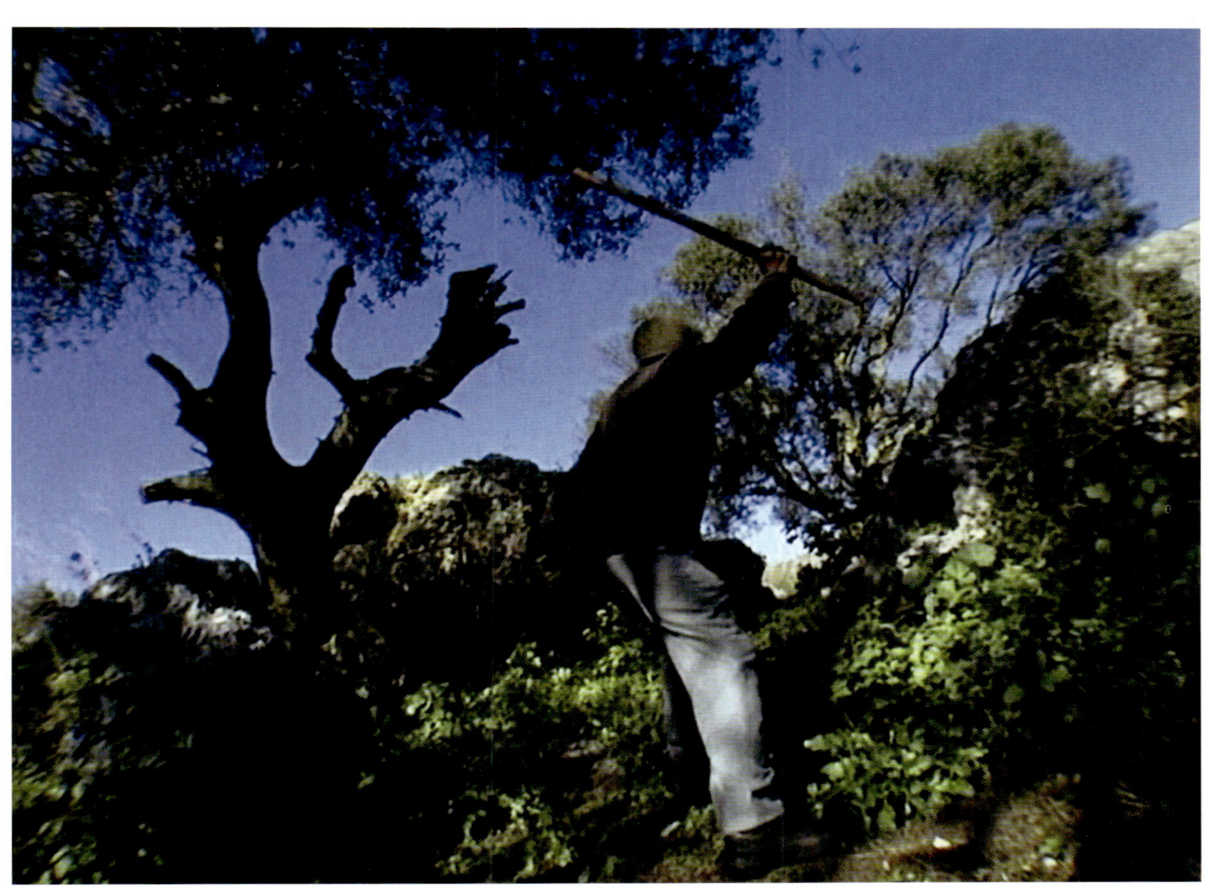

*Tarrafal*, 2007. Film still

# A Group Exhibition. 70s. Photography and Everyday Life

## Horizons of a New Photographic Geography

One of the most recognisable qualities of photography is its capacity to induce and confer interest upon the most unexpected subjects. In fact, the singularity of photography derives from this ability to reshape relatively insignificant events and matters, thus affording them an aesthetic and conceptual value. Throughout history, this reshaping ability has exerted a crucial influence on our individual and collective imaginations, broadening the range of subjective expressiveness and enabling us to gain another perception of everyday life. Due to this photogenic effect, the most common and banal aspects of daily life can acquire an unprecedented importance, forming one of the axes through which people experience reality, in the space between what is factual and what is fictional.

Yet, what then are the reasons for this focus on the 1970s? What is its singularity in comparison with other moments in recent history? We shall begin by acknowledging two of our most immediate motivations: the 1970s were marked by a series of changes and social reflections that had decisive effects on our ways of understanding and dealing with living conditions and lifestyles, with the questions that were raised about individual identity and with many of the characteristic and structuring aspects of modernity; and, correlated with this, the panorama of image-making practices, in particular the production of photographic images, adapted to, incorporated and reflected these societal phenomena, giving rise to other artistic and communicational horizons for photography. At the same time, this exhibition seeks to signal *a certain inflection towards the photographic*, also marked by the appearance of a common platform (rarely found before then) between the more specific medium of photography and the multidisciplinary field of the plastic and other visual arts. It can therefore be said that, in this decade, it was possible to detect a relative narrowing of the gap between the so-called "photographer-artists" and the "artists who make use of photography", and that one of the factors behind their coming together in this way was their growing need, motivation and attention for dealing with the instants, objects and places of everyday life.

*The 1970s. Photography and Everyday Life* is a group exhibition bringing together 23 photographers who, in their differences and points of affinity, make it possible to compose a broad spectrum of images and conceptual, technical and aesthetic attitudes, framed within the context of a new social and artistic outlook on photography and everyday life. And it is also important to recognise that this spectrum remains significant and up-to-date, a fact that also makes this retrospective look at the subject highly relevant to us nowadays. Without indulging in nostalgic feelings or revisionist impulses, recentring our attention on the 1970s is a way of understanding recent genealogies in which a new geography of the photographic is defined, made of advances and retreats, dynamic conflicts and creative proximities. In short, a moment when what was at stake was the status and scope of photography as a medium.

All of the works that are exhibited here were produced in this decade, a period that also corresponded to the full artistic affirmation of most of the photographers taking part. In some ways, this is also an exhibition about the *emergence of a generation*. In this exhibition, we find many different methods and types of images: ranging from the most diverse (re)affirmations of the documentary, passing through the practice of appropriating pre-existing images (from public and private archives), and through staged images and documents of performative gestures, to works that combine both image and text.

**Photographs by Laurie Anderson, Claudia Andujar, Christian Boltanski, Victor Burgin, Sophie Calle, William Eggleston, Hans-Peter Feldmann, Alberto García-Alix, David Goldblatt, Karen Knorr, Viktor Kolář, Ana Mendieta, Fina Miralles, Gabriele & Helmut Nothhelfer, J.D. Okhai Ojeikere, Carlos Pazos, Anders Petersen, Eugene Richards, Allan Sekula, Cindy Sherman, Malick Sidibé, Ed van der Elsken & Kohei Yoshiyuki**

Consequently, this is a group of artists engaged in the reformulation and reinvention of the visual arts in the context of a renewed faith in the art that witnesses and is inextricably involved with social reality, or, in other words, these are image-making practices that call into question the conventions of the history of art and photography and that, simultaneously, open up a space and channel our attention to individual experience, affirming their differences, singularities and idiosyncrasies.

Returning to the 1970s is, in some ways, akin to reviving a moment that is not very far removed from our history, in which we can identify a significant series of changes at the level of mentalities and social attitudes that, at a more local or global level, had repercussions on cultural, ideological and civilisational imaginations. At this level, let us begin by highlighting the phenomenon of social fragmentation, which accompanied the increased public protagonism of identities and sub-cultures that had previously been repressed or marginalised. Amongst the questions that were raised about gender, sexual orientation and ethnic and racial characteristics, multiple sensitivities and discursive fronts were organised, affording concrete expression to a vast and effective process of decentring identity and, consequently, giving rise to a new posture of the subject in relation to himself, in the light of his own singular conditions and predispositions, as well as his relationship with society.

In the field of the visual arts, this was also a period of important changes. From the criticism of modernism to the rejection of the conventions of modern art, "post-modern" art was projected upon a more heterodox, transgressive and transdisciplinary horizon. And it was within this framework of opportunities and deconstructions that an ever greater number of artists burst forth, more permeable to, and engaged with, their social time and ready to accept the possibility of asserting their identity as both individuals and artists. The rejection of both disciplinary purisms and a certain timeless and strictly aesthetic conception of art drove several artists to recognise that it was essential to recreate and recentre their creative universes on the basis of gestures that were more closely bound up with their experiences of reality and with the languages of daily life. It was therefore a question of constructing a vaster and more decentred context of discursive competencies for visual artists in their forms and strategies of representing the instants, objects and places of everyday life. It was in such a context that photography gradually took shape as a privileged medium and a flagship culture for the artistic panorama of the 1970s.

This means that the connection between photography and everyday life was seen as a way of re-establishing a proximity, which modernism did not fulfil, between artistic practice and social reality. Yet, in turn, the inflection of art towards the photographic, and the reflexive and critical impulse that this provoked, also led to a clarification of the potentialities and limitations of photography. It is within this framework that both the works and the photographers featured in this exhibition are intended to signal a historic moment when photography became the model of an art that "faced the world head on".

[Sérgio Mah]

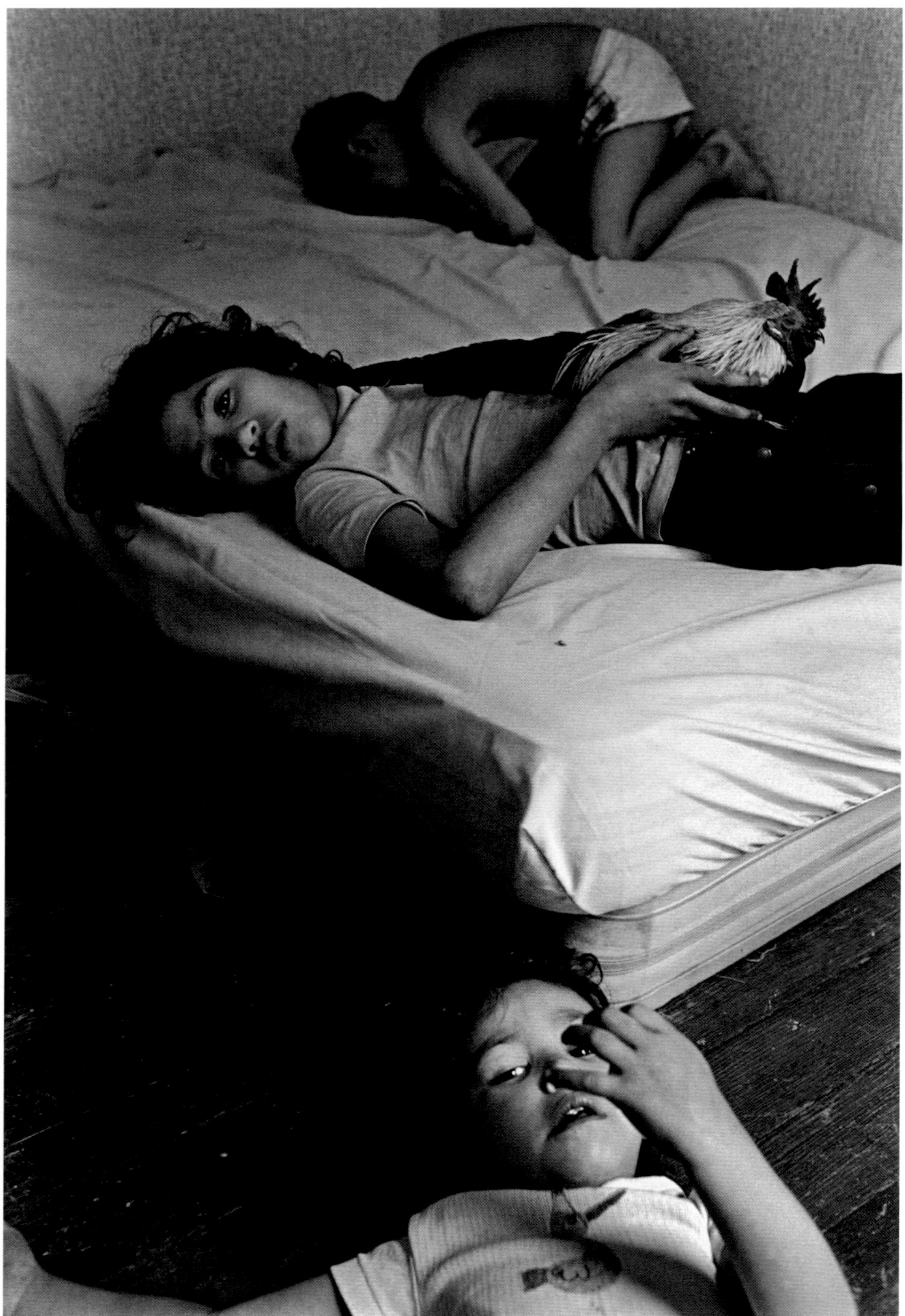

**Eugene Richards**
From the series *Dorchester Days*, 1977-1999
Courtesy of the artist

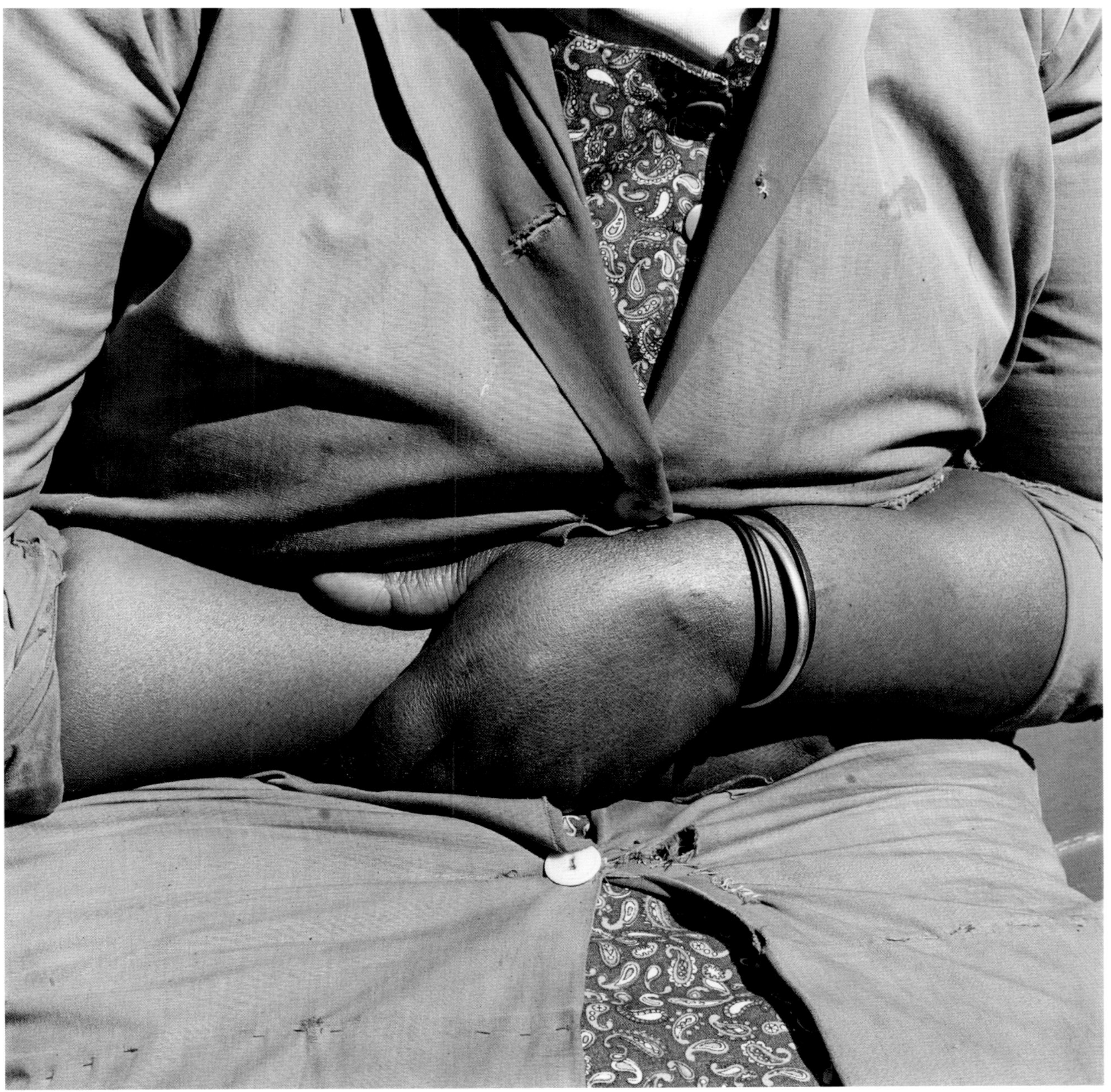

**David Goldblatt**
*Child Minder, Joubert Park, Johannesburg*. From the series *Particulars*, 1975
Courtesy of the artist; Michael Stevenson Gallery, Cape Town; Elba Benítez Gallery, Madrid

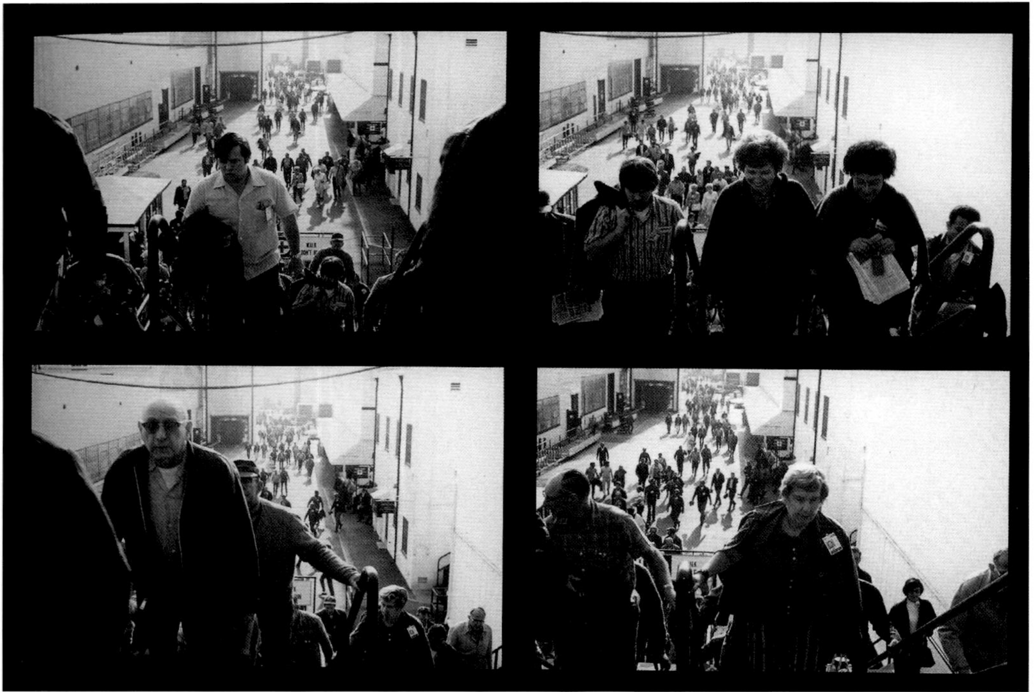

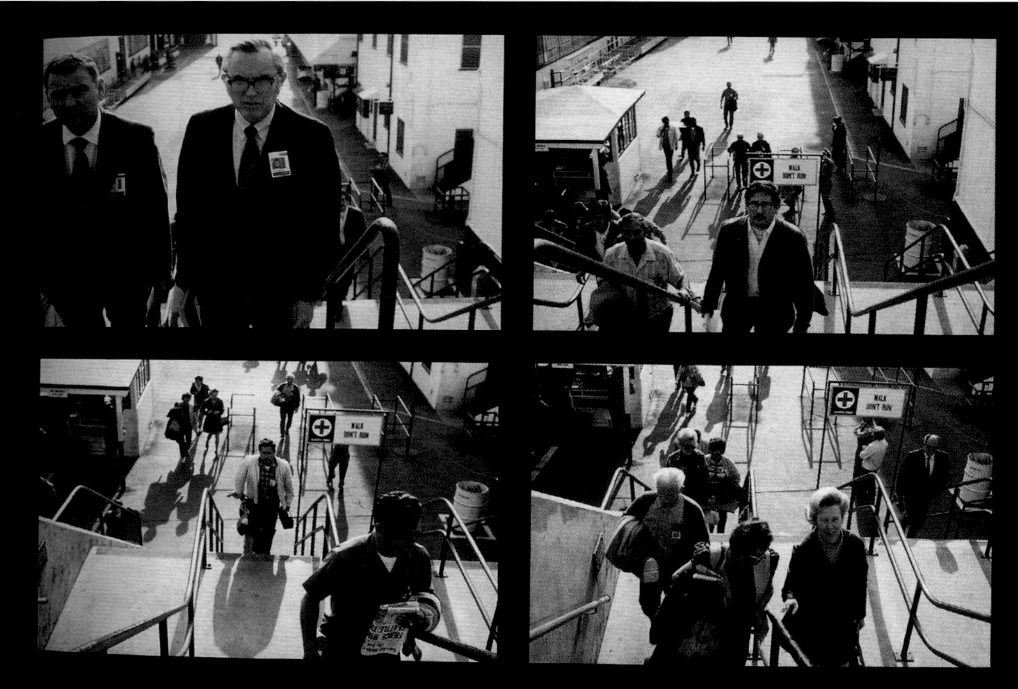


**Allan Sekula**
*Untitled Slide Sequence*, 1972
Courtesy Ellipse Foundation. Contemporary Art Collection, Cascais
© Allan Sekula

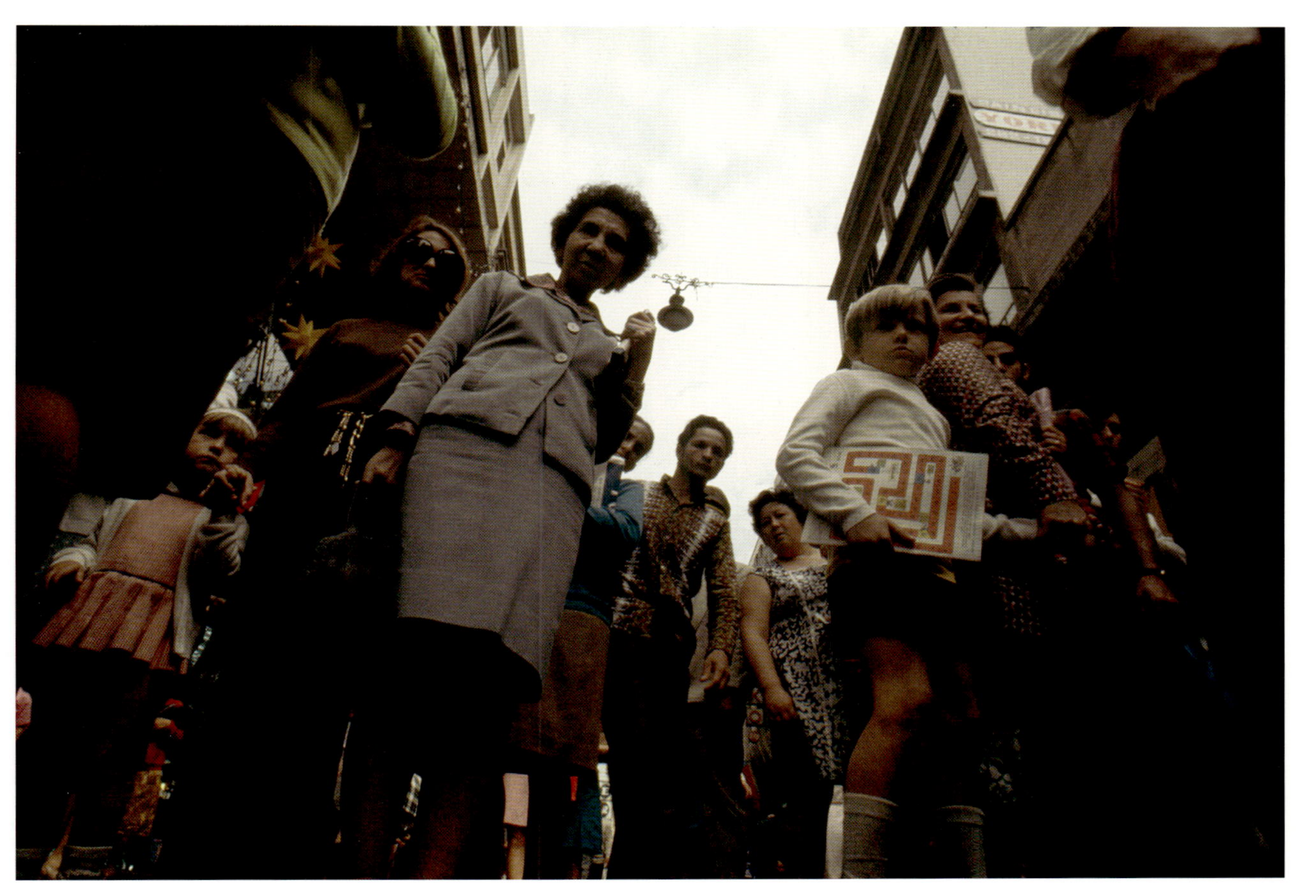

**Claudia Andujar**
From the series *Rua Direita*, 1970
Courtesy Vermelho Gallery, São Paulo, Brasil
© Claudia Andujar

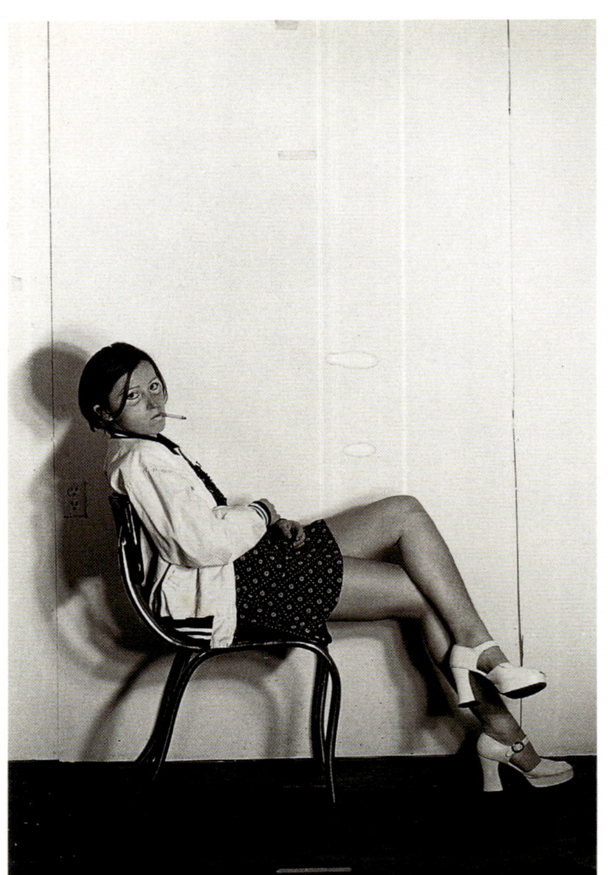

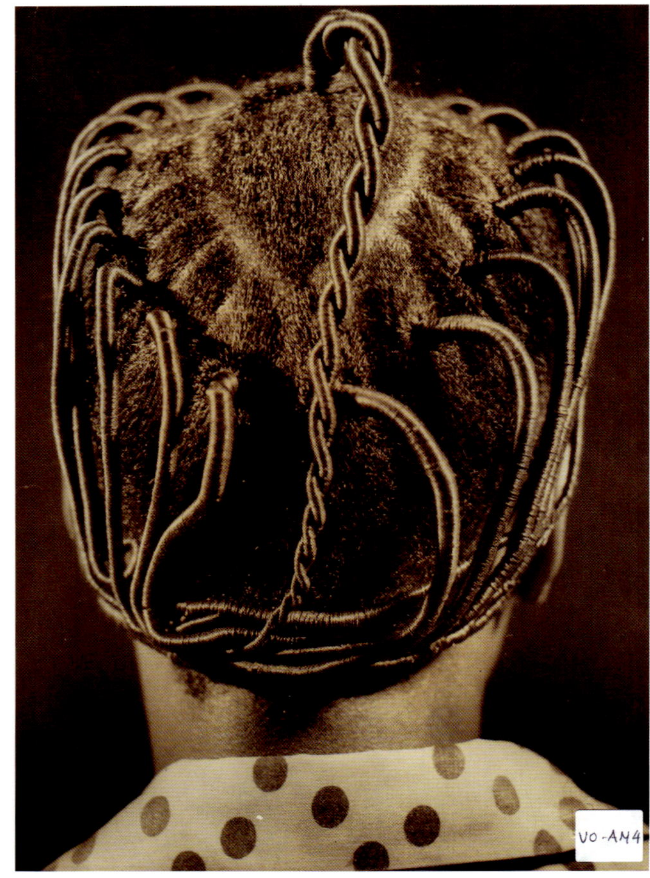

**Cindy Sherman**
Untitled. From the series *Bus Riders*, 1976
Courtesy Centro de Arte Contemporáneo de Málaga
© Cindy Sherman

**J.D. Okhai Ojeikere**
Untitled (Hair Style)
Courtesy Fifty One Fine Art Photography
© J.D. Okhai Ojeikere

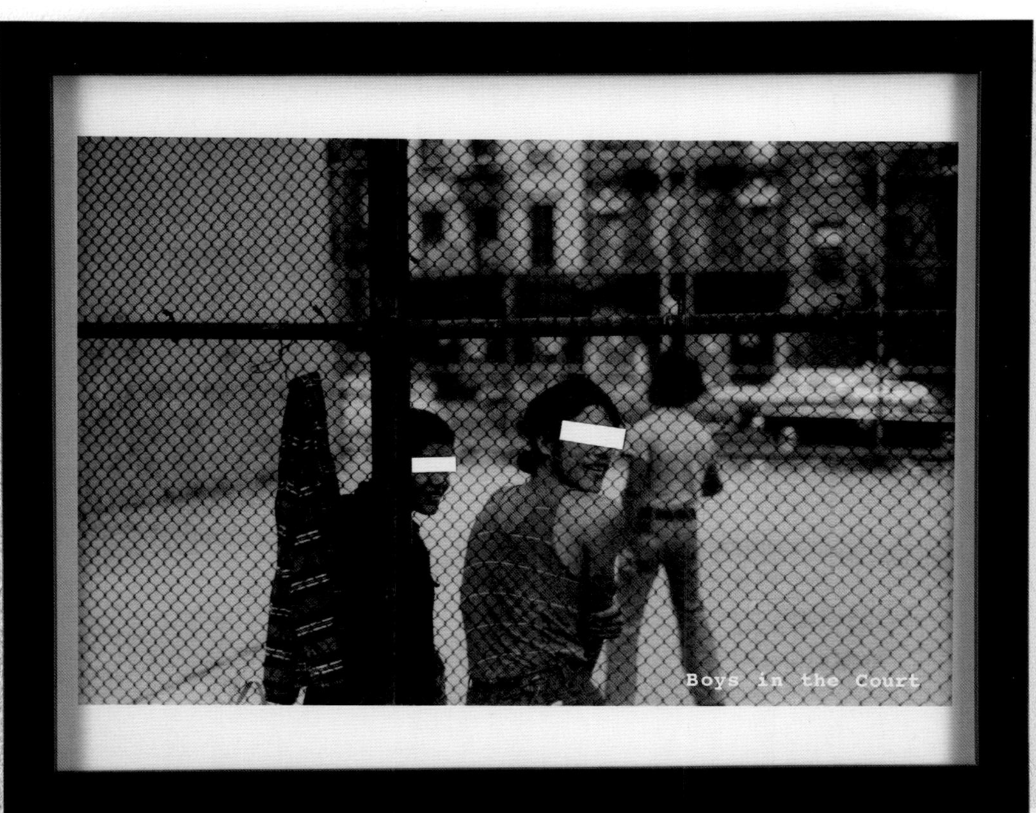


This boy and his girlfriend were watching a basketball game on Houston Street when I walked by. "I'd like a piece of you baby," he said. When I asked to take his picture, he smiled and his girlfriend said, "He don't mean nothin'. He says that to all the girls".

**Laurie Anderson**
*Fully Automated Nikon (Object / Objection / Objetivity)*, 1973. Detail
Courtesy Sean Kelly Gallery, New York. Photography Jason Wyche

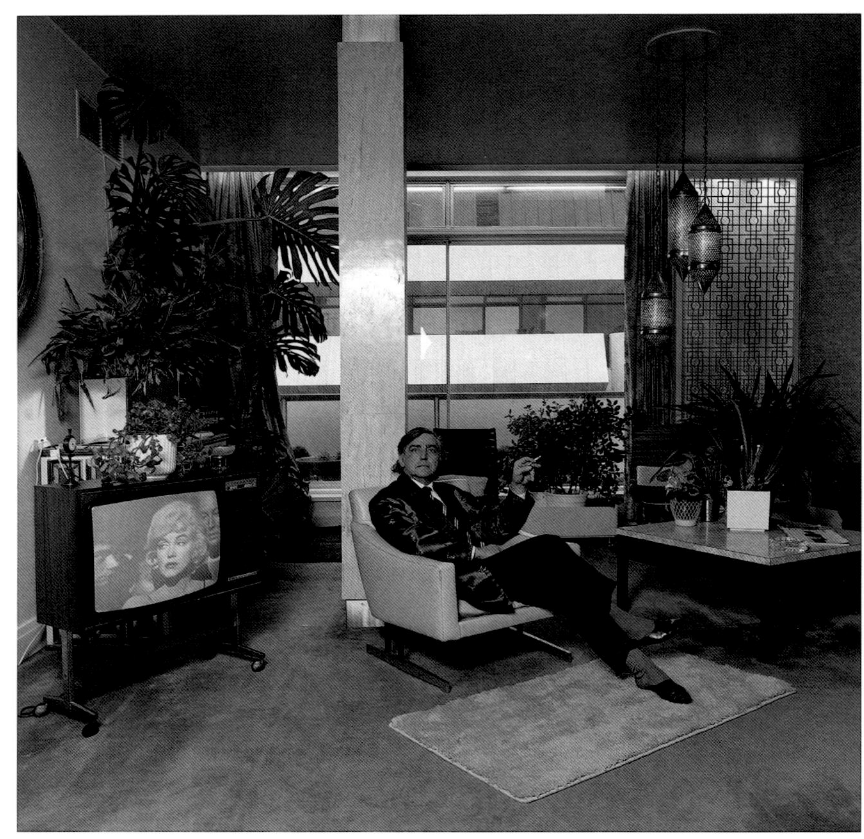

The ideal Woman must be
a mirror reflection of myself.

**Karen Knorr**
From the series *Belgravia*
Courtesy Louise & Eric Franck, London

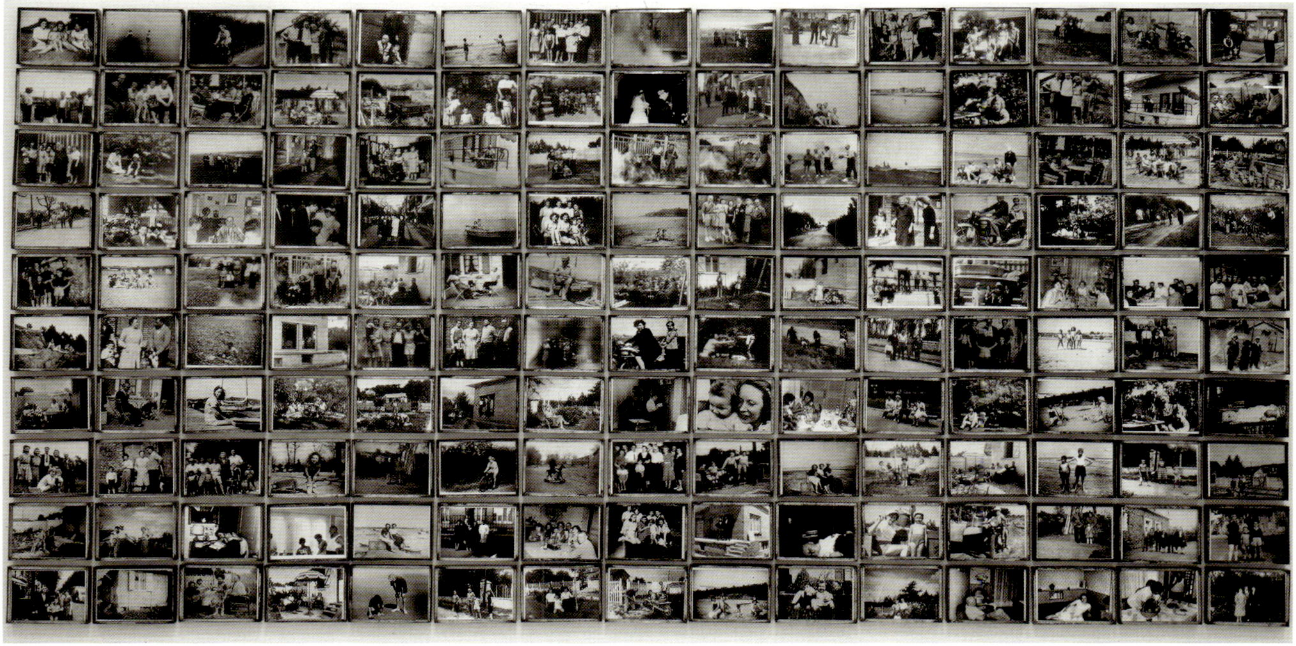

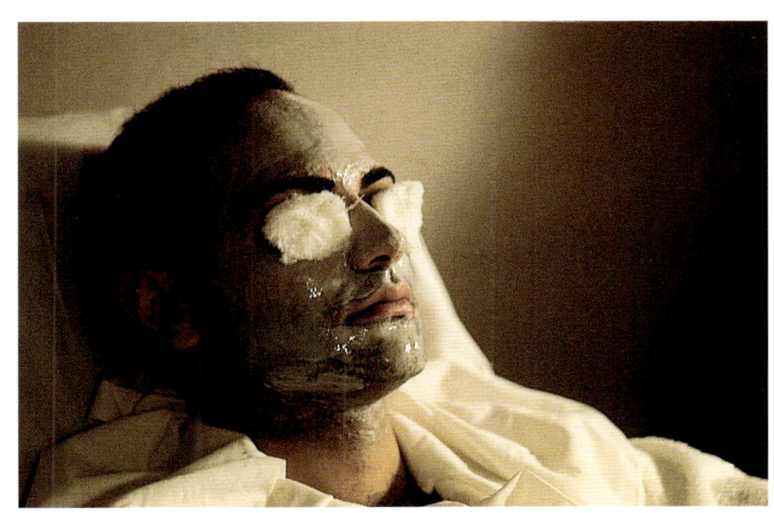

**Christian Boltanski**
*The D. Family Album*, 1971
Courtesy Collection Rhône-Alpes. Institut d'art contemporain, Villeurbanne/Lyon
© Yves Bresson, Musée d'art moderne Saint-Etienne Métropole

**Carlos Pazos**
*In Privacy*, 1977
Courtesy MACBA. Museu d'Art Contemporani de Barcelona
© Carlos Pazos

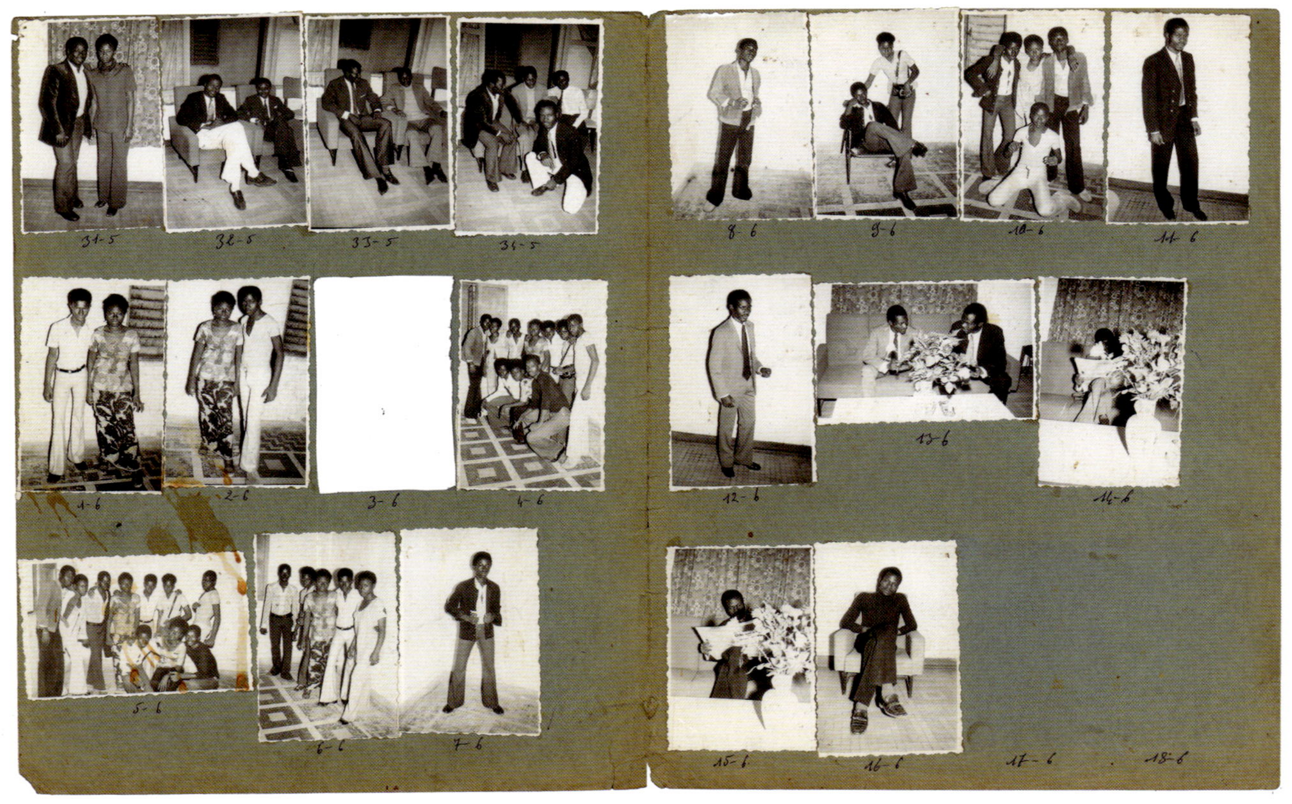


**Malick Sidibé**
*Chemises* Album, page 8
Courtesy GwinZegal Plouha

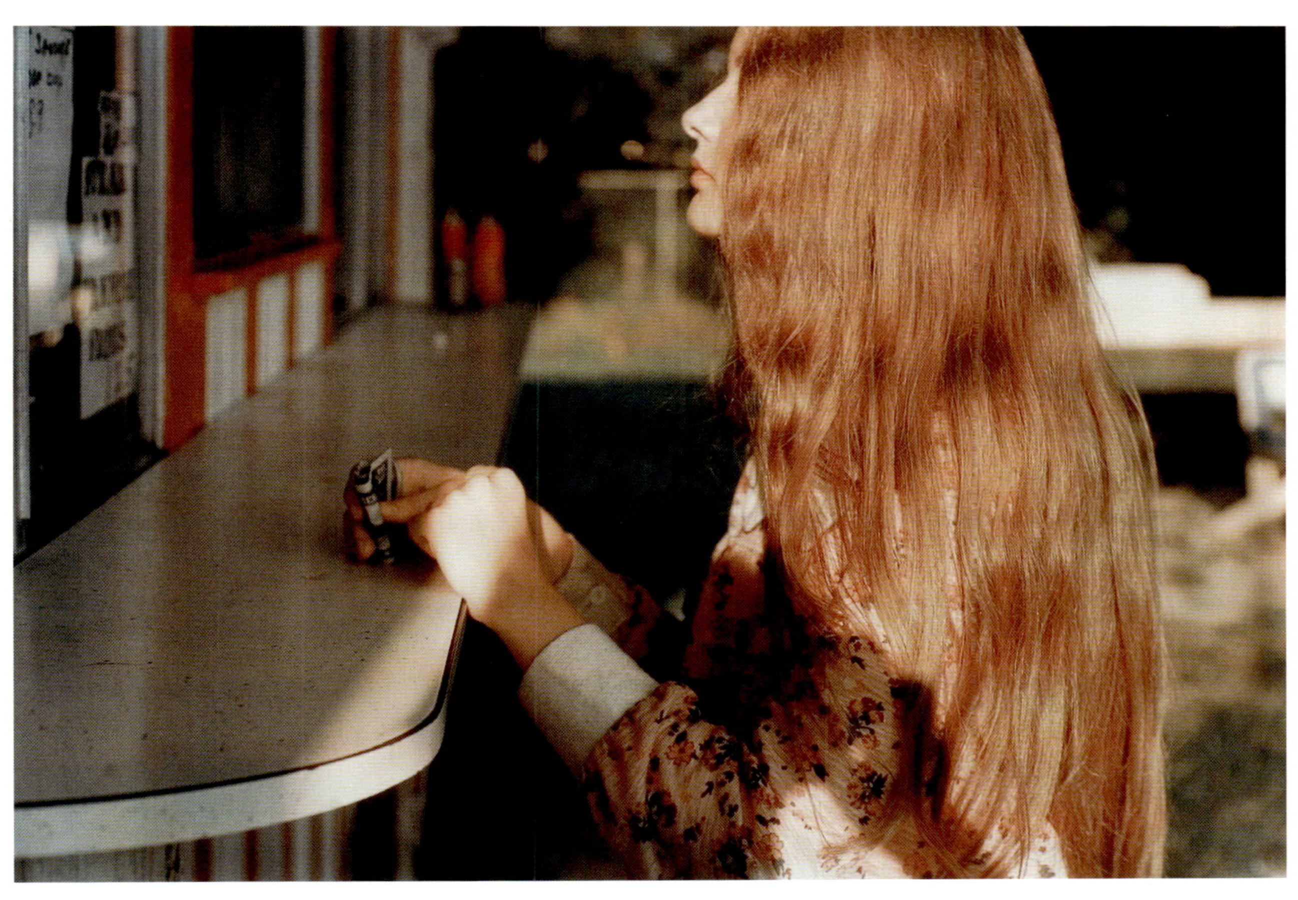

**William Eggleston**
From *The Seventies: Volume Two*, circa 1970s
Courtesy Cheim & Read, New York

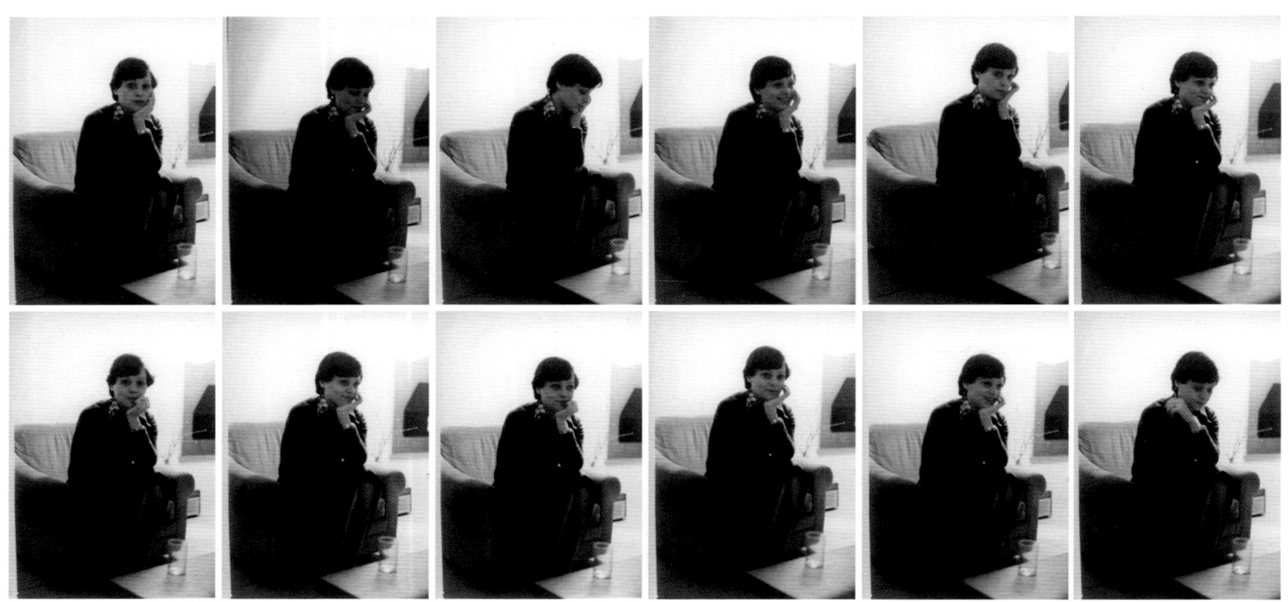

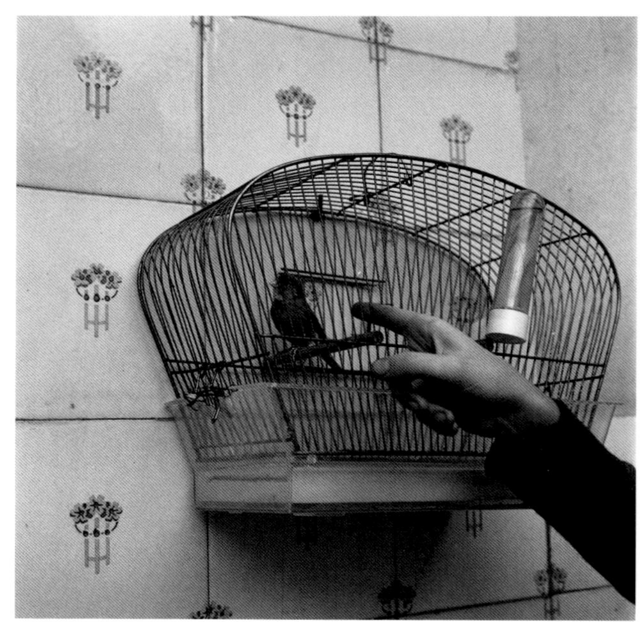

**Hans-Peter Feldmann**
*Rosanna*, 1972. From the series *Time*


**Fina Miralles**
*Relationships. The relationships between the human body and natural elements during day-to-day activities: to touch the bird (document of the work)*
Courtesy Museu d'art de Sabadell

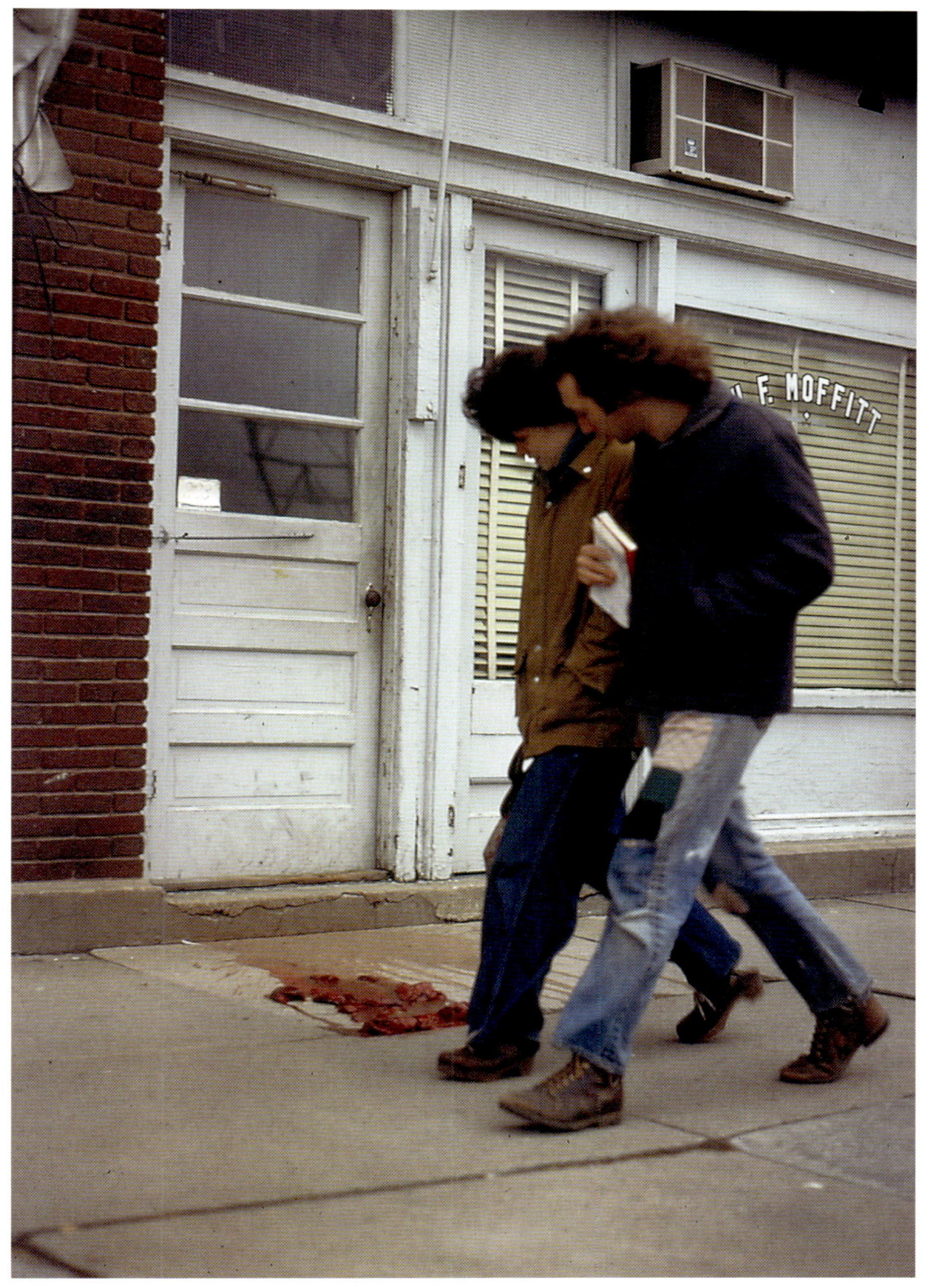


**Ana Mendieta**
From the series *People Looking at Blood, Moffitt*, 1973
Courtesy The Estate of Ana Mendieta and Galerie Lelong, New York

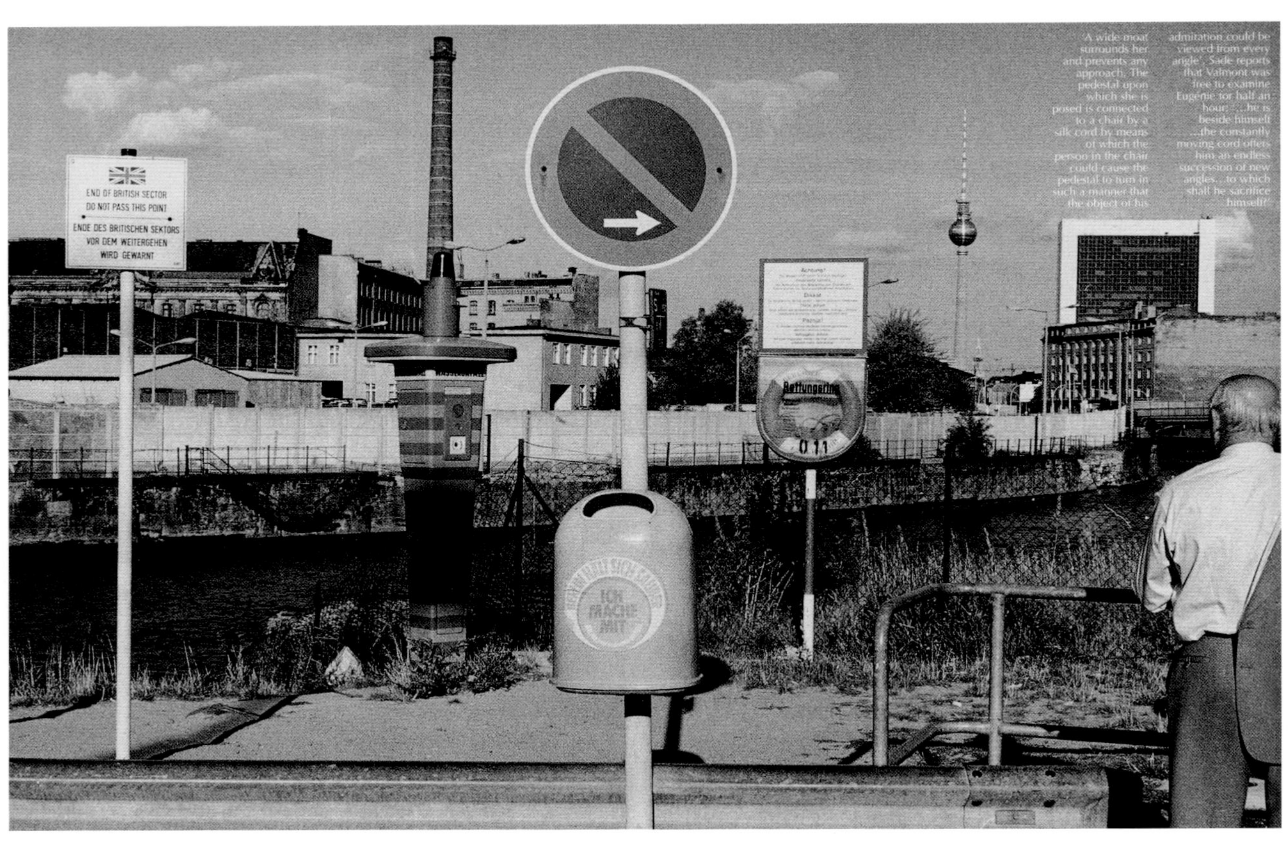


**Victor Burgin**
From the series *Zoo 78*, 1978
Courtesy Collection Eva Felten
© Victor Burgin

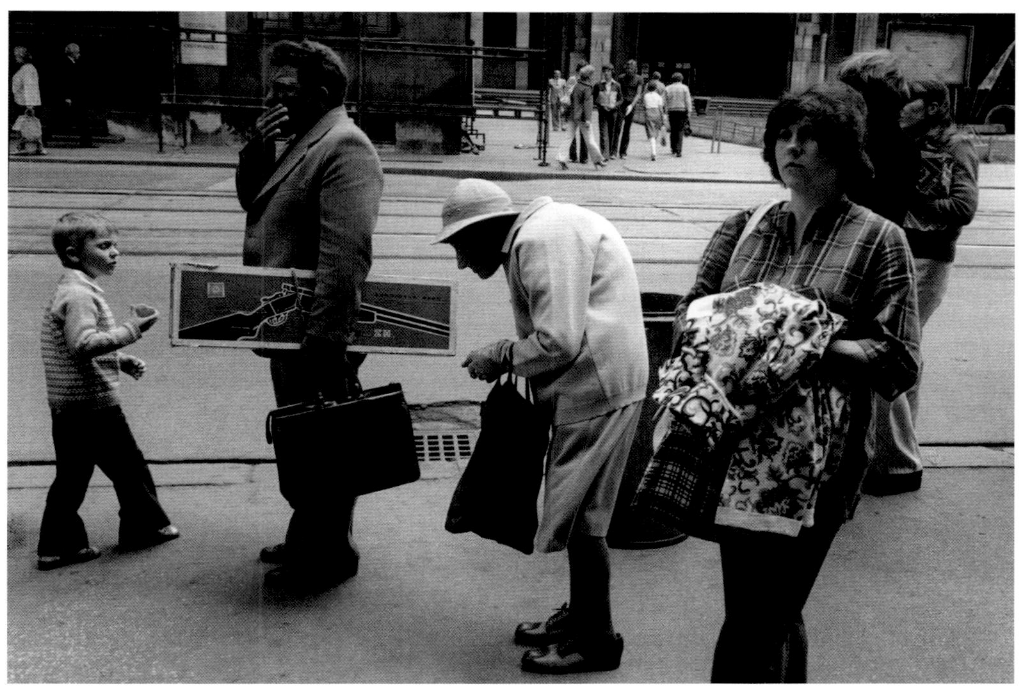

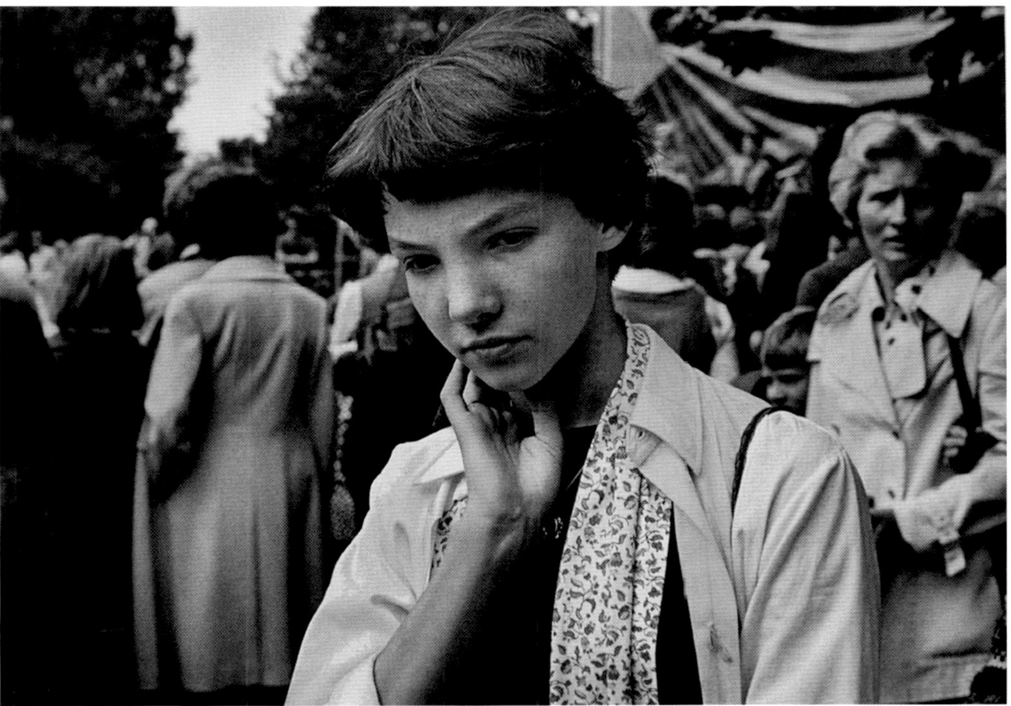

**Viktor Kolář**
From the series *Ostrava*, 1979
Courtesy of the artist


**Gabriele and Helmut Nothhelfer**
*Girl at the Protestant Church Congress in Tiergarten, Berlin*, 1978
Courtesy Galerie Berinson, Berlin

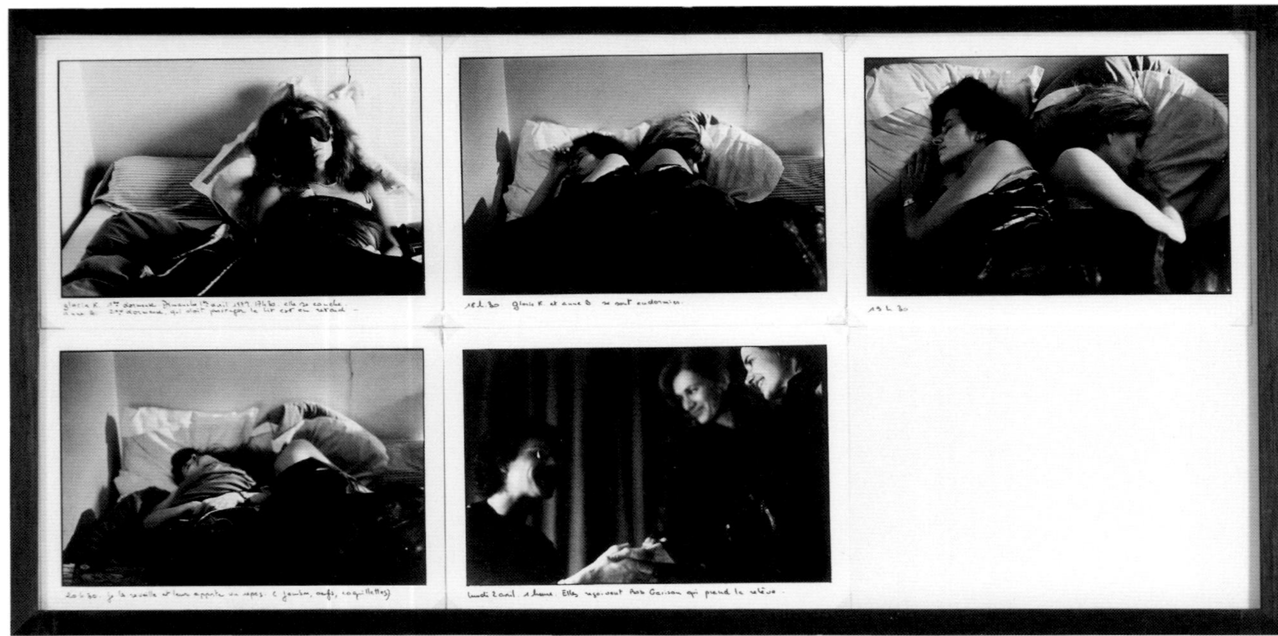

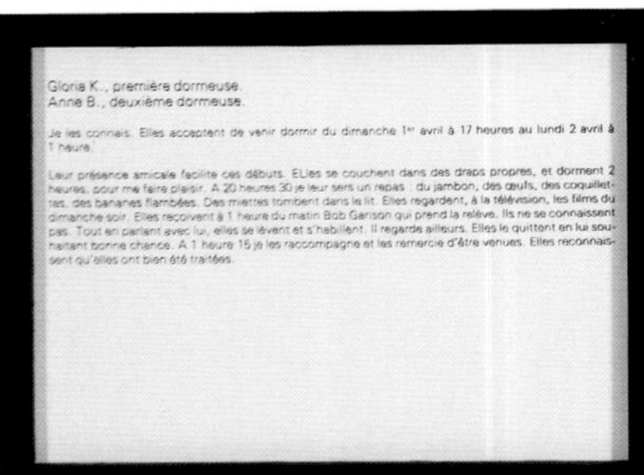

Gloria K., première dormeuse.
Anne B., deuxième dormeuse.

Je les connais. Elles acceptent de venir dormir du dimanche 1er avril à 17 heures au lundi 2 avril à 1 heure.

Leur présence amicale facilite ces débuts. ELles se couchent dans des draps propres, et dorment 2 heures, pour me faire plaisir. A 20 heures 30 je leur sers un repas : du jambon, des œufs, des coquillettes, des bananes flambées. Des miettes tombent dans le lit. Elles regardent, à la télévision, les films du dimanche soir. Elles reçoivent à 1 heure du matin Bob Garison qui prend la relève. Ils ne se connaissent pas. Tout en parlant avec lui, elles se lèvent et s'habillent. Il regarde ailleurs. Elles le quittent en lui souhaitant bonne chance. A 1 heure 15 je les raccompagne et les remercie d'être venues. Elles reconnaissent qu'elles ont bien été traitées.

**Sophie Calle**
*The Sleepers* [Les Dormeurs], 1979. Detail
"Gloria K., first sleeper.
Anne B., second sleeper.
I know them. They agree to come and sleep from Sunday 1st April at 5pm to Monday 2nd April at 1pm.
Their amicable presence makes the start easy. The get into bed in the clean sheets, and they sleep for two hours to keep me happy. At 8:30pm I serve them a meal: ham, eggs, pasta shells, flambéed bananas. Crumbs dropped onto the bed. They watch Sunday evening films on the television. At 1 am they receive Bob Garison who is taking over. They don't know each other. While talking to him, they get up and get dressed. He looks elsewhere. They take their leave wishing him luck. At 1:15 am, I see them out and thank them for coming. They say that they've been well looked after."
Photo by David Huguenin
Courtesy Fonds national d'art contemporain (Cnap). Ministère de la Culture et de la Communication, Paris. 2494.
Deposited at Carré d'Art - Musée d'Art Contemporain, Nimes

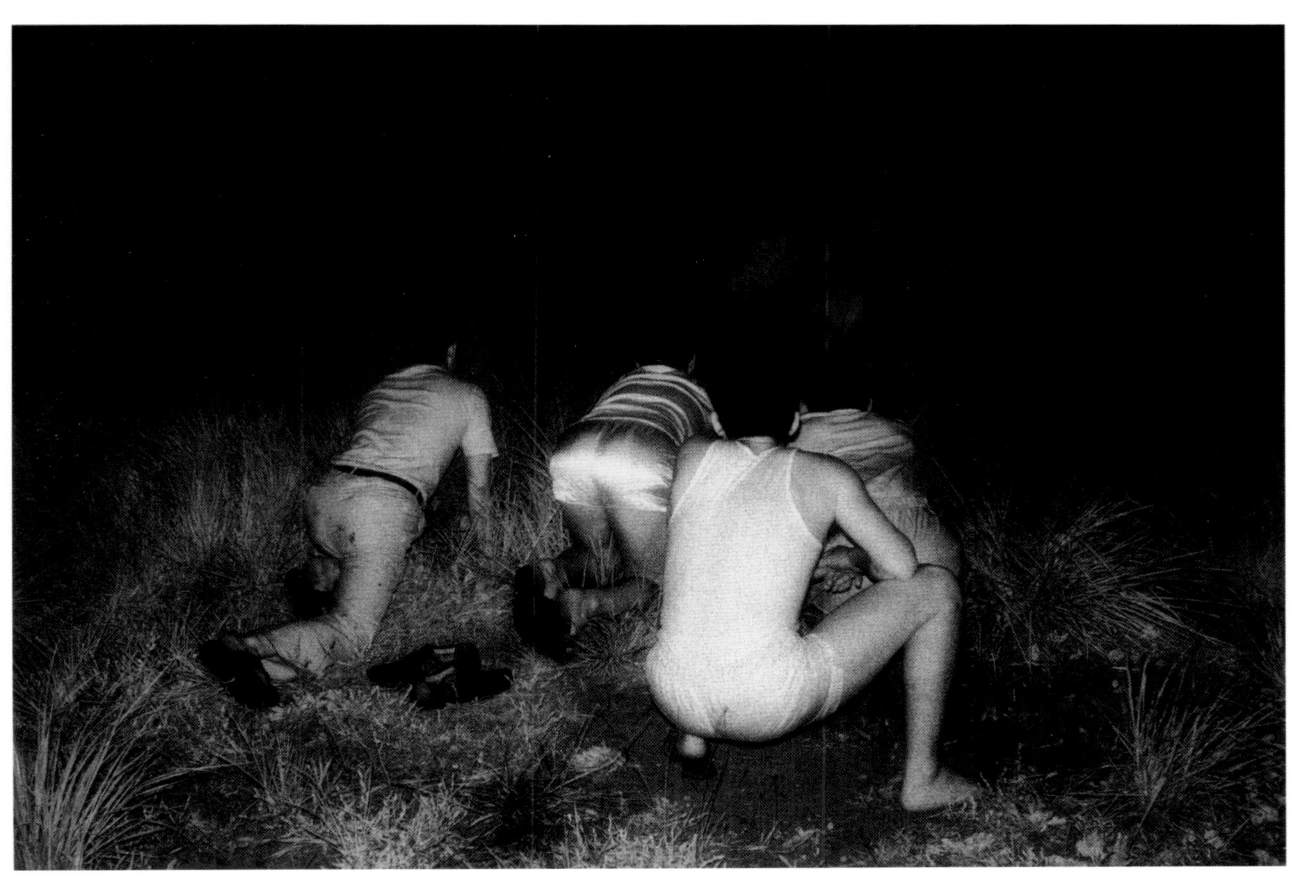

**Kohei Yoshiyuki**
Untitled, 1971. From the series *Park*
Courtesy Yossi Milo Gallery, New York

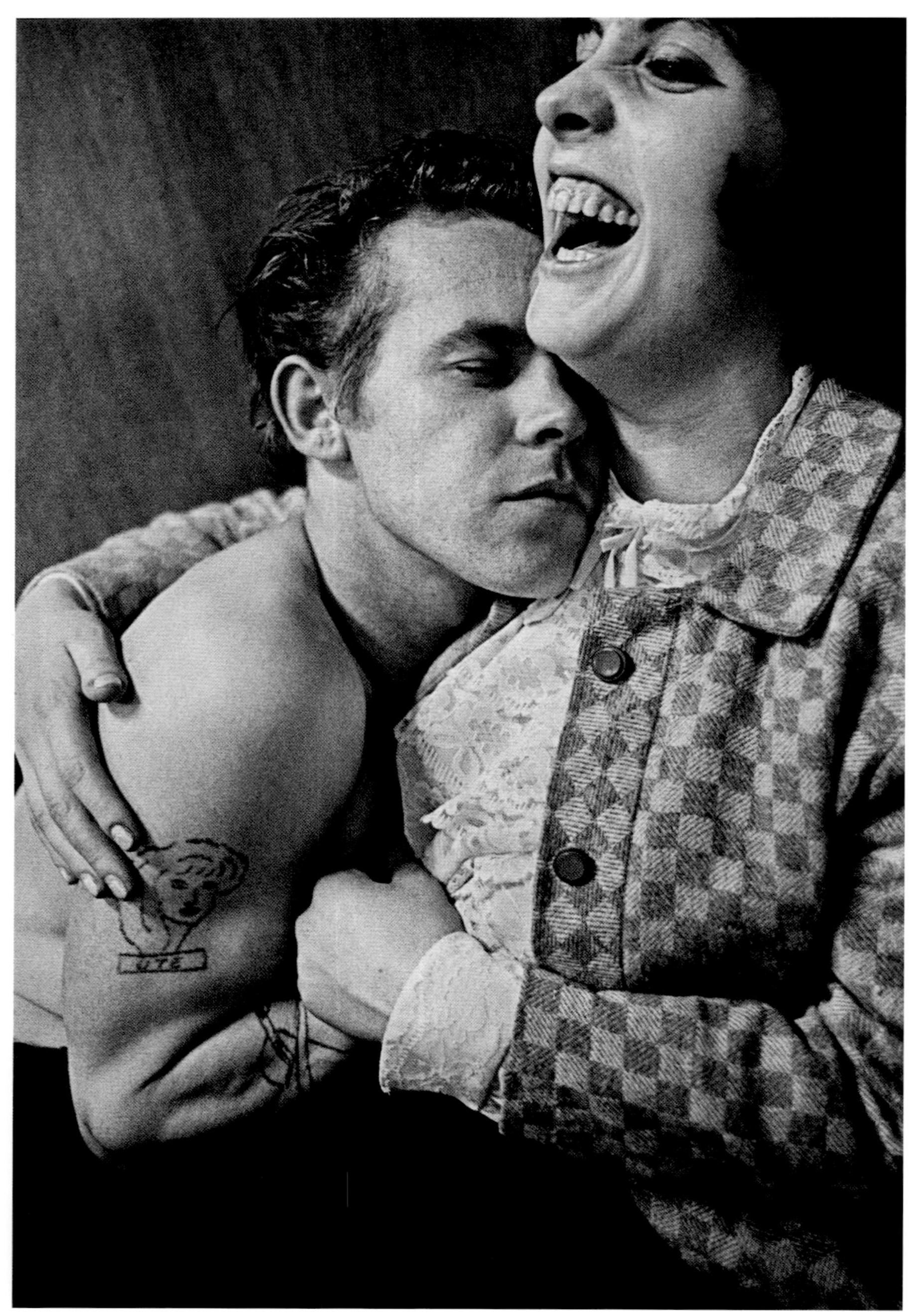

**Anders Petersen**
Untitled. From the series *Cafe Lehmitz*, 1977
Courtesy of the artist
© Anders Petersen

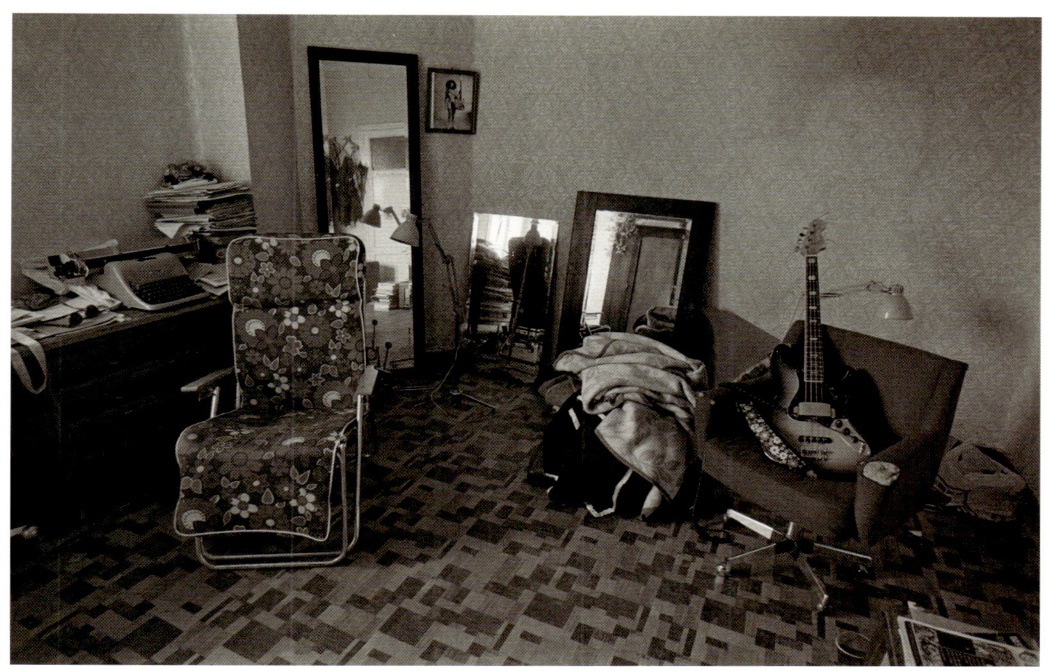

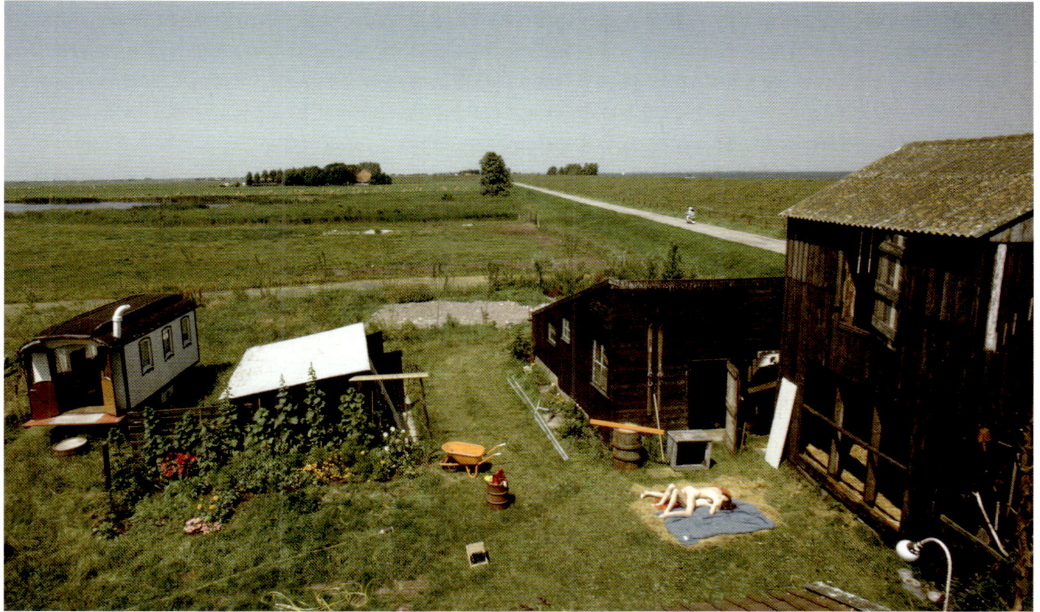

**Alberto García-Alix**
*Room at Paseo Imperial*, 1978
Courtesy of the artist


**Ed van der Elsken**
*Couple making love, Edam*, 1970
Courtesy Nederlands Fotomuseum, Rotterdam / Annet Gelink Gallery, Amsterdam

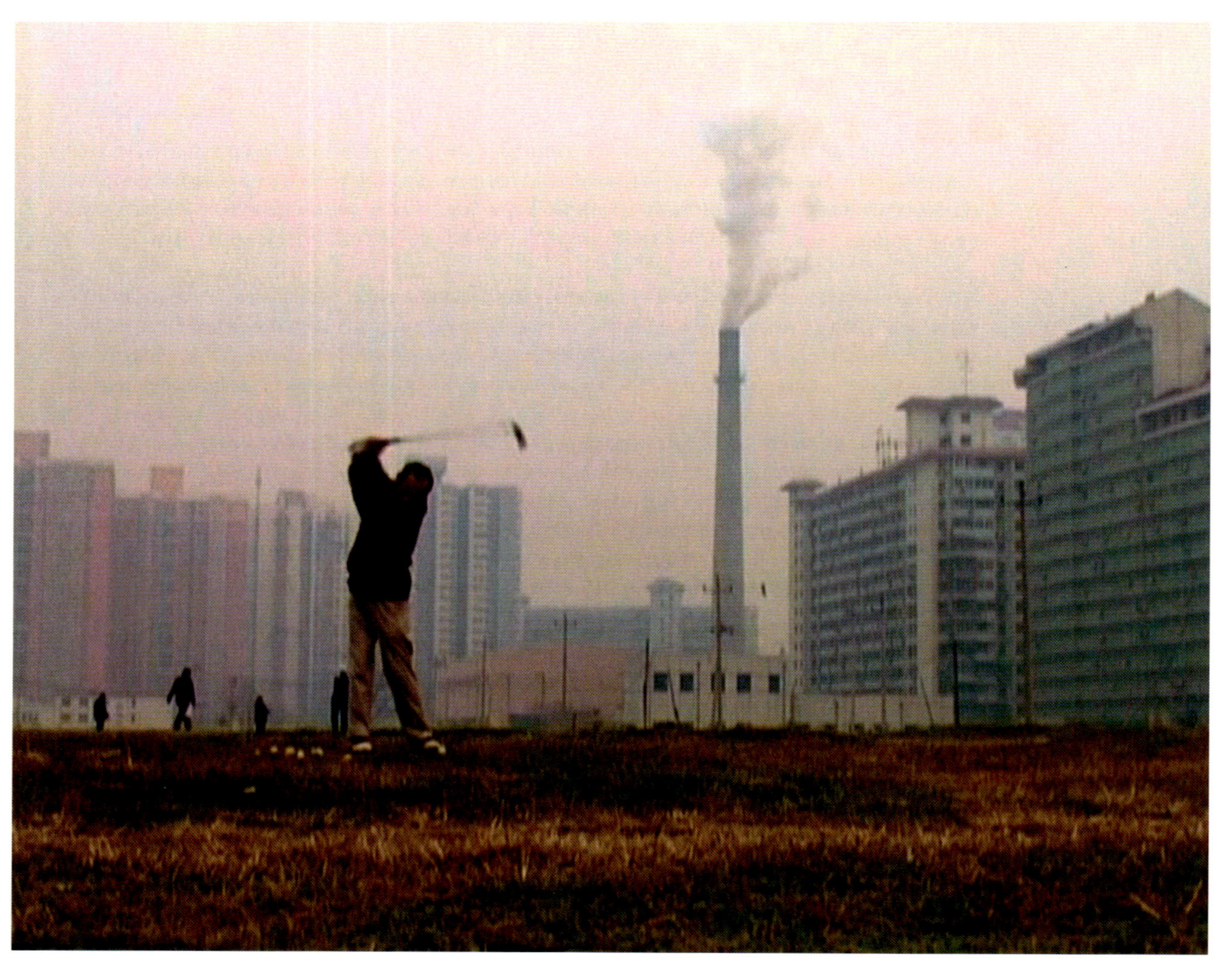

*City Scene*, 2004. Film stills
Courtesy L.A. Galerie - Lothar Albrecht, Frankfurt

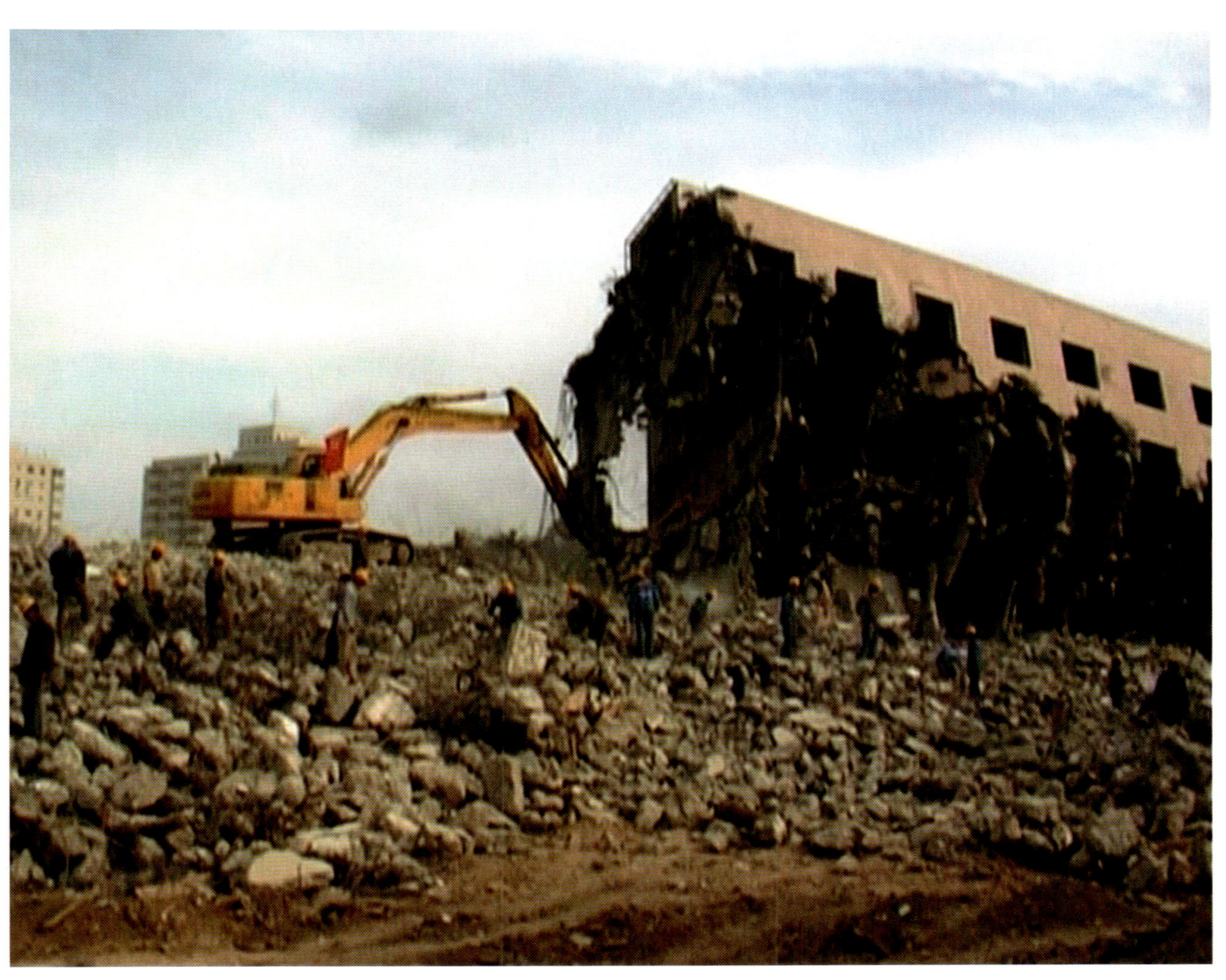

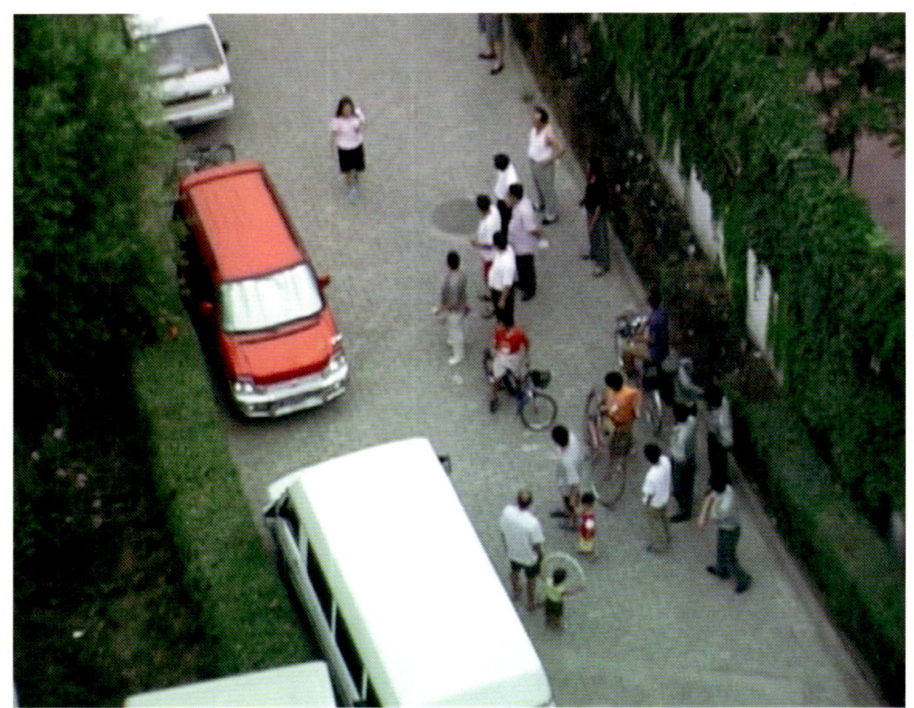

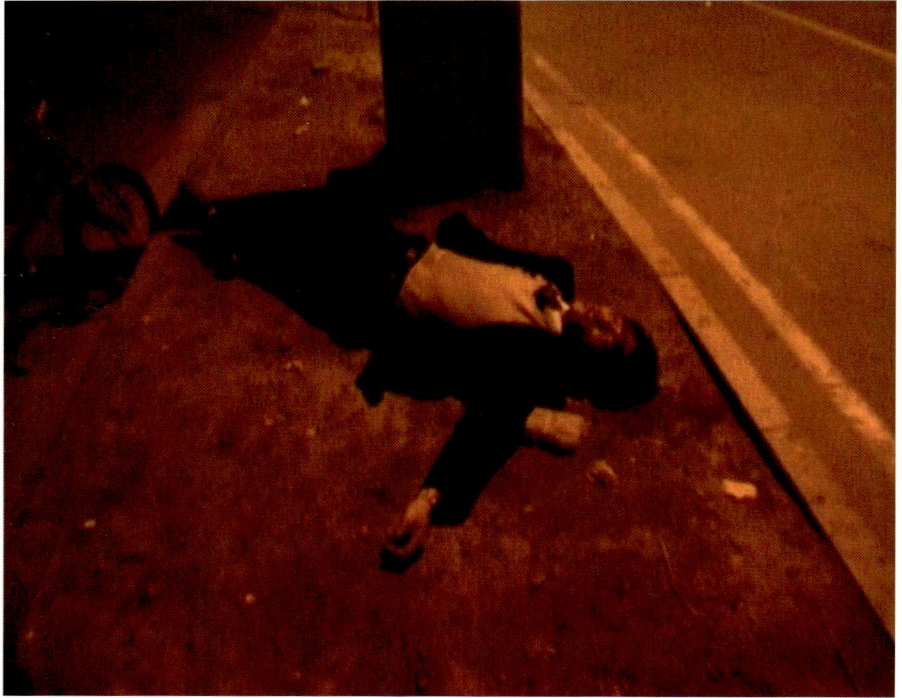

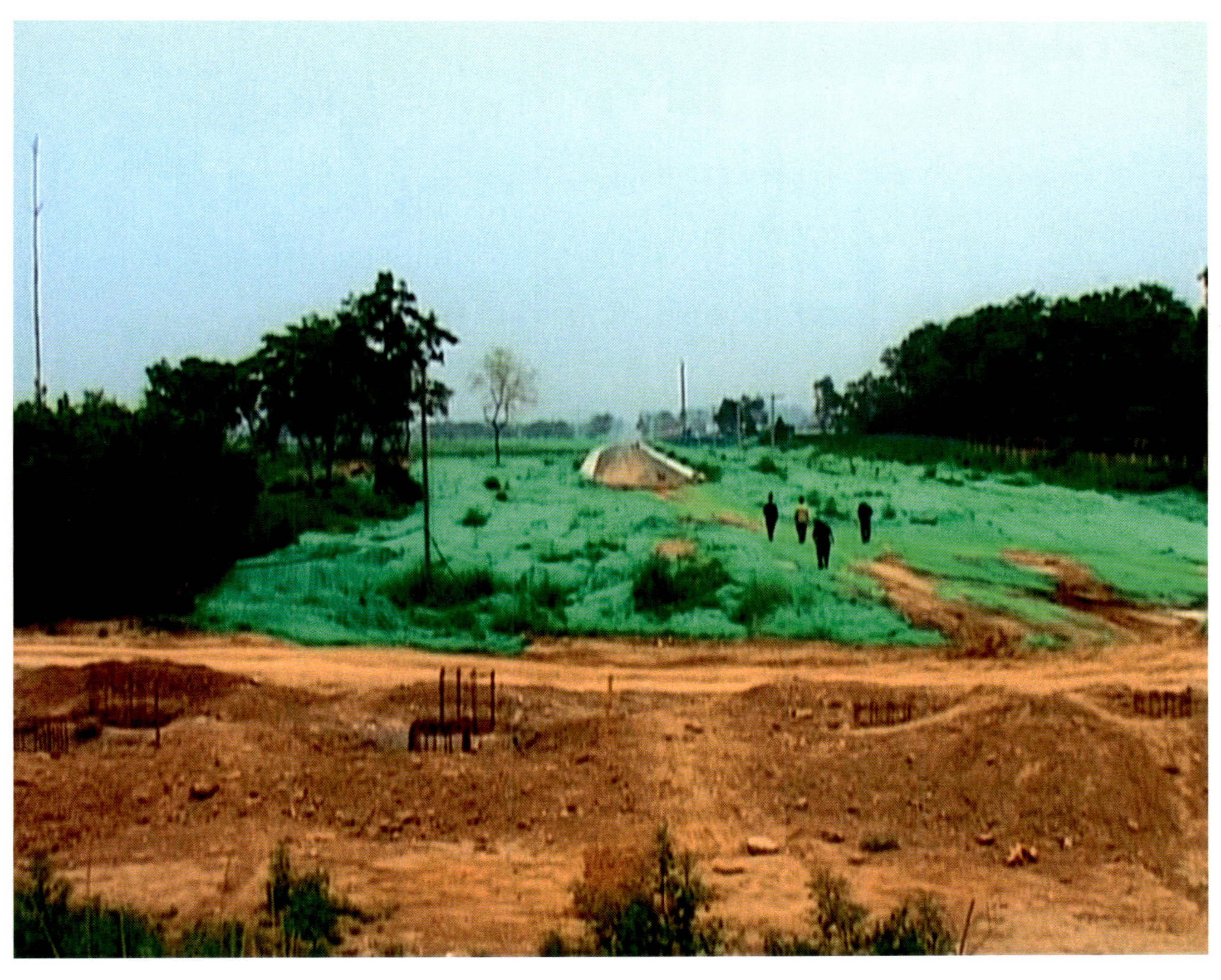

*City Scene*, 2004. Film stills
Courtesy L.A. Galerie - Lothar Albrecht, Frankfurt

# Dorothea Lange. The Crucial Years

## Commitment and propaganda

The nineteen thirties and forties were fundamental in the development of Dorothea Lange's work. During this time she produced an oeuvre unique in that one of its main characteristics was its relationship with the everyday, with the life of the inhabitants of her country. It was also during these decades that her great documentary style, of an overwhelming strength and depth, reached maturity. An outstanding feature of this style was her empathy for the people she photographed, something that has made her a major point of reference in documentary photography.

At the beginning of the thirties, Lange began to document the difficult situation her country was experiencing due to the Great Depression of 1929. From her studio she observed the increasing number of unemployed workers who wandered through the streets of San Francisco. She grabbed her camera and decided to go out and photograph the lines at soup kitchens, the May 1st demonstrations, dock strikes and the hoboes produced by the Great Depression. Some of her most famous photographs date from this period, such as *White Angel Breadline, 1933*, in which her skill at concentrating attention on one face, detail or figure in the midst of the masses was already evident as well as what were to become some of her hallmarks: a deep sympathy for the dispossessed and empathy for the unfortunate. These photographs caught the attention of Paul S. Taylor, a professor at the University of California Berkeley. Impressed by the strength and dignity that Lange was capable of giving to her subjects, he invited her to work with him illustrating an article he was going to publish in the *Survey Graphic* magazine. This was the beginning of a series of collaborations, and *An American Exodus. A Record of Human Erosion*, published in 1939, is outstanding among them.

In an attempt to alleviate extreme rural poverty, the Federal government created the Resettlement Administration (RA) in 1935 as part of Franklin D. Roosevelt's New Deal. The RA, which became the Farm Security Administration (1937-1942), appointed Roy Stryker head of its Historical Section. A photography lover who was aware of the medium's capacity to convey values, Stryker employed a large group of photographers with the mission of documenting the rural world and the actions undertaken by the RA to save agriculture from the crisis and improve the life of farmers and farm workers. Lange worked for these government agencies and for the BAE until 1942. Later, she also worked for the OWI, 1942-1943, and for the War Relocation Authority, Japanese-American Evacuation and Resettlement (WRA).
During those years, she travelled throughout the country with tireless dedication and passion. Often in collaboration with Taylor, the artist documented the exodus of farm families toward the West in search of work. This was a milestone in her career and the source of images, such as *Migrant Mother* (1936), that were to become true symbols.

One of her most interesting assignments in the forties was for the War Relocation Authority, created in 1942, which lasted until 1946. This measure was taken a few months after the Japanese attack on Pearl Harbor on December 7th 1941, in the context of intense anti-Japanese sentiment. The almost 120,000 citizens interned in the camps represented a wide spectrum of the Japanese-American community. Lange was invited to take the photographs that documented both their evacuation and relocation.

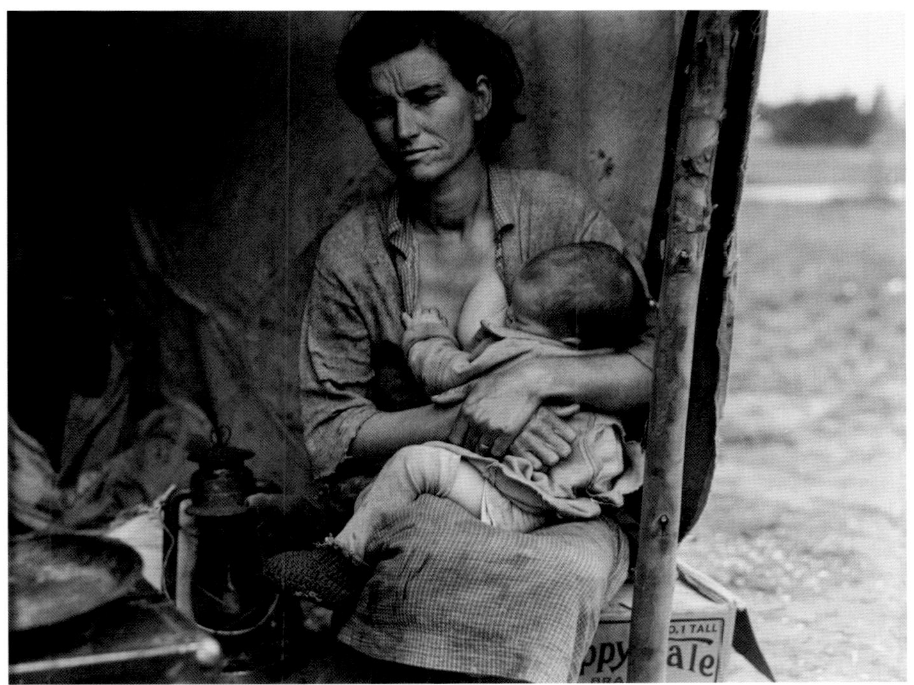


Some of her images evoking the horror of a community taken from their homes and submitted to harsh living conditions in the camps were censured by the U.S. Army. Thanks to Lange, we can relive the difficult moments that Japanese-American citizens had to endure. We see the streets and houses where they lived; the going-out-of-business sales in their stores; the lines they had to form when registering in the pertinent offices after being summoned to evacuate; their farewells to friends and neighbours; the interviews prior to evacuation; the check-ups; the vaccines they had to take before evacuation; the instructions they received; their waiting in the streets with their suitcases and other belongings for the buses that were to take them to the camps; the trucks that picked up their belongings; the barrack huts in which they were accommodated, and daily life in the internment centres.

Lange's images transport us to the years in which the United States suffered the most intense crises of its history. Many of them will remain in our memory as true icons, but beyond that they will continue to be an example of the capacity for empathy that photography can convey and of Lange's approach to the underprivileged and the subjects of daily life.

[Oliva María Rubio]

*Nipomo, Calif. Mar. 1936. Migrant agricultural worker's family. Seven hungry children. Mother aged 32. Father is a native Californian*, March 1936
Courtesy Museum of Contemporary Photography. Columbia College Chicago. Museum purchase from the Library of Congress

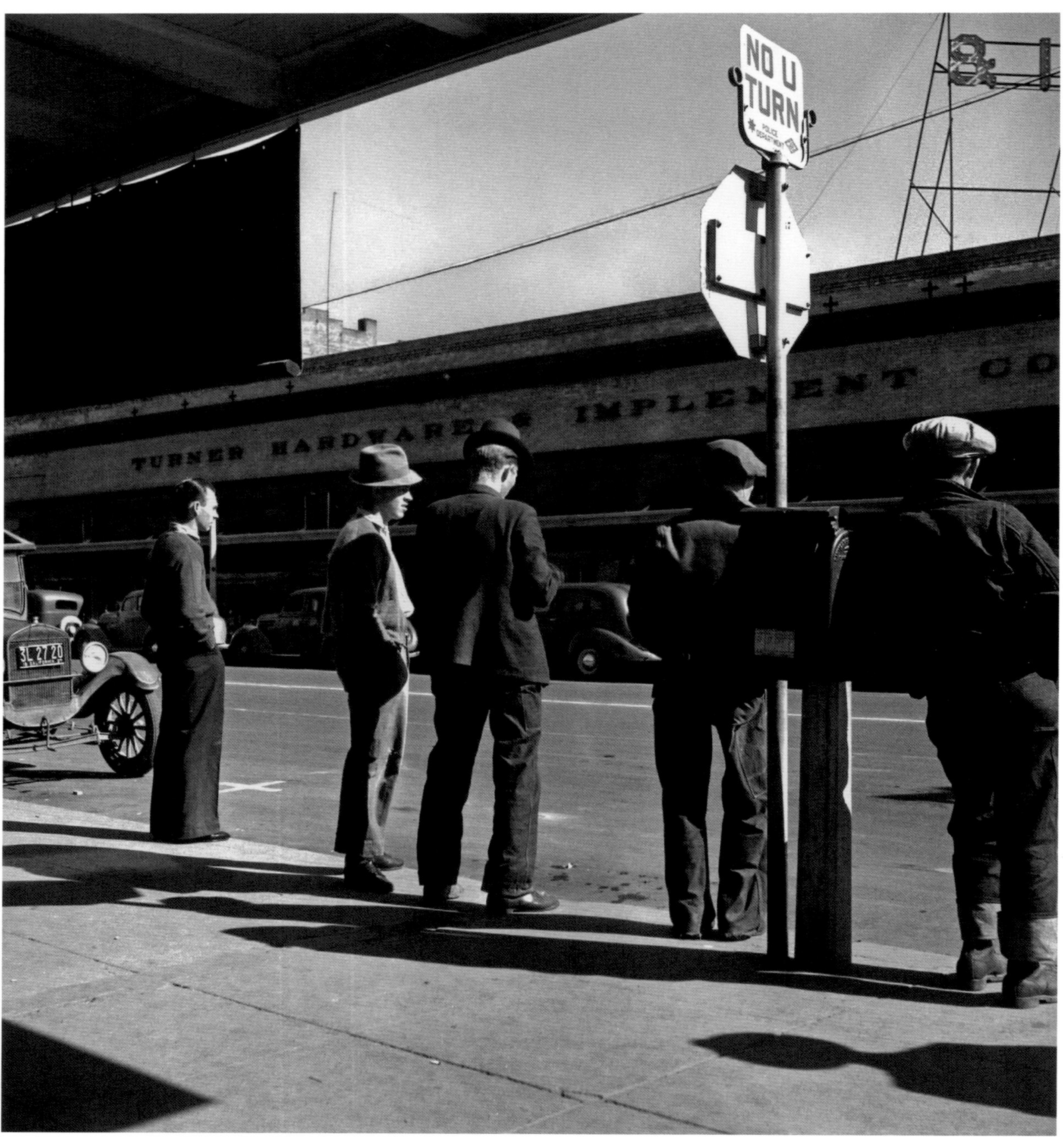


*Men on Skid Row, Modesto, California*, 1937 Mar.
Courtesy Library of Congress, Prints & Photographs Division, FSA/OWI
Collection LC-USF34-016386-E


*Street Meeting. San Francisco, California*, August 1936
Courtesy Library of Congress, Prints & Photographs Division, FSA/OWI
Collection LC-USZ6-1025

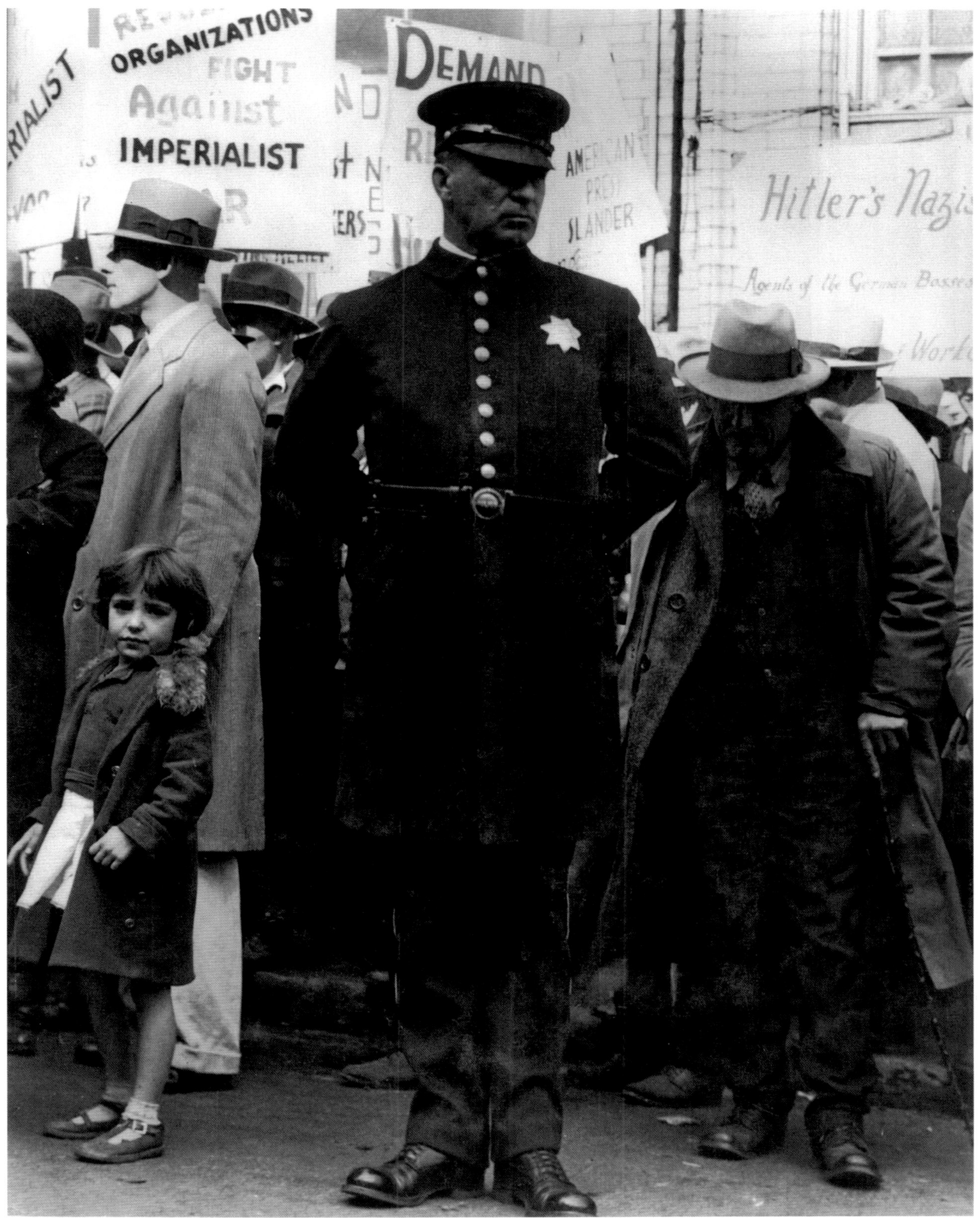
ORGANIZATIONS
FIGHT
Against
IMPERIALIST
DEMAND
SLANDER
Hitler's Nazis

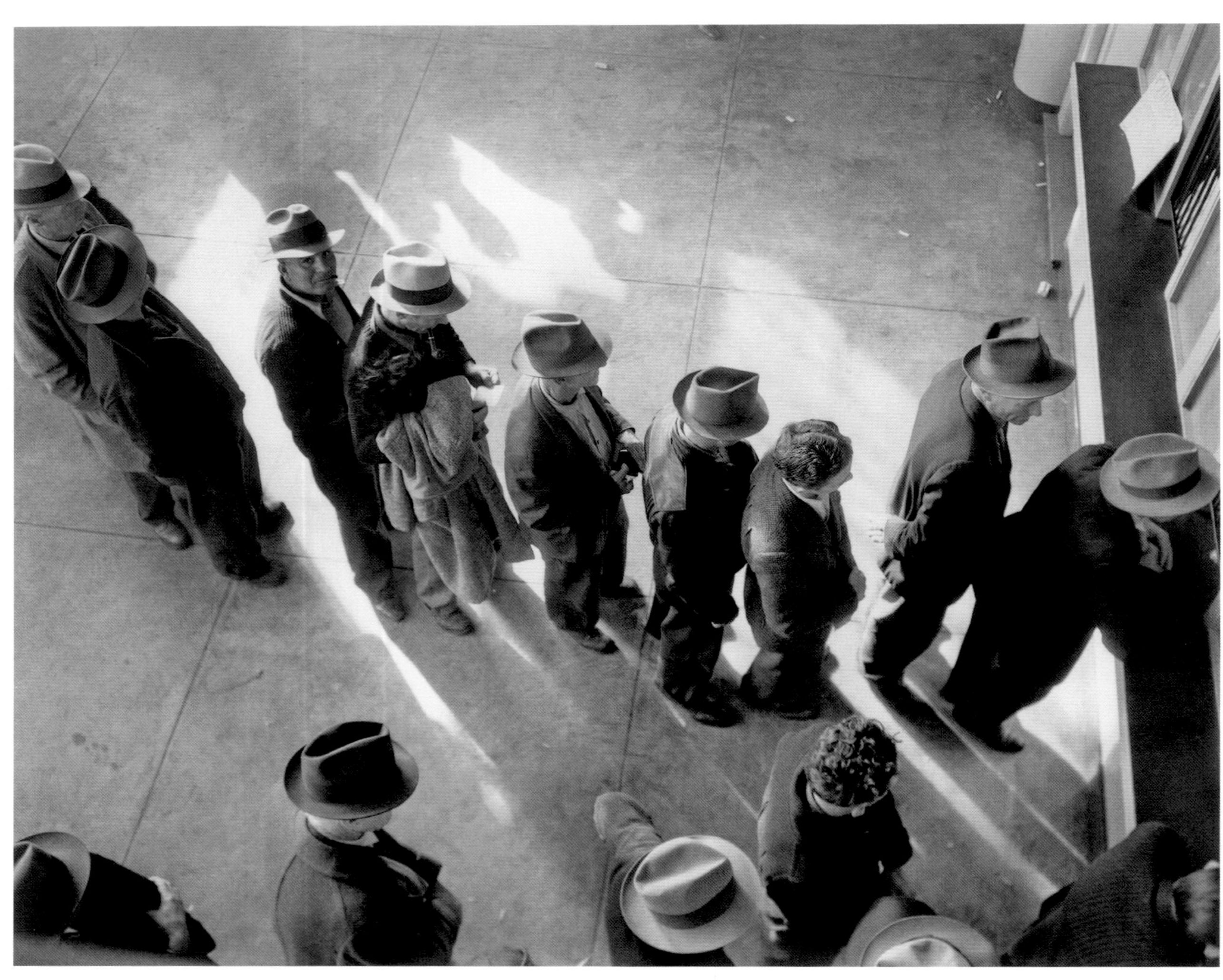

*Unemployment benefits aid begins. Line of men inside a division office of the State Employment Service office at San Francisco, California, waiting to register for benefits on one of the first days the office was open. They will receive from six to fifteen dollars per week for up to sixteen weeks. Coincidental with the announcement that the federal unemployment census showed close to ten million persons out of work, twenty-two states begin paying unemployment compensation*, 1938 Jan.
Courtesy Library of Congress, Prints & Photographs Division, FSA/OWI Collection LC-USZ62-99723

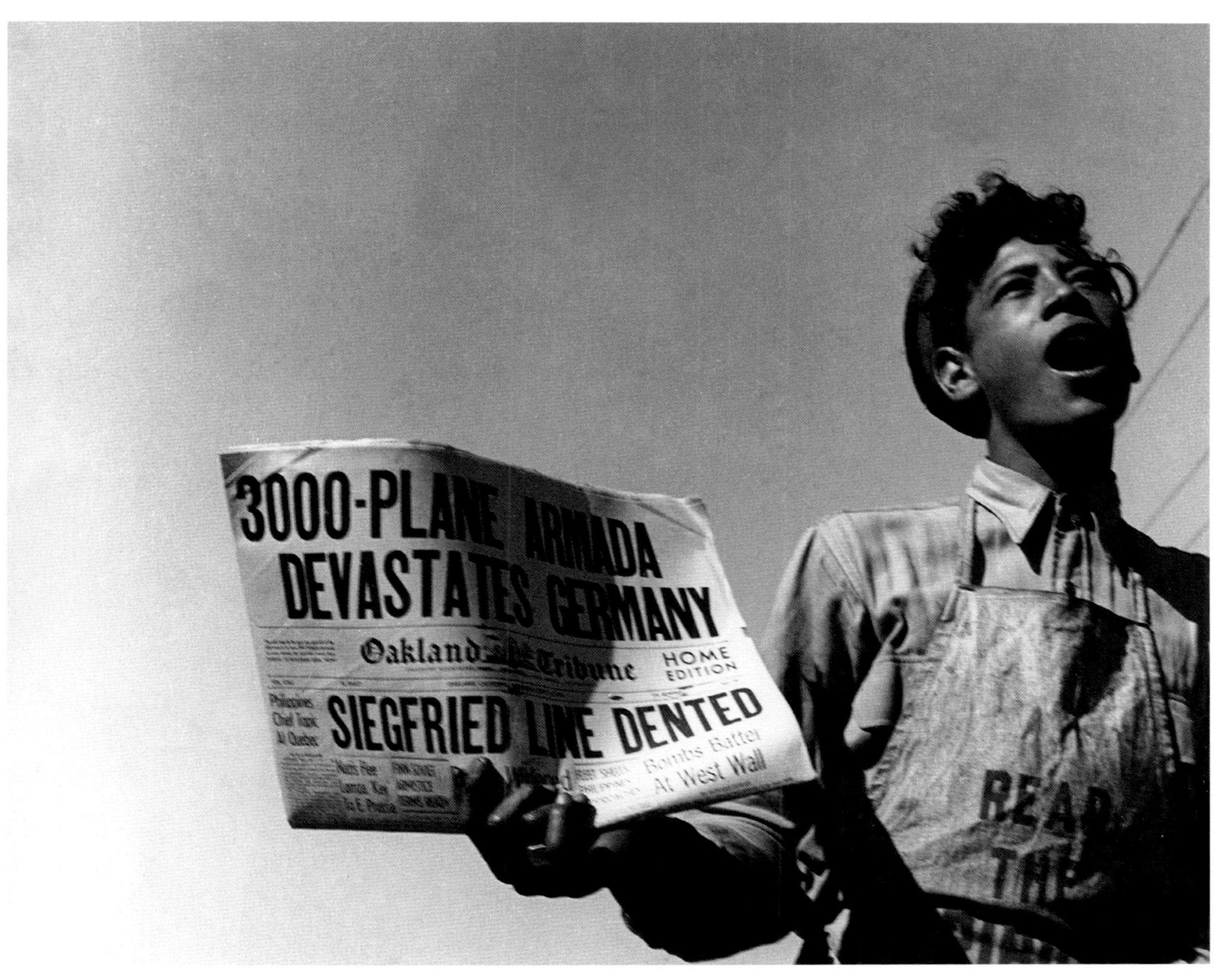


*Richmond General Scenes, "Planes Devastate Reich" 1944, Signs of the Times*, 1944
Courtesy Museum of Contemporary Photography. Columbia College Chicago. Gift of Katharine Taylor Loesch

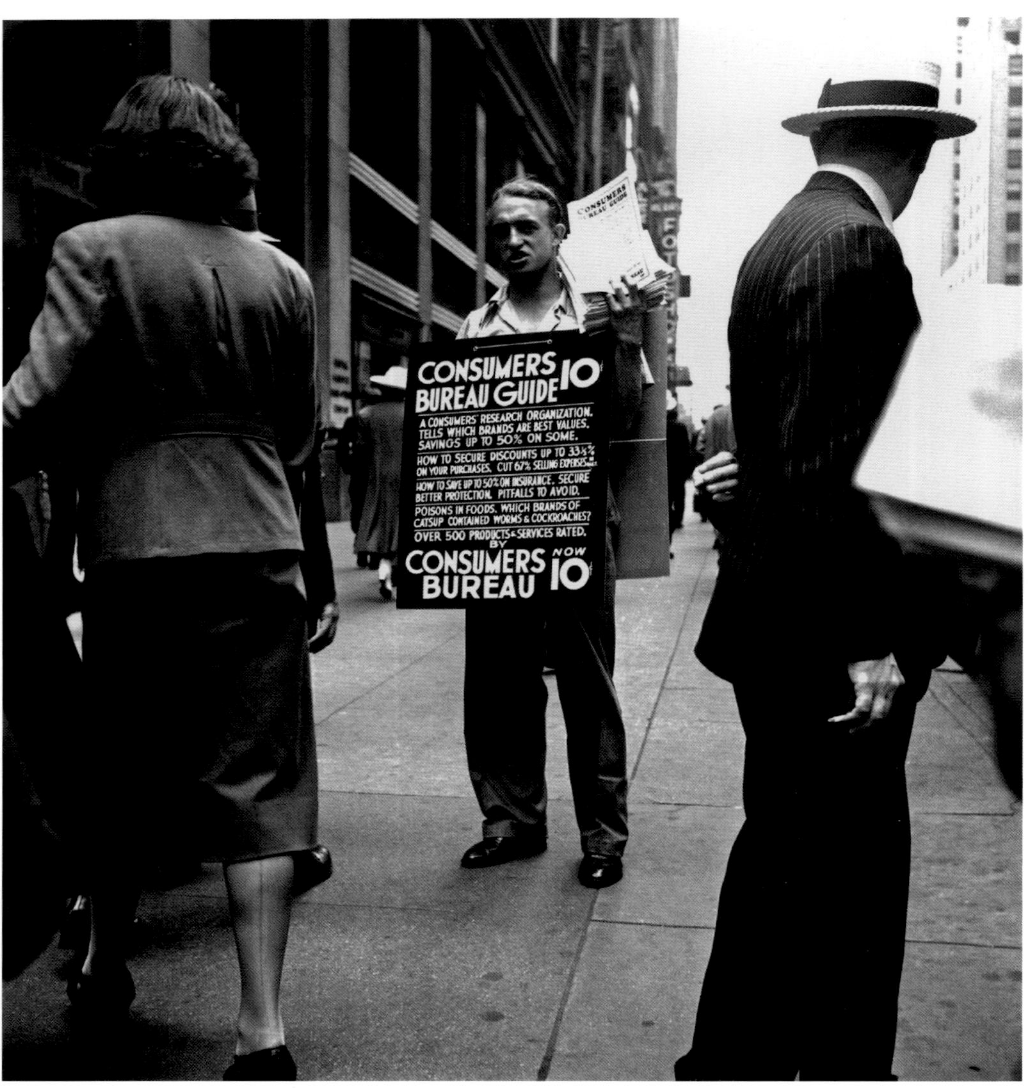


*42nd Street and Madison Avenue. Street Hawker Selling Consumer's Bureau Guide, New York City*, 1939 July
Courtesy Library of Congress, Prints & Photographs Division, FSA/OWI Collection LC-USF34-019830-E

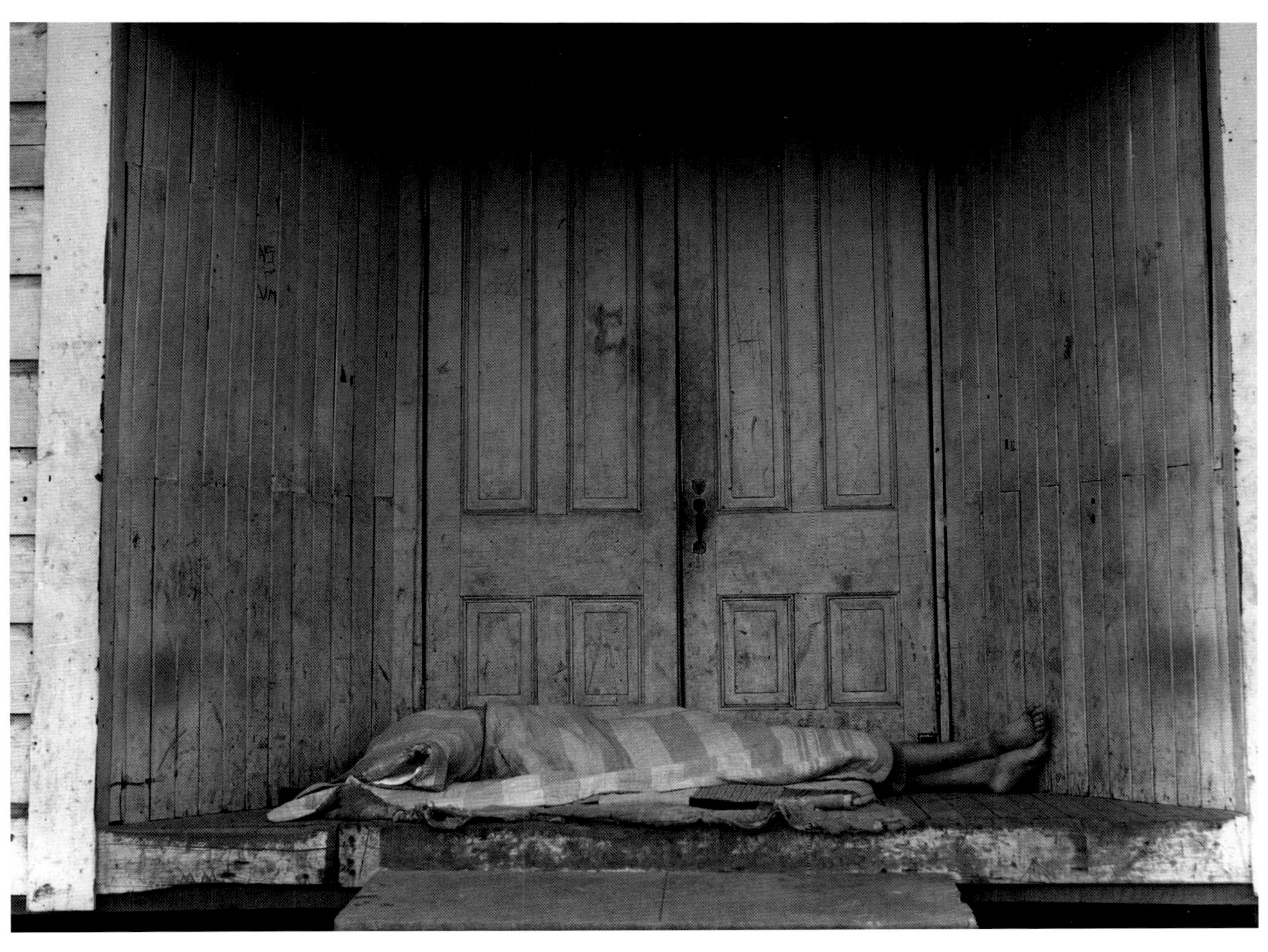

*Death in the Doorway. San Joaquin Valley, California*, 1938 [MOCP, SFMOMA] April 20, 1939 [OMCA]
Courtesy Museum of Contemporary Photography. Columbia College Chicago. Gift of Katharine Taylor Loesch

# Sergey Bratkov. Glory Days

## Pitiless Report

In a collection of essays entitled "Back to the Future", Boris Groys sums up the historic dilemma of realpolitik in the former Soviet states: "Communism, for so long an intellectual construct and a political vision, held out the promise of a future utopia. Now that Communism is a thing of the past," he argues, "the very fact that it is over testifies to its reality."

The bulk of Sergey Bratkov's work was created during these years of unbridled confusion at the loss of a previously stable world order, and the promise of a better, freer, more individualised future. The wild, even lurid, photographs, picture cycles and videos, verging at times on the very limits of good taste, form the expressive core of his prodigious and extensive output. Bratkov works in the media of photography and video, whereby it is not so much the camera itself that stakes out the communicative framework as Bratkov's own insatiable curiosity about the individuals he encounters, with whom he engages both personally and with an eye for their social conditions. Bratkov scratches the surface of the collective body, questioning and challenging it phenomenologically.

Following an exceptionally productive period around 2000-2001, in which he created such important cycles of portraits as *Kids* or *Soldiers, Fighters Without Rules, Secretaries* and the *Army Girls*, Bratkov has more recently concentrated primarily on panoramic photography. In contrast to his portraits, which are based on a more or less open agreement between photographer and sitter, the horizontal scanning of the outside world in the *My Moscow* cycle (2003) appears like a documentary construct, a panopticum of unhierarchically juxtaposed social and historical phenomena of the city. The countless private celebrations and semifolkloristic occasions flag up an ideological interpretation of "post-Communist" life in which the Russian "soul" still yearns deeply for the warmth and comfort of nestling in the lap of the collective, in spite of the political sea-change. Bratkov, utterly fascinated, tracks down the phenomenon of how people move in public spaces and occupy them anew. Spaces, for instance, that only recently were platforms for political insignia and symbolism: streets, marketplaces, racetracks, parks.

Financial constraints forced Sergey Bratkov to supplement his art by taking on commercial work in his home town of Charkov, Ukraine, where he lived until moving to Moscow in 2001. This included working for magazines and advertising agencies as well as for friends and acquaintances. But rather than seeking to keep these two visual worlds strictly separate, he found intelligent and subversive ways of activating aspects of these commercial photographic jobs to serve his own artistic ends. For the series *Birds* (1997) he photographed children in an orphanage on behalf of prospective adoptive parents, most of them American. The *Secretaries* (2001) series was based on the actual selection process for the post of personal assistant to a Caucasian businessman.

Sergey Bratkov has described his collaboration with Boris Mikhailov in 1994, which led to a series of performative actions in the *Fast Reaction Group* from 1994 to 1997, as a formative experience for him as an artist. Bratkov and Mikhailov, later joined by the artist Sergey Solonsky and Mikhailov's wife Vita, developed programmatic manifestos in which they deliberately provoked the establishment with their rapid actions and reactions and their illicit interventions. In this approach of guiding situations in certain directions or responding to certain external circumstances by means of well-aimed interventions and manipulations, we find – as in Boris Mikhailov's *Case History* (1997/98) – an important key to understanding Bratkov's subsequent work. Neither his *Sailors*, nor his *Kids*, first shown in 2000 at the Regina Gallery in Moscow, would have been conceivable without this programmatic foundation. In *Kids*, Bratkov to some extent appropriates the gaze of the parents who wanted their young daughters to be photographed for a children's modelling agency. But this approach, parasitic as it may be, is not sexually exploitative. Rather, the inscrutable expressions of the girls are child-like reflections of the clichéd ideas projected by the none-too media-aware parents who accompanied them to the shootings and even dressed them that way. Writer Boris Buden refers to this in terms of the ideology of the "post-Communist" gaze that looks out of the re-evaluated photographs. At the same time, he questions the supposed objectivity of this gaze on grounds that it is all too easy to perceive in his photographs a state of "no-longer" and "not-yet" when they are seen from the secure viewpoint of the (capitalist) winners – a viewpoint that, as he puts it, "cannot recognise these individuals without depriving them of a voice". However radical, unsettling and strident Sergey Bratkov's compositional approach may seem to be, what it offers is, above all, an open, unsparing and ultimately honest report on the state of a social order whose heights and depths are still being plumbed. The protagonists in Sergey Bratkov's works are heroes of time – "back from the future".

[Thomas Seelig]

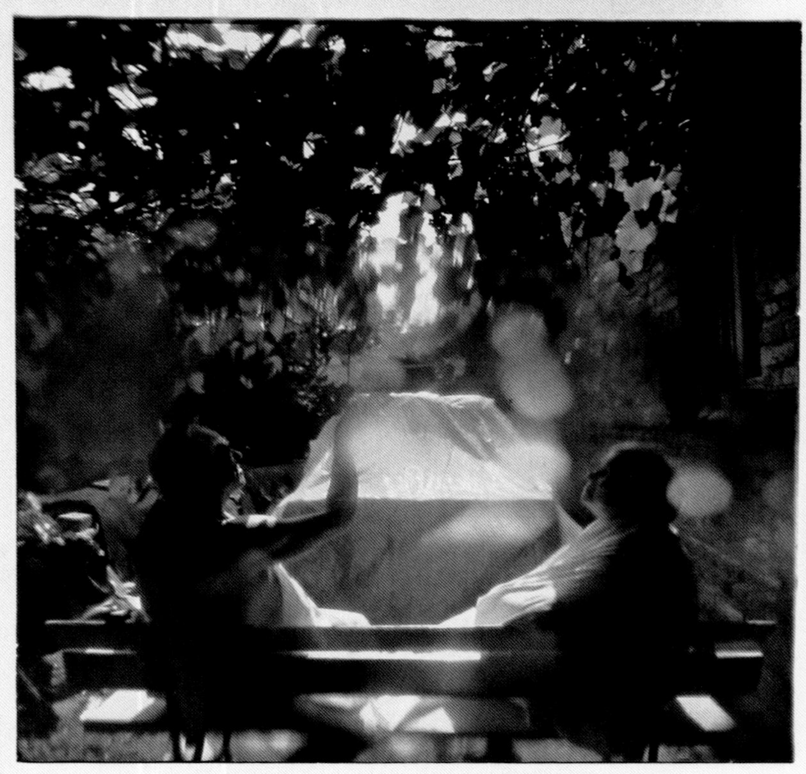



From the series *No Paradise*, 1995
© Sergey Bratkov

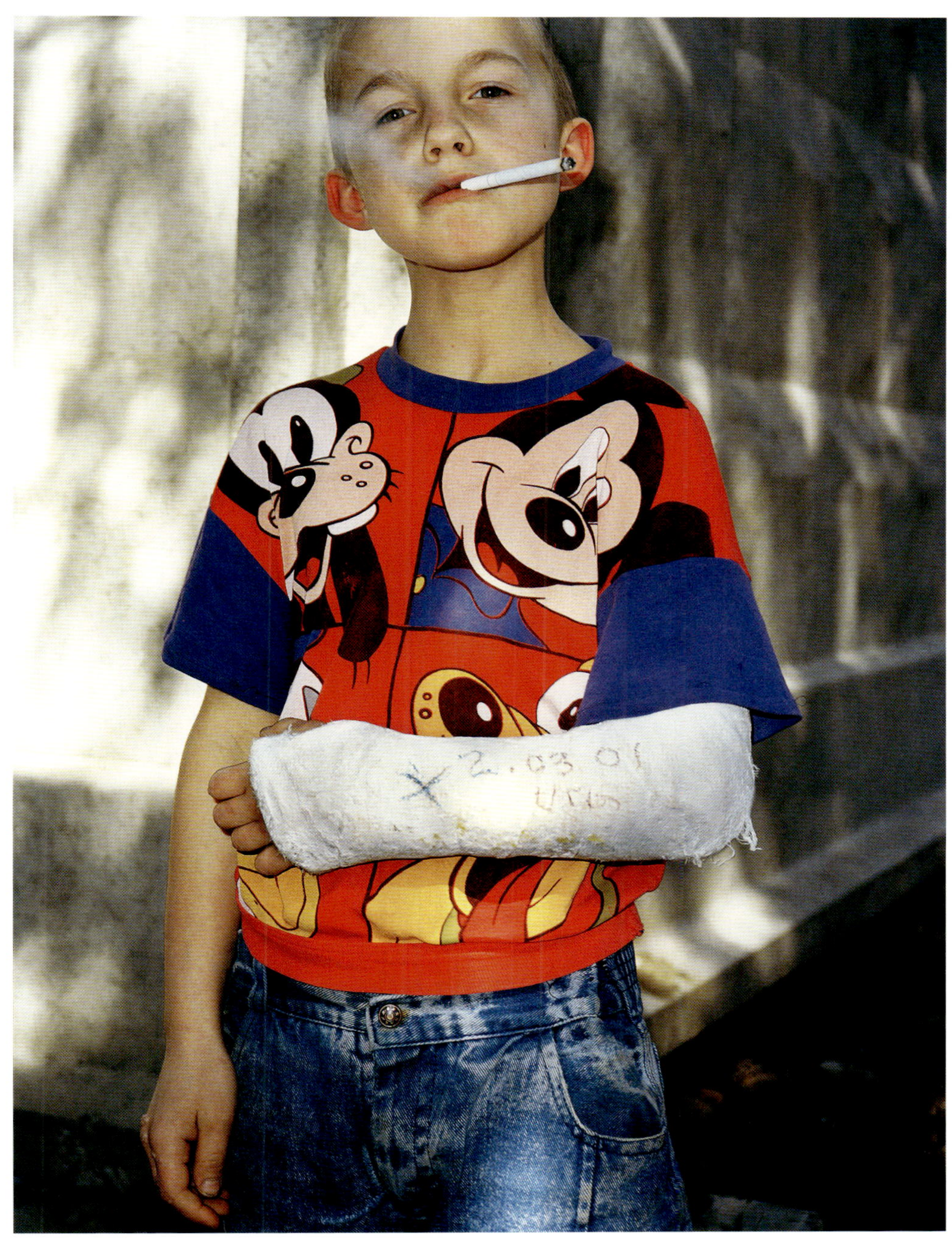

*Mickey Mouse*. From the series *Juvenile Detention*, 2001
Courtesy Regina Gallery, Moscow

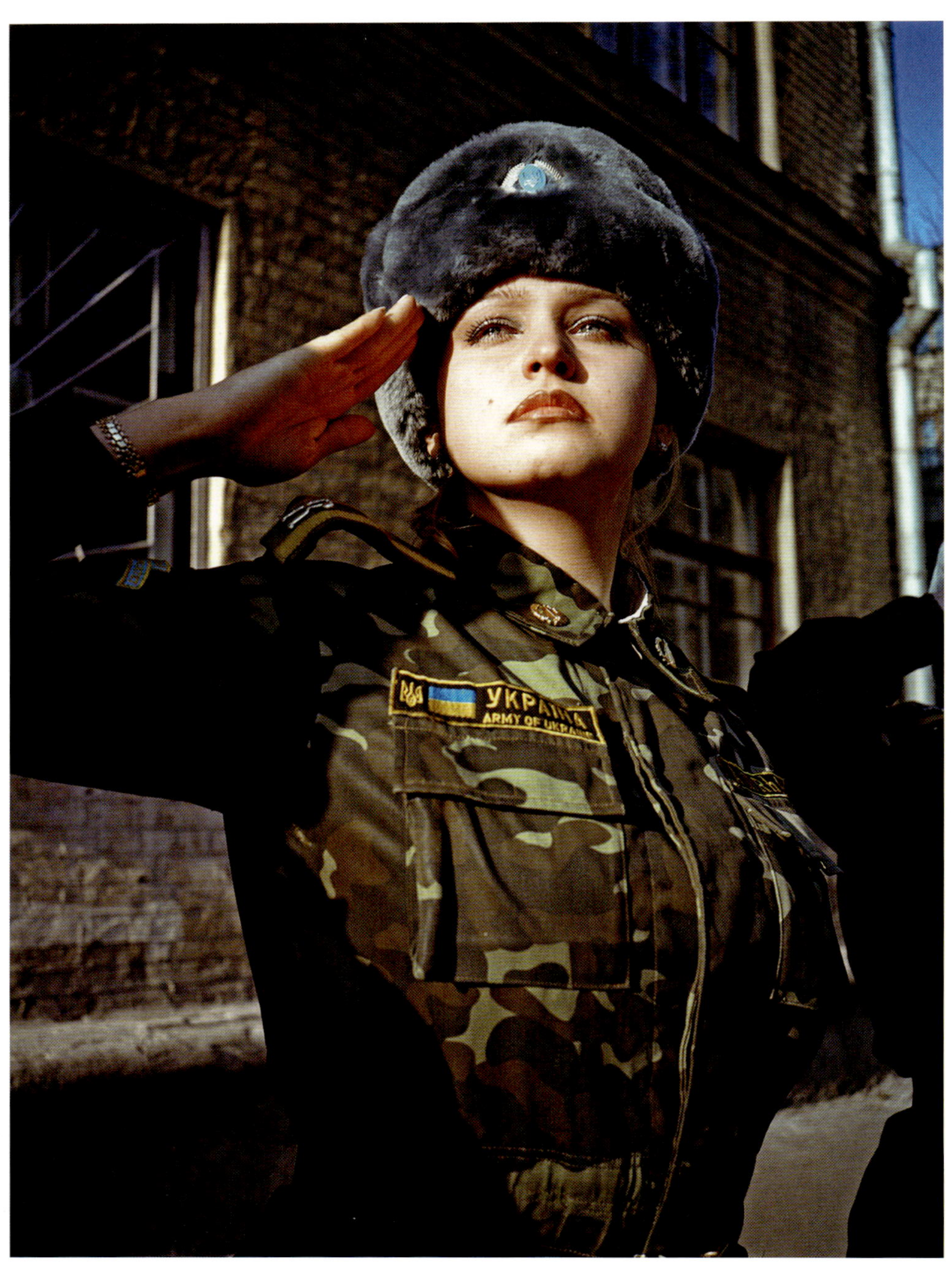

From the series *Army Girls*, 2000
Courtesy Regina Gallery, Moscow
© Sergey Bratkov

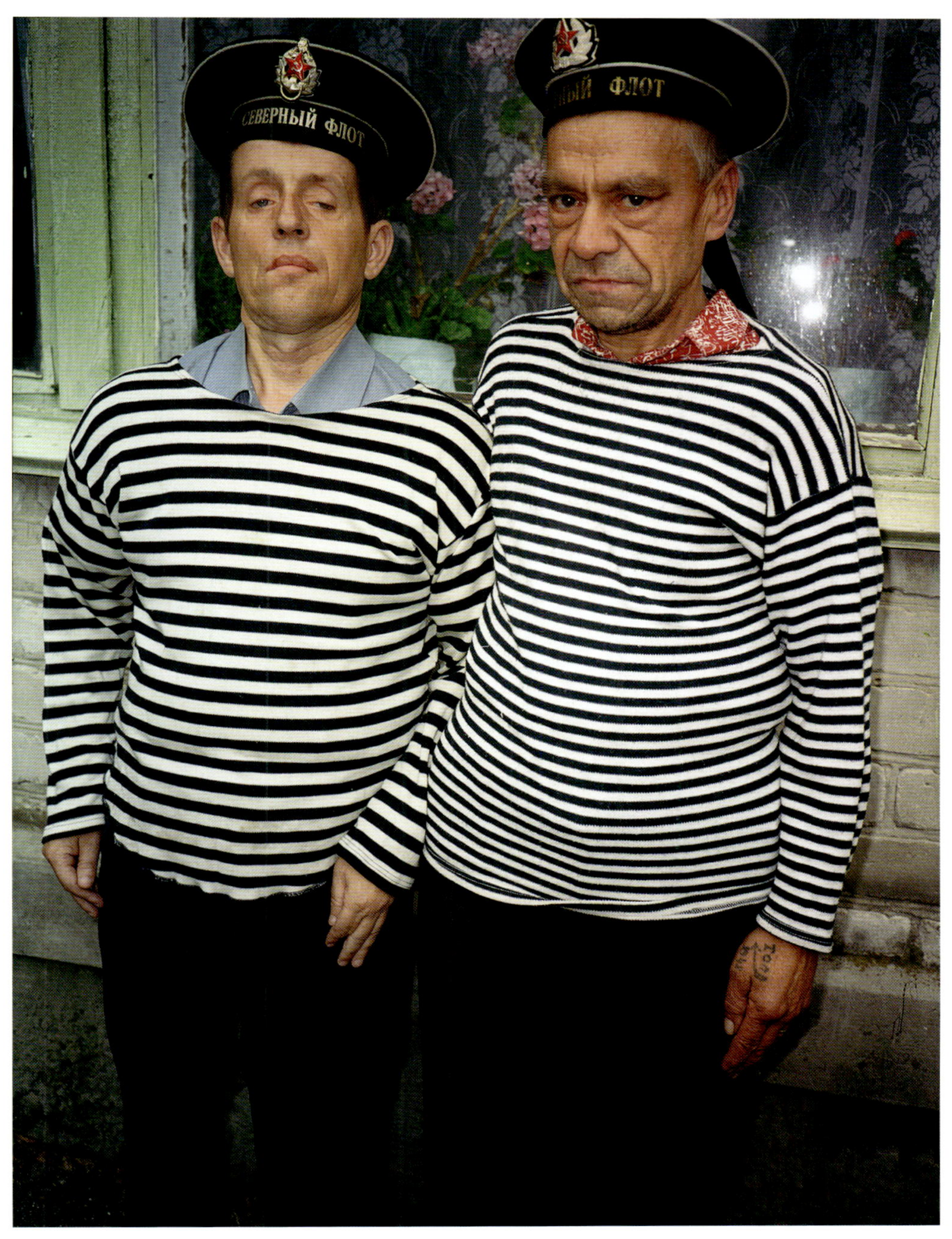


From the series *Sailors*, 2001
Courtesy Regina Gallery, Moscow
© Sergey Bratkov

# Íñigo Manglano-Ovalle. Nocturne... (in real-time)

## The Artist as a Systems Administrator

When Íñigo Manglano-Ovalle (Madrid, 1961) participated in the *Culture in Action* programme held in 1993 in Chicago, the city where he had grown up, he developed *Tele-vecindario* (Tele-Neighbourhood). This audiovisual project, made in collaboration with the city's Chicano youth, enabled this small group to deploy modes of visibilisation in order to make their interests and concerns public and generate a social network endowed with a certain identity. Nothing indicated that the programme in which the project was inserted, curated by Mary Jane Jacob, would provide the culture medium on which subsequently and to the displeasure of many of its participants including Manglano-Ovalle, the denomination "new genre public art" was created, a term that to some extent preceded the hackneyed "relational art" and the problems, obvious today, inherent in both nomenclatures.

While the project carried on after this artist's participation,[1] the doubts generated about the denomination of an artistic practice using social networks were well founded. It would seem logical, therefore, to believe that this was not a demand for the umpteenth deconstruction of the artist's role, but that new forms of conceiving artistic work were really being tested: a new approach in which in addition to social involvement certain other already existing fields were revealed that the artist could modify by giving them depth, confusing them, altering them or alluding to qualities that, after being short-circuited by the artist, can undoubtedly only reveal their most unexpected dimensions. In some way, these fields similar to the disciplines mentioned by Foucault could be considered pre-established "systems" from which unexpected associations are made to come forth.

Íñigo Manglano-Ovalle has shown extreme skill in introducing and modifying these systems. Thanks to this type of intervention, the Monumental bullring in Mexico was turned into an enormous radio antenna similar to those used to listen for improbable waves sent from alien planets (*Search/En búsqueda*, 2001). Obviously the fact that the legal status of immigrants in the United States requires their obtaining the so-called "Alien Card" underlies the entire scene. In the same way, all the rational meticulousness of Mies Van der Rohe's architecture and the utopian connotations of modernity that his building implies showed the driving dimension it can have through the only action permitted by cultural heritage conservation regulations: window washing (*Le Baiser/The Kiss*, 2000).

The two works presented in the Espacio Abierto x Obras space in Matadero, *Sonambulo III* (Sleepwalker III) and *Nocturne (White Poppies)*, follow this same principle by which various elements from different origins are combined to show surprising relationships. In both works, night vision cameras seem to set up a game that, easily following Paul Virilio, we could call "war machine". Just like so many other military inventions, the images produced by these devices have become so widely known that it is very hard to stop thinking of them without the connotations imposed by their origin. Nevertheless, Manglano-Ovalle produces a sharp contrast of sensations for the occasion that shows, as if in a photograph to which time has been added, a recording of his son sleeping in *Sonambulo III* and the real-time representation of some white poppies that also occupy the installation space in *Nocturne*. In this second case, various cameras arranged in the form of a cross project images on several screens that debate between the beauty of the flowers and the greenish tones that irremediably suggest that threatening quality to which the wars of Iraq and Afghanistan have already

1. See Javier Rodrigo, "De la intervención a la articulación. Trabajo colaborativo desde políticas culturales", en AA.VV. *Activismo /Transformación social*, pp. 88-93. (www.idensitat.org/blog/document/IDENSITAT%20cast%20part03%20-%20activismo-transformacion.pdf).

accustomed us. A special interconnection seems to exist between the two works: as is widely known, the poppy is the source from which heroin is extracted. In its natural state, it has a soporific effect that seems to have affected the artist's child's sleep in *Sonambulo III*. The audio track filling the exhibition hall, a kind of relaxing music, belongs to the second work and also echoes these unexpected relationships when we realise that, far from audible repose, the music comes from having slowed down the sound of a gunshot.

While this has been the most widely published interpretation[2] of Manglano-Ovalle's works, they can also be considered in the light of the everyday that concerns this event, an interpretation that thanks to rhythm analysis illustrates in a different way the deviations that at first glance seem present in his work. It was Henri Lefebvre[3] who proposed that the everyday was a diffuse atmosphere in which rational rhythm (the linear temporality inherent to modernity and ruled by consecutiveness and progression) and cyclical rhythm (centred in the founder repetition both of boredom with the everyday and with historical cycles) converged. In this sense, Manglano-Ovalle's oeuvre and particularly the works we consider herein seem to combine this double temporality in which ordinary acts, situations and places are displaced to territories that seem to uncover their most unexpected implications. In this process, it is difficult to eliminate the meanings found both in the banal and in the extraordinary even though they also seem to intertwine so that both spheres appear blurry, as if what we take for granted were revealing its artificial condition. After all, the everyday is historically determined in spite of the fact that its production conditions are no longer clear to us. The relationships on an ideological level that are exposed thanks to this procedure should not be overlooked when showing the ease with which the violence of a war-like visuality becomes integrated into social imagery.

[Iñaki Estella]

2. See Ralph Cristofori (Org.), *Íñigo Manglano-Ovalle*, Barcelona, La Caixa, 2003.
3. Henri Lefebvre, *Critique of everyday life Vol. II. Foundations for a sociology of the everyday*, Verso, London and New York, 2002, pp. 340 et seq. (Trans. John Moore).

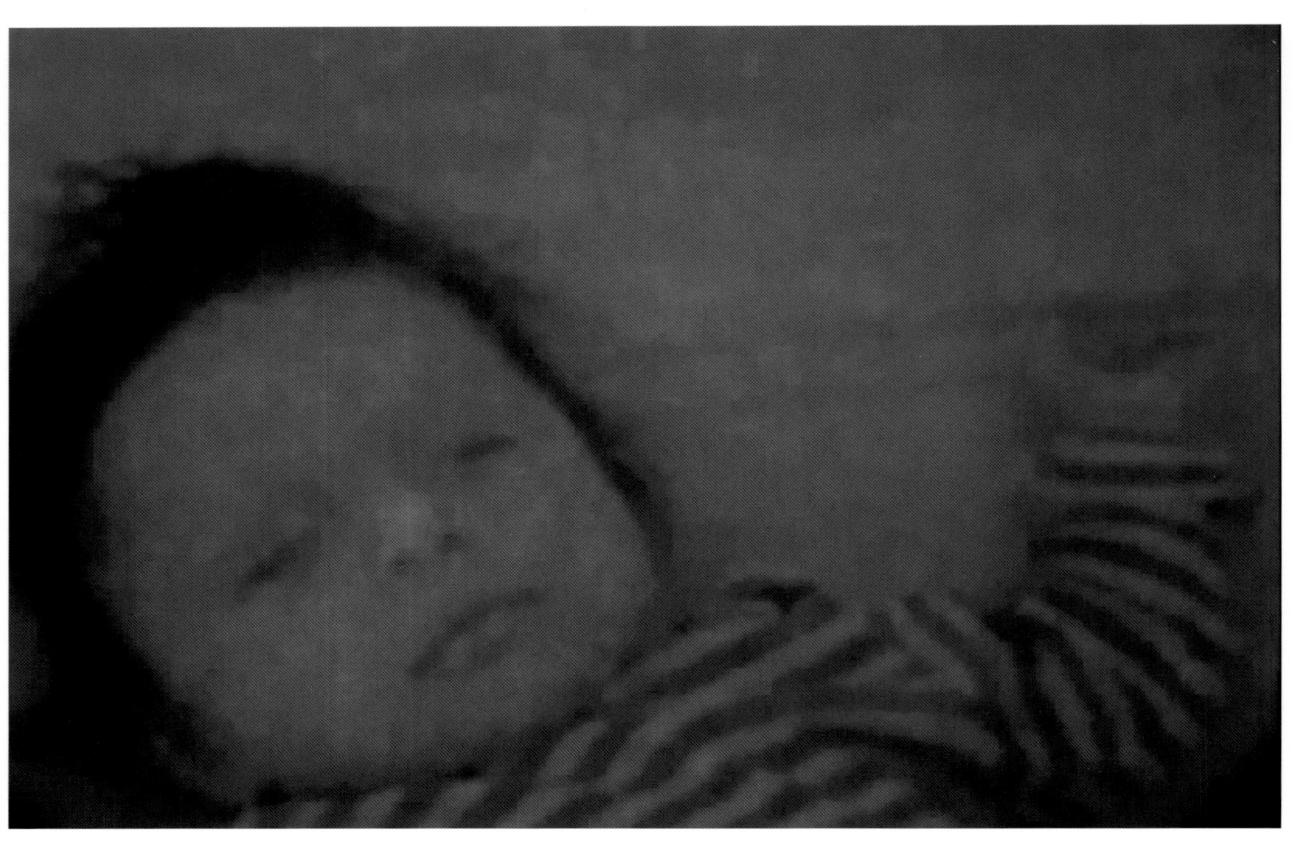

*Sleepwalker III (infrared), 2003*
© Íñigo Manglano-Ovalle

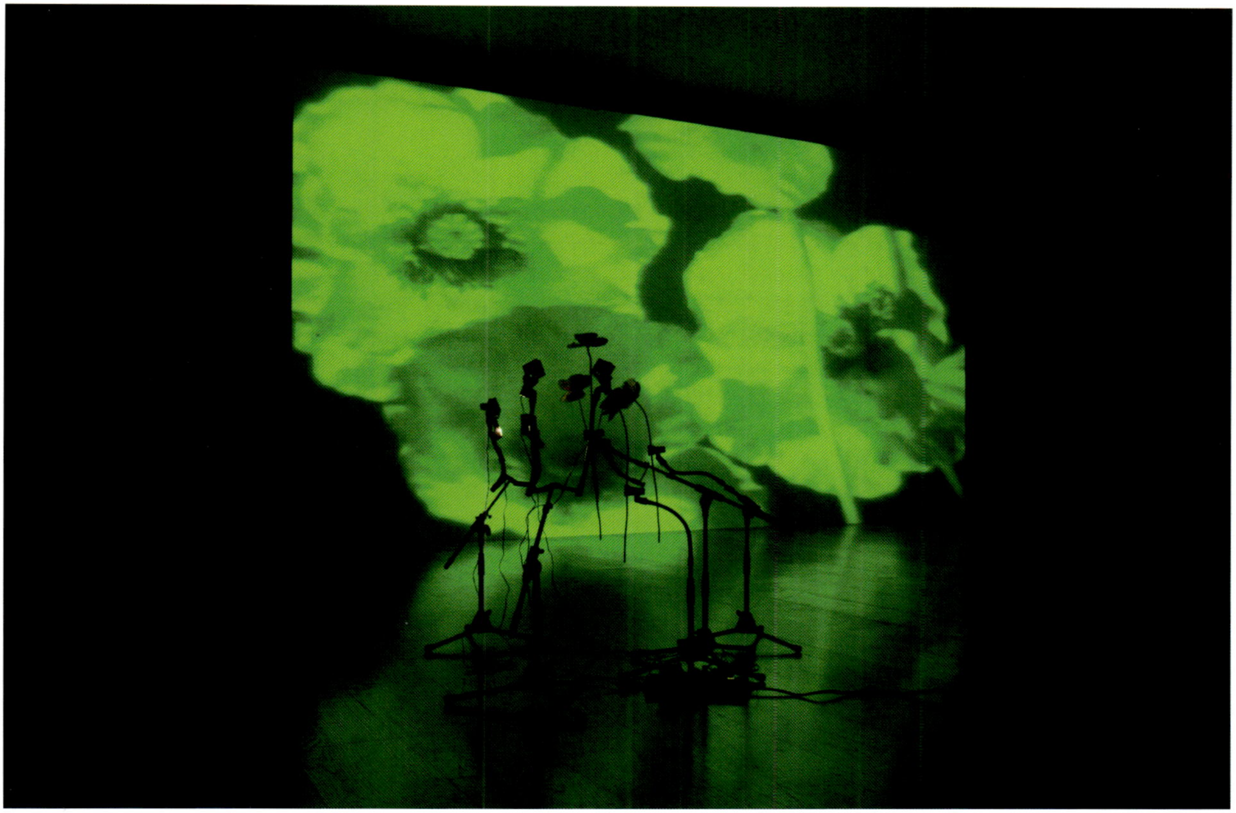

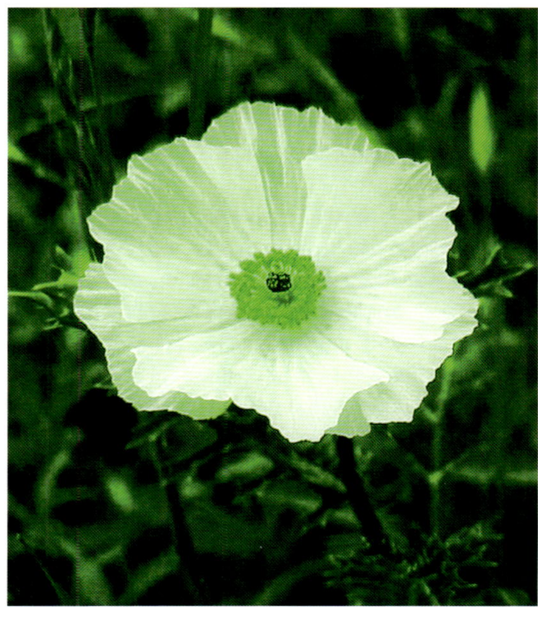

*Nocturne (White Poppies)*, 2002
© Íñigo Manglano-Ovalle

*Nocturne (detail)*, 2002
© Íñigo Manglano-Ovalle

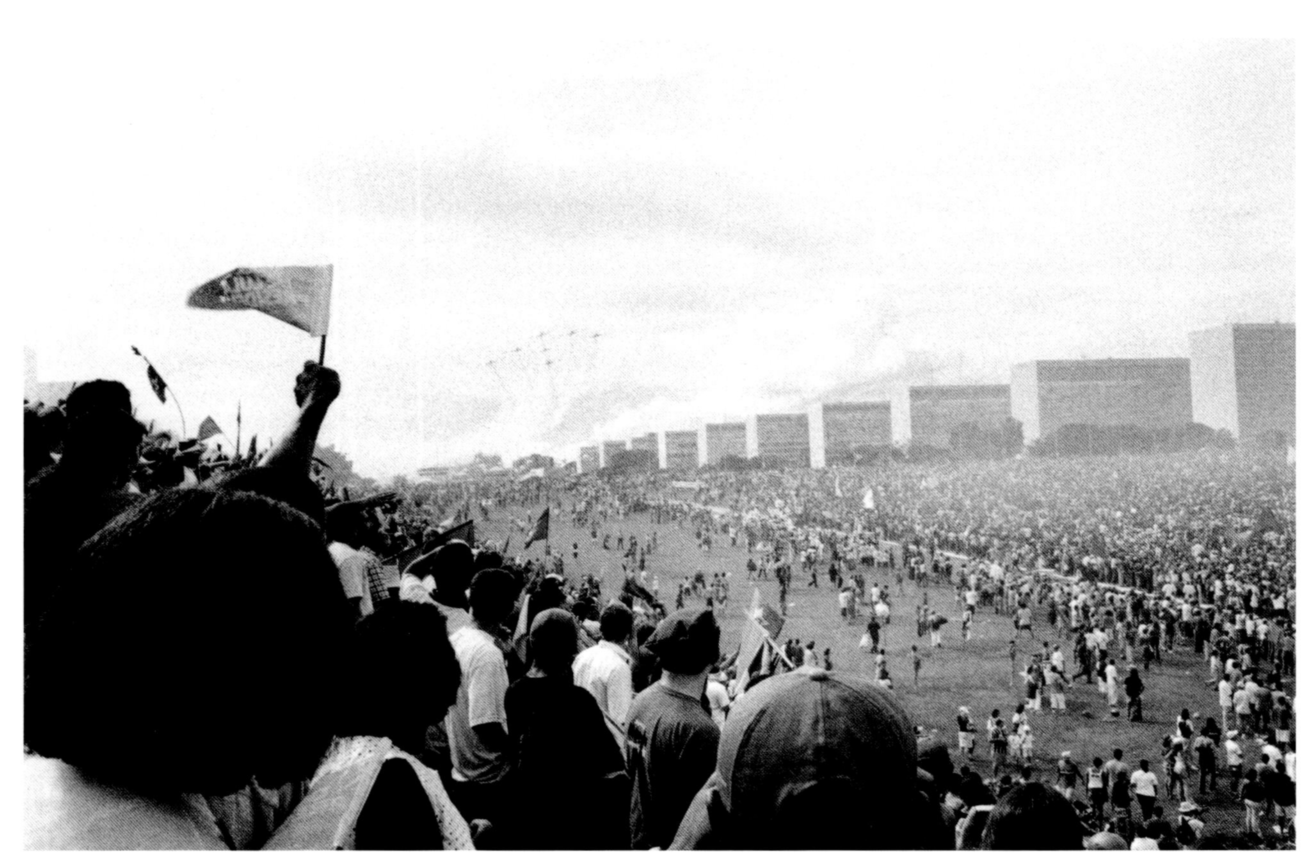

*Investiture #9* [Empossamento #9], 2003
Courtesy Coleção Inhotim, Brumadinho, Minas Gerais
© Mauro Restiffe

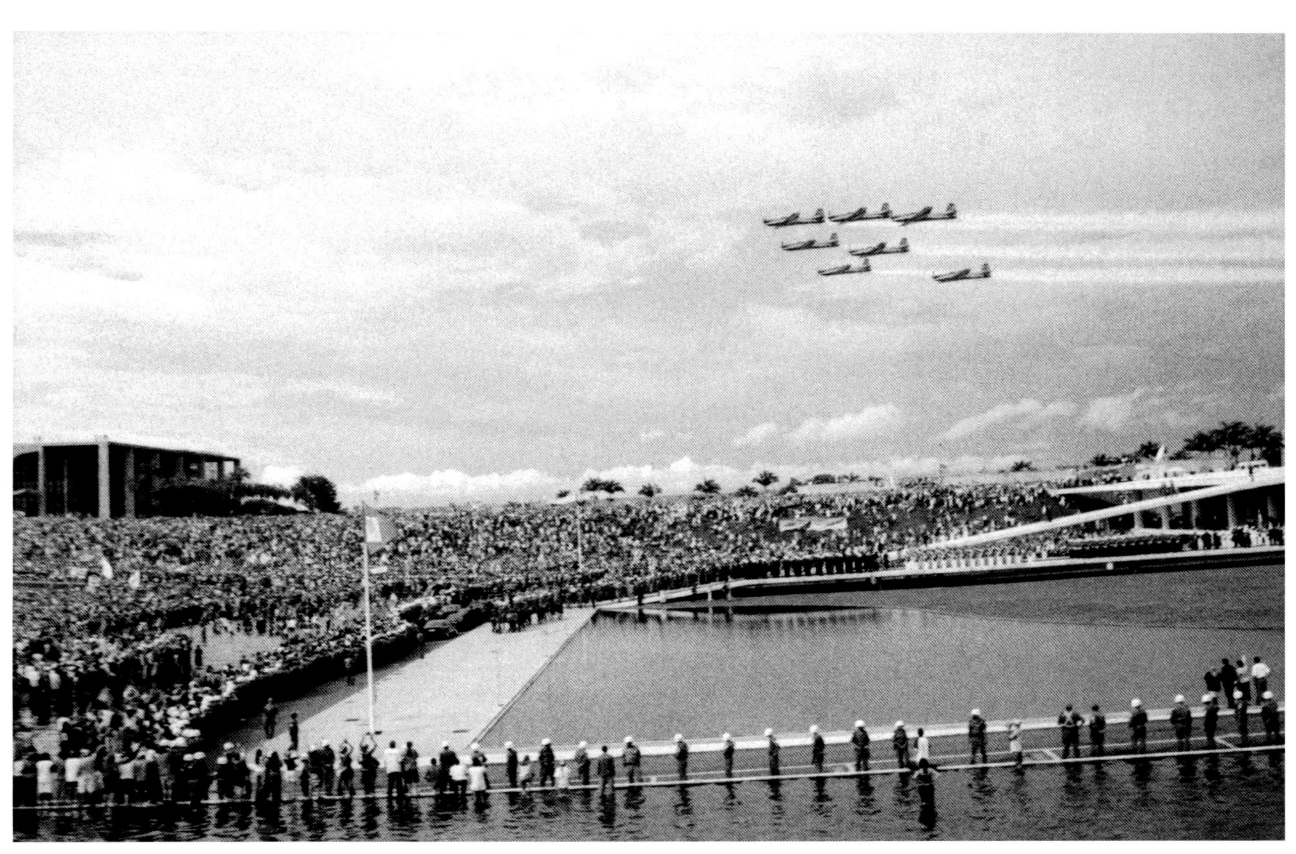

*Investiture #2* [Empossamento #2], 2003
Courtesy Galeria Fortes Vilaça, São Paulo
© Mauro Restiffe

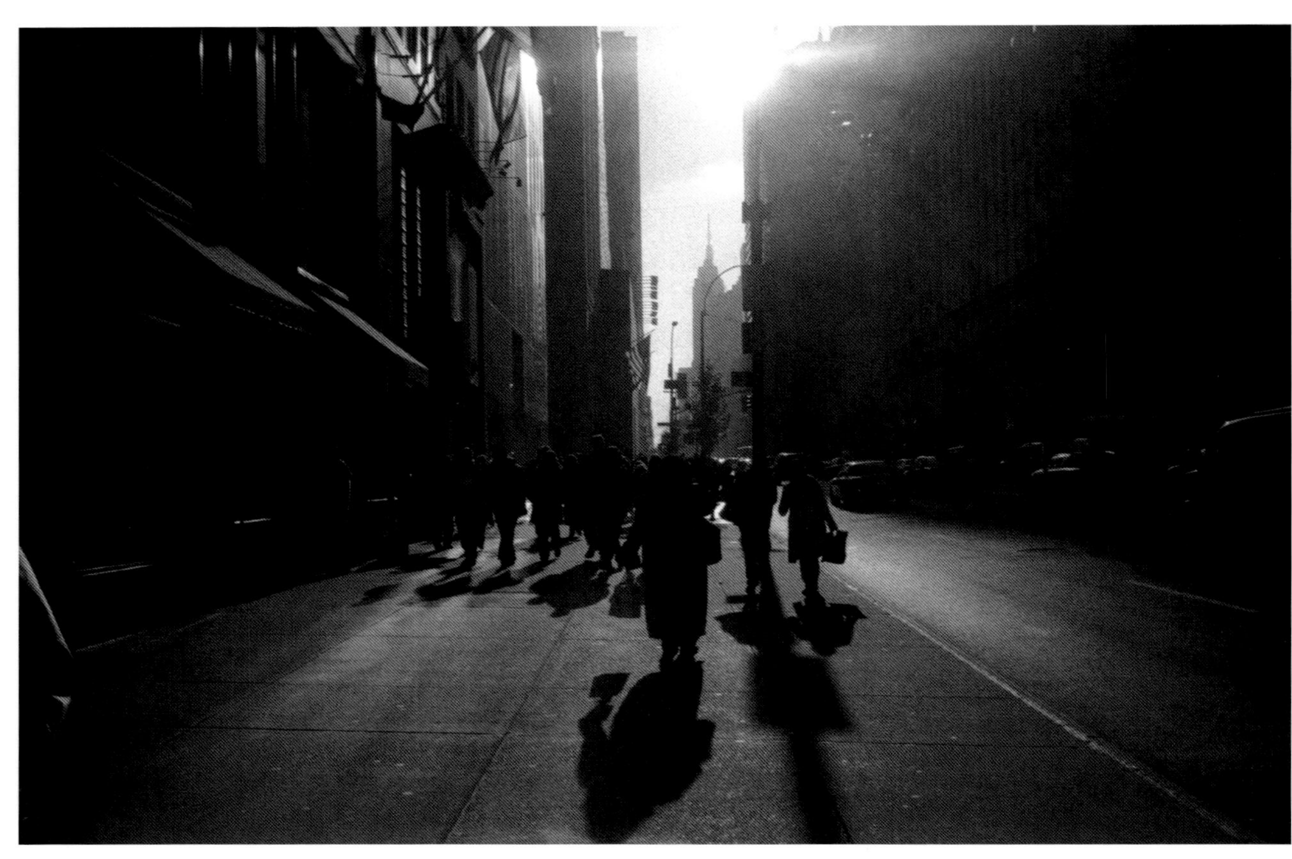

*Five on 5th*, 2008
Courtesy Galeria Fortes Vilaça, São Paulo

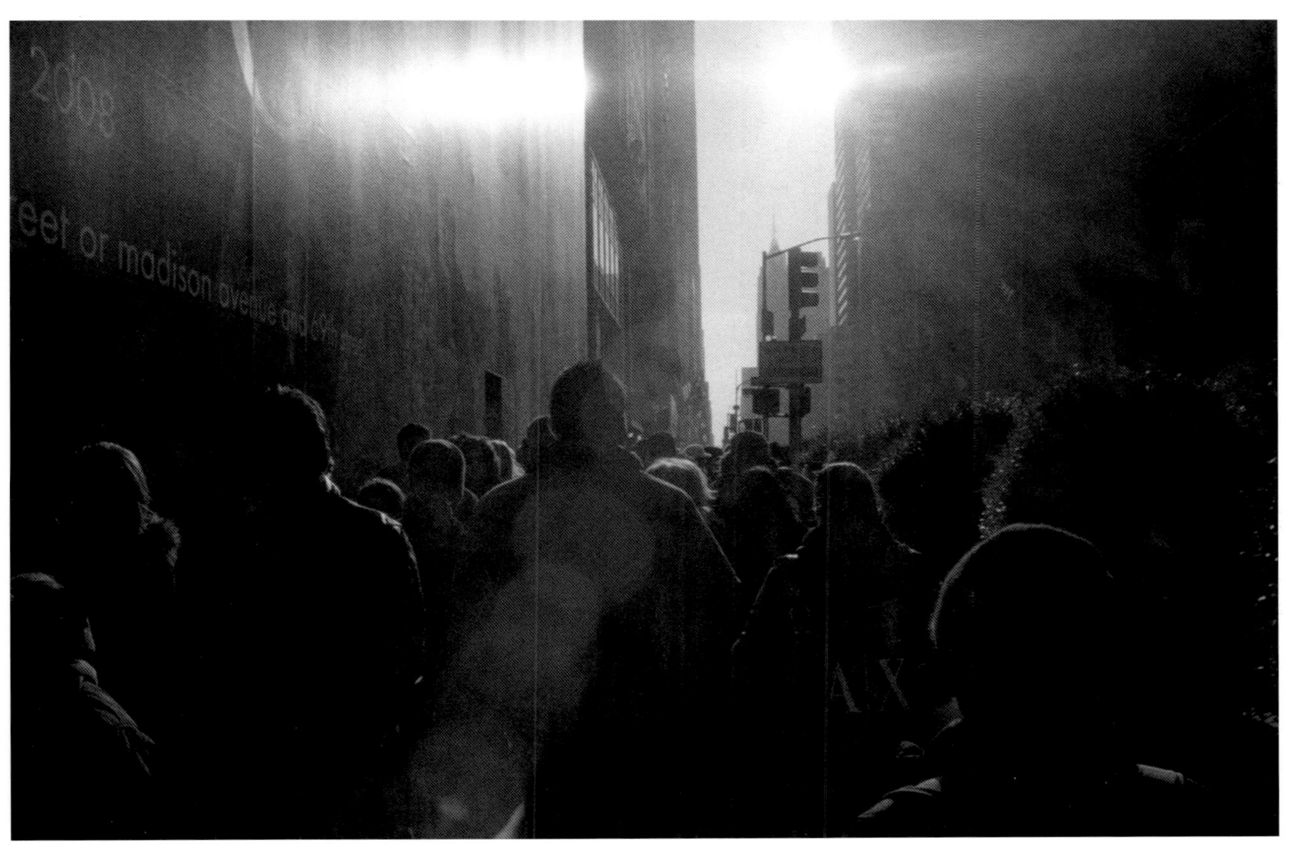


*Five on 5th*, 2008
Courtesy Galeria Fortes Vilaça, São Paulo
© Mauro Restiffe

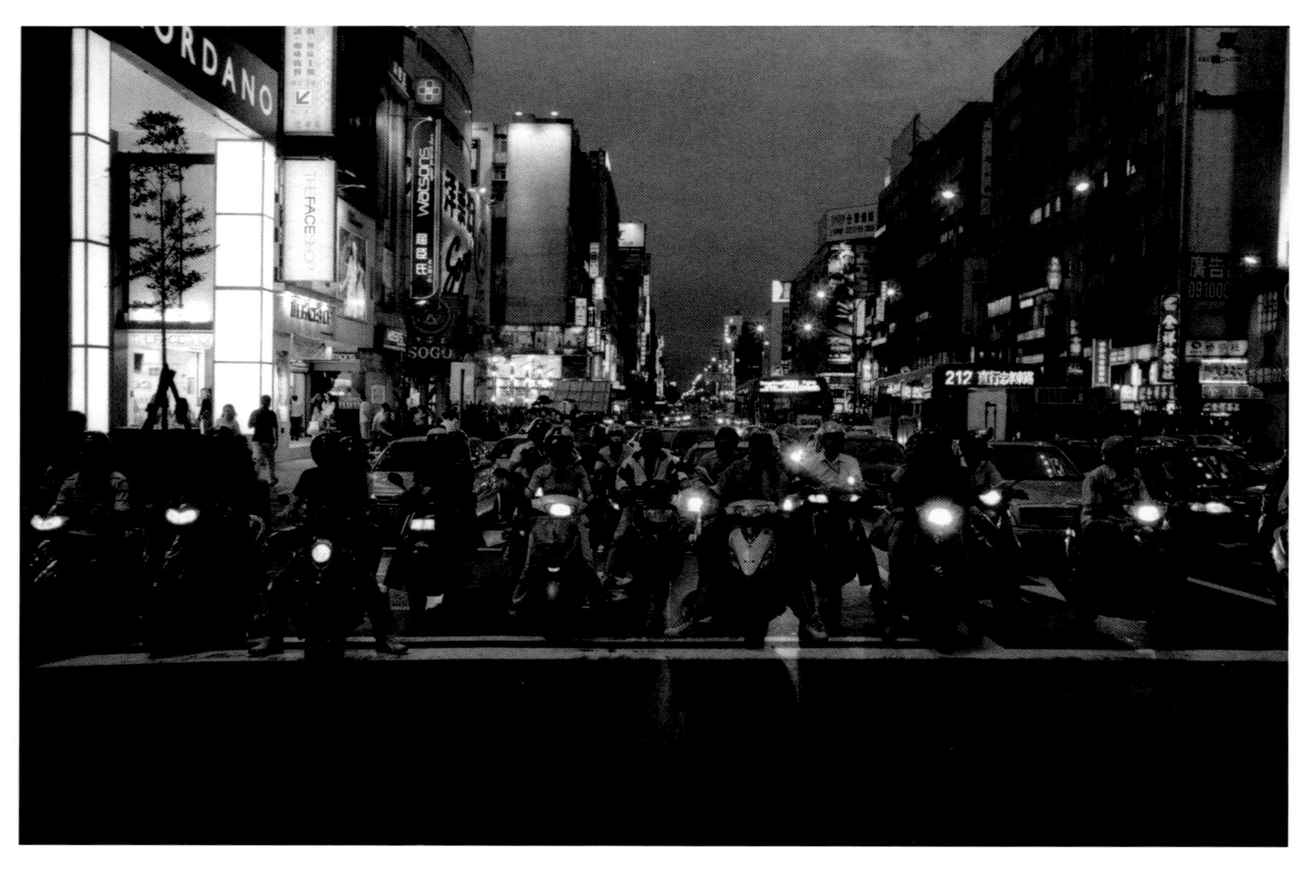


*Red Light Portrait #16*, 2006
Courtesy Galeria Fortes Vilaça, São Paulo
© Mauro Restiffe

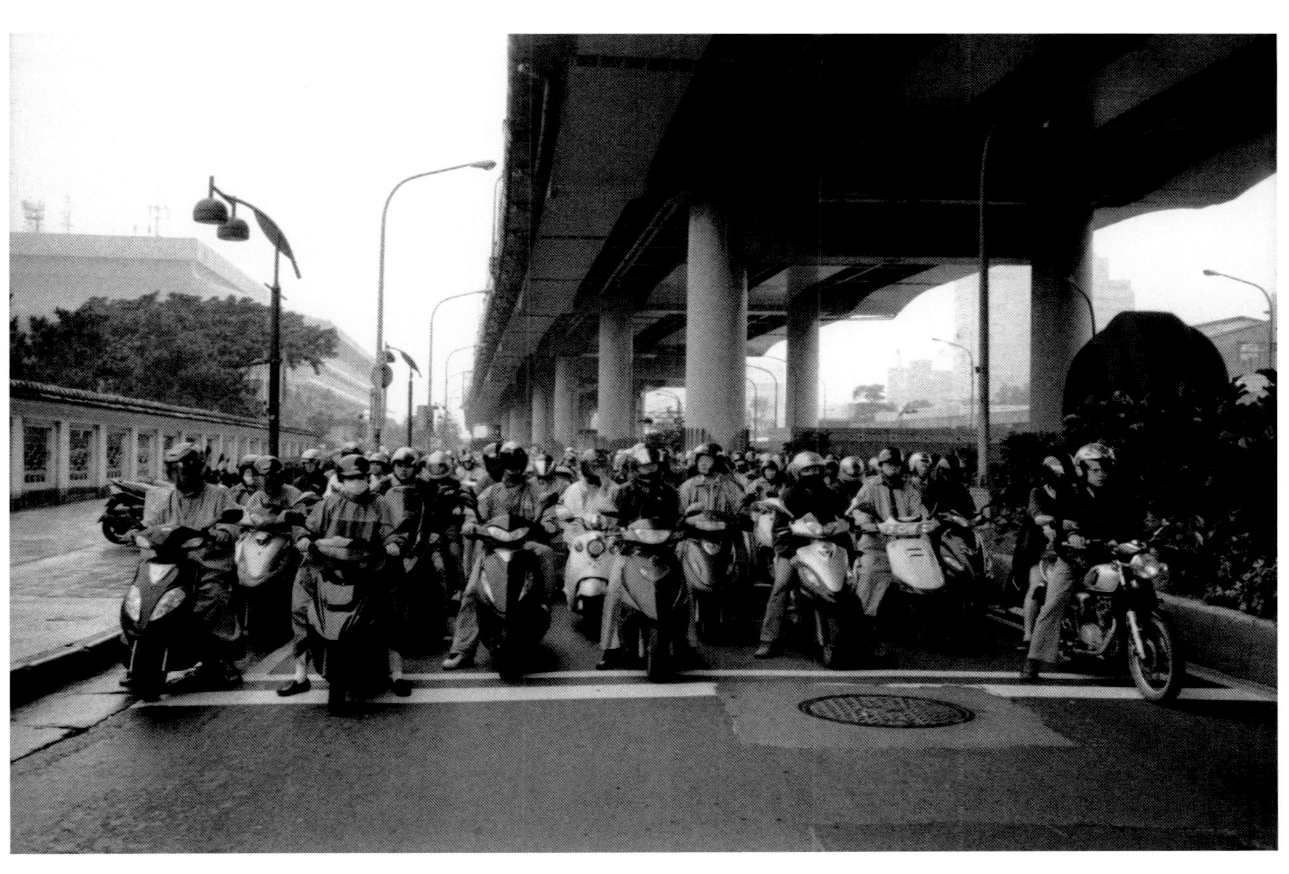

*Red Light Portrait #19*, 2006
Courtesy Coleção Sérgio Carvalho, Brasília

## Mabel Palacín

### Critique of Pure Image

Some artists are like that. Just like some of the key philosophers of modernity, it seems that their whole work evolves around a fundamental issue. Despite consciously using a variety of media, Mabel Palacín is conceptually a minimalist.

As we will see, the course set by this artist within a body of work produced with different media is essentially related to a single issue: what is the role of the image, in general, in contemporary societies?

The question is as old as the answer is intangible. What makes the construction of this project truly unique is its questioning evidence, in opposition to the moralist temptation that frequently structures theoretical or poetical propositions that take on this type of subject.

The first thing to consider when looking at the work of Mabel Palacín is the fact that the artist works essentially with the moving image, namely, with techniques and concepts that derive from the cinematic tradition. The inscription of critical revisions of models, structures, and modes of filmic creation in the universe of contemporary art has reached, in the past few years, an absolute point of no return, in that the main preoccupation, in most cases, is not as much related to the repercussion of cinema on society in general, which was problematized by Walter Benjamin in a paradigmatic way, as it is with what Jan Debbaut designated as *cinematic grammar*, in an eminently deconstructive process.

Thus, to the trivialization of the image and consequent crisis, which emerged from the numbing effect or the commercially targeted models imposed by the movies and marketing industry, and also, to say the truth, by a substantial part of contemporary artistic production, some artists responded with projects that create moments of suspension in the load of the entertainment business that seems to permeate everything. Curiously, this occurs largely through a sort of return to documentary, mirrored in projects such as the ones from Hito Steyerl, the deviant narratives of Tacita Dean, or in the radicalization of the filmic essence in Pedro Costa's cinema. In an opposite field, the critique gains form from the miscegenation of imagery traditions (from the so called fine arts, to photography, cinema and television), where authors such as Jeff Wall or the most recent Jean-Luc Godard are major examples. In this way, the directed attention, as opposed to the eminently dispersive nature of pure entertainment, would be established based on a vital self-referenciality or trans-referenciality.

Mabel Palacín positions herself in this second field. *La distancia correcta* is, in this respect, a paradigmatic work. Conceived as a double video projection, the first element to take into account is the plasticity inherent to the way in which it is presented. Although this work clearly guides us with assertiveness into the cinematographic universe, its perception is based on the tradition of video installation: the reception space was carefully thought out by the artist, and instead of the frontal omnipresent single screen, the two suspended screens let the viewer move around and even behind the screens, an openness that points towards the idea of the projection light as a material.

Basically, what we see in the two screens during the eight minutes and thirty seconds of the piece, are the actions of a character arriving at a sort of basement or garage where he gets ready to build a device that we soon associate with an explosive device. From the first moment, however, we are plunged into an environment that dislocates the action spatially towards an undetermined level, in which the narrative mingles with the history (or histories) of cinema: the first sound of the soundtrack – a decisive moment in the construction of the environment of this piece – is, symptomatically, the sound of a filmstrip passing through a projector. And the first images are images in which the character establishes a relation with background images that show excerpts of several "classic" movies. One should note the complexity of the procedure: this interaction originates both from the spaces, props and actions of the films, and from what is happening on the set. On the other hand, the narrative does not spread from one screen to the other. On the contrary, what we see in the right hand screen is a sort of flashback of what has happened in the left hand screen, where repetitions, anticipations, reverse shot details and still images that bring to mind a photographic memory instead of a clarification of the narrative, seem to thicken its hermeneutical opacity.

A crucial question is put forward: what is the basis of truth in the narratives intersected here? Doesn't the cinematographic memory configure a piece of our reality that is as valid as what has been *experienced*? In exalting the interaction between the character of *La distancia correcta* (The Correct Distance) with the movie excerpts that populate our imagination in a more or less significant way, the artist establishes this project in a territory where the reception, the a-perceptive modes in which the viewer is confronted with the work, is decisive. And in this case, as already mentioned, the manner in which the author clearly constructs a physical space for the reception of the work, granting it an eminently sculptural presence, is not innocent – and is further enhanced by the plasticity of the soundtrack that seems to earn a personality of its own within the narrative plot. Thus, just like the main character searches for a putative distance between the camera, the space in which the images are shot, and the images that flow on the background, so the spectator is invited to find the correct distance for the reception, both physically and psychologically.

This takes us back to the starting point: what is the status of the image in our contemporary society? Or rather: what is the origin of what is called the *construction of memory*? Is it intentional, or is it inevitably culturally determined, in the exact measure in which we move more or less critically through the flow of the real and the fictional with which we are confronted?

*Hinterland* and *Las puertas españolas* close the exhibition. In the same way as in *La distancia correcta*, Mabel Palacín creates a series of conceptual devices that short-circuit the transparency of the proposed images. In the first case, we see a video where the camera meticulously travels over a landscape; however, the naturalistic potential of this procedure is booby-trapped, for that which serves as the base for the filmed image is not nature, but a photographic representation of that same nature. The truth of the image has its origin in the technologically assisted representation of the real.

In the still brief history of the photographic and the moving image, something seems to strangely prevail: we are quicker to associate the moving image with the real, and more easily concede a memorial credibility to still photography. *Hinterland* works, thus, as an allegory for the reconstruction of memory through the still image, in this case in an inverted exercise because of being manipulated through the editing of the moving image.

In *Las puertas españolas* the artist turns this strategy upside down, composing four photographic sequences that are threefold recombined. Edition and montage, central concepts for the structuring of cinematic discourse, are transported into the context of photography. The origin of these images is filmed material, but it is in their interstices and in their sequencing that the recombination becomes meaningful, reiterating the role of the reception in the devices that the artist skilfully manipulates.

But let's return to the beginning: like the philosopher who operates in the territory of concepts, Mabel Palacín uses the image as a conceptual construct in order to better dissect its essence. Like the philosopher, the artist knows she may not reach a final conclusion; however, what truly interests her, and what decisively and positively affects the reception of her body of work, is precisely the process of disturbing the notion of image as an entity *free of risk and free of harshness*, as Catherine David has put it. This project is, thus, an eminently political project, or at least repeatedly questions the politic(s) of the image.

[Miguel von Hafe Pérez]

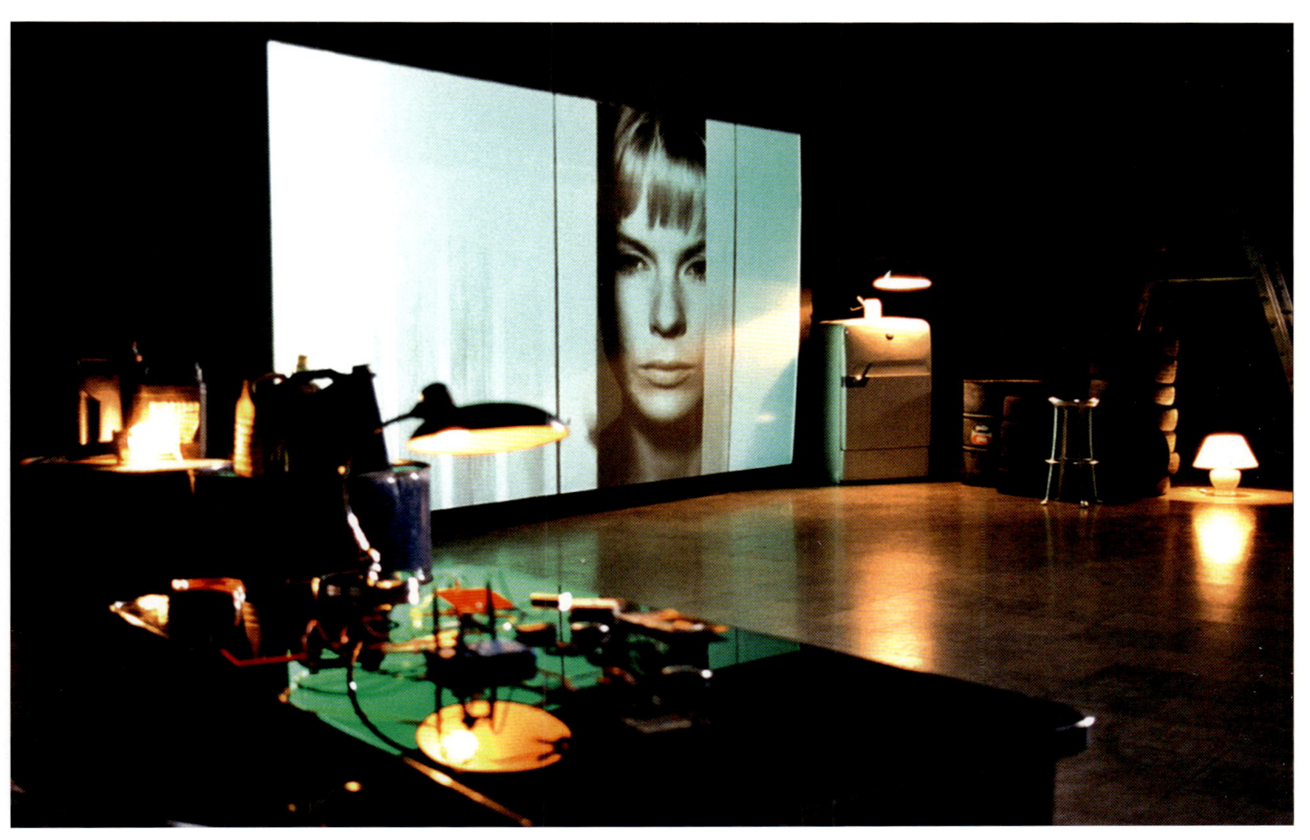

*The Right Distance*, 2002-03. Video show
© Mabel Palacín

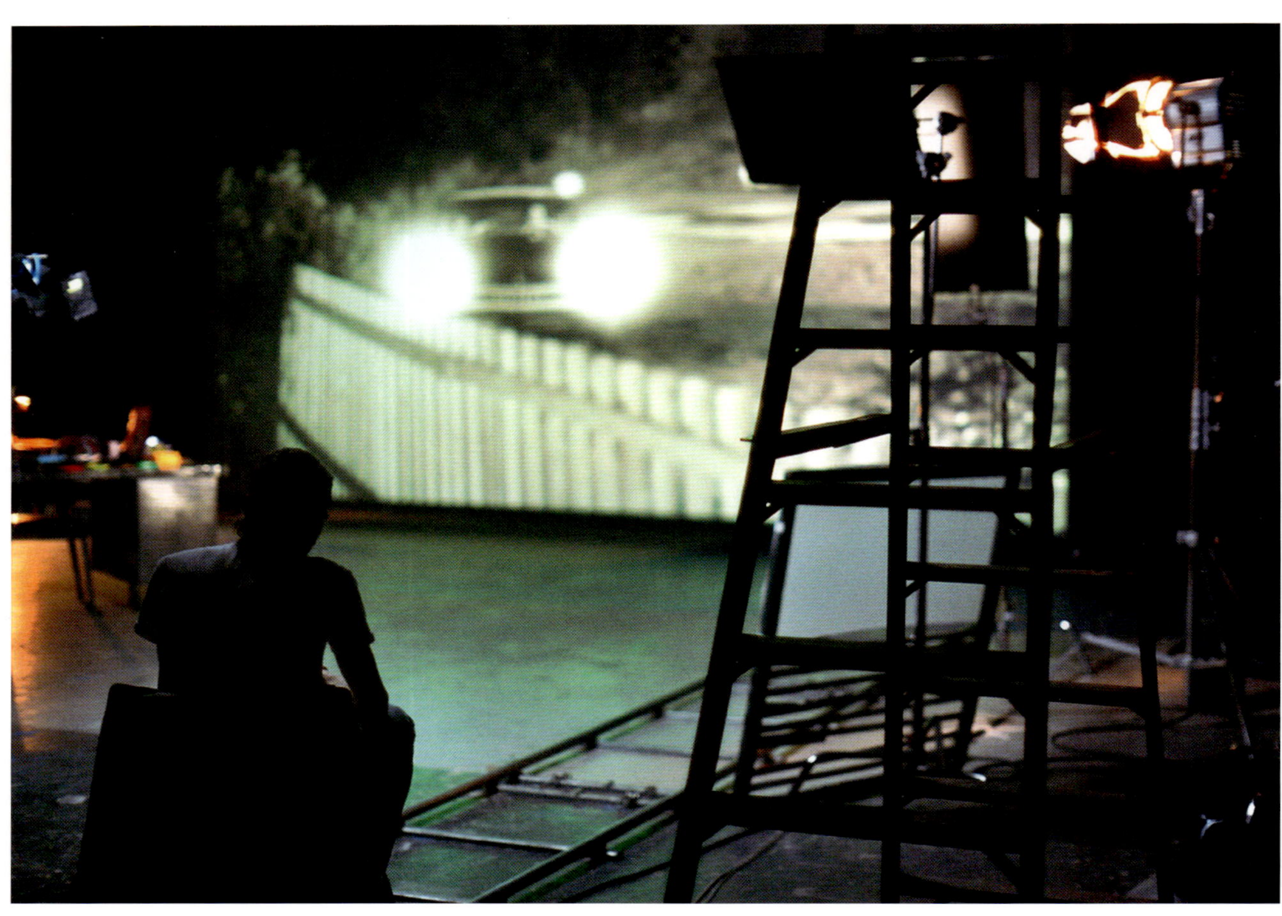

*The Right Distance*, 2002-03. Video show

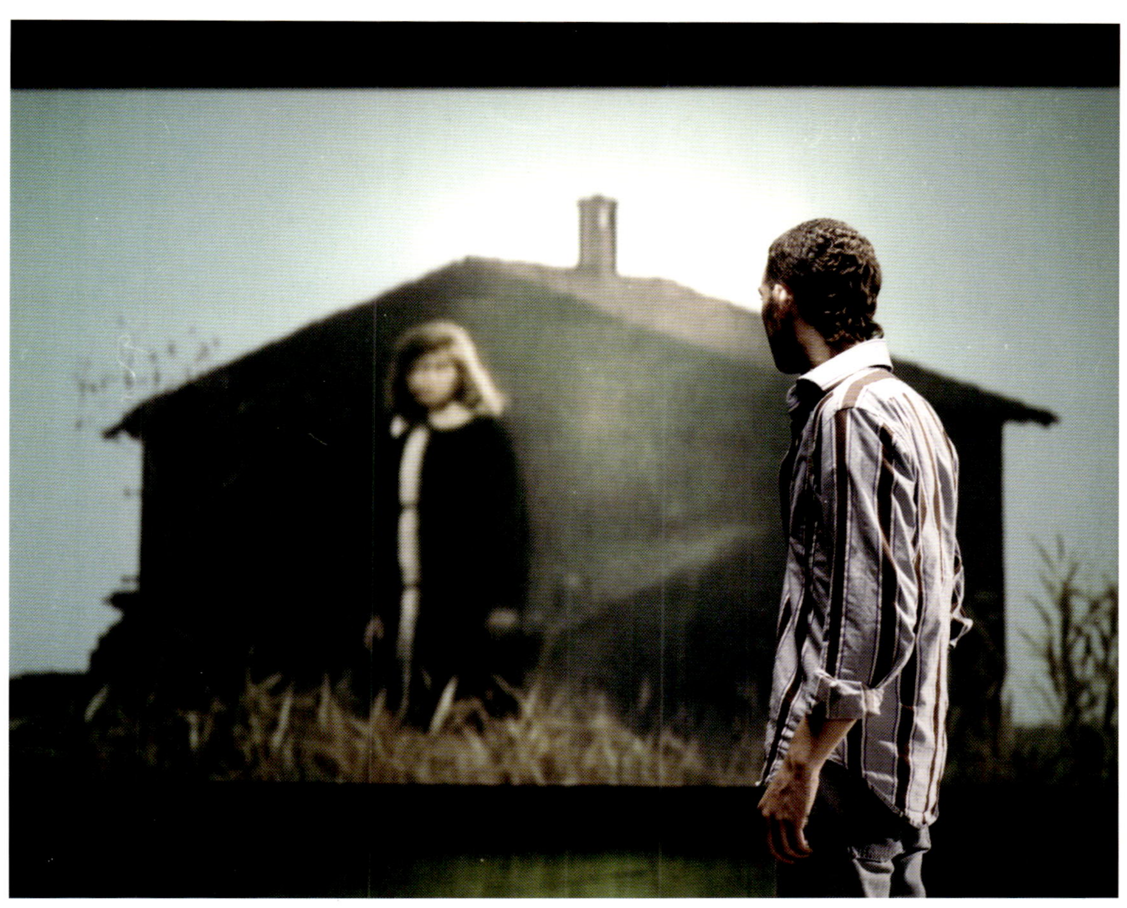

## Ugo Mulas

### Thought by Thought, Shot by Shot

Few authors have contributed as much to the evolution of photographic language as Mulas, and perhaps no one else has studied and experimented with all the possible registers offered by this art, which is simultaneously ambiguous and strikingly precise. Mulas was deeply aware of the specificity of the instruments of photography. So much so that he delved into the depths of every intellectual concept with his work *Verifiche (Verifications,* 1968-72), after a career in which he had already been a key figure in news, portrait, fashion, advertising and art photography and its research.

From his very first photographs in the 1950s to his premature death in 1972, Mulas was able to demonstrate how much potential was hidden within photography as a medium and a language, and he stimulated thought within the world of contemporary art that he frequented, analyzed and masterfully documented.

It was precisely his persistent visual documentation of his artist friends and above all his 1965 trip to see the burgeoning Pop Art phenomenon in New York, which brought him fame not only as an extraordinary portraitist, but also as a one of a kind art critic. He confronted the essence of the work in all its implications, and never stopped at the documentary function of a shot. Umberto Eco has no doubts that Mulas, as a photographer, went far beyond the emotional impact of the figure, of the work and of his study: "It is about a discourse on the strategy of the piece, and the working artist is present only when his gesture is part of that strategy."[1]

Mulas' start in photography was based entirely on self-taught skills and lasted just twenty years. During that period he produced a startling number of photographs, covering a wide range of terrain, but injecting each work with a subtle ability for innovation, the fruit of constant research, insurmountable curiosity, profound culture and a superior intelligence.

He was studying law in Milan when his relentless attraction to art drew him to nearly camp out in the Bar Jamaica, a dairy bar near the Brera Fine Arts Academy and local hang out for artists and intellectuals. It was there that someone put a camera in his hand and said simply, "One one-hundredth eleven in the sun, one twenty-fifth five-six in the shade." Mulas always insisted on the fact that he began by chance, but actually everything about him was predisposed to this means of expression, as he wrote in one of his revealing texts: "I was not even an amateur photographer. The first photo I made, I immediately sold."[2] At that period in history, "authentic" photography was photoreporting, as involvement with the surrounding reality was, for many, a moral imperative. So in 1953, riding on the wave of neorealism that tinged all artistic expression in the post-war period, Mulas developed a project on the outskirts of Milan. "Those old neorealist style photos are dear to me; they are my first attempts at establishing photographic contact with a real life situation. I wanted to put a message into focus, a message that I felt I had to bring, and at the same time I wanted to single out the common thread that connected the people, the episodes, the facts and the places."[3]

A constant tension arises from the drive to understand reality in order to understand himself. This tension is present in all the photographic genres Mulas took on, and he took them all on together, simultaneously, and did so professionally in every field. Surely this was most salient when he addressed the universe of contemporary art. "It is also true that for many years I went around photographing painters. The hidden

1. *Fotografare l'Arte*, pictures by Ugo Mulas, work by Pietro Consagra. From the *Introduction* by Umberto Eco, Milan, Fratelli Fabbri Editore, 1972.

2-7. Ugo Mulas, *La fotografia*, edited by Paolo Fossati, Turin, Giulio Einaudi editore, 1973.

drive was the idea that through painting and painters I would have been able to grasp something more than painting alone and I would be able to understand myself."[4] The extraordinary encounters he had while frequenting the Venice Biennales and spending time in the studios of Italian and international artists, often turned into very special relationships, in which collaboration, trust and friendship mixed together creating fertile occasions for dialogue. Calder, Duchamp, Fontana, Burri and Consagra, and then the Americans, from Jasper Johns to Roy Lichtenstein, from Warhol to Rauschenberg, all felt understood by Mulas, "as though it were a session of psychoanalysis," as Umberto Eco suggests in the introduction to the book on the sculptor Consagra.

His skill in controlling the camera and above all within the dark room was equal to his elegance as a theorist of the photographic language. This meant the entire creative process was carried out with an awareness that was rare at the time: "... My point of view is not only optical, but spiritual as well."[5]
The *Verifiche* which were made shortly before his death were nothing more than an organization of the reflections that Mulas had elaborated with regard to his intense relationship with photography. In them he analyzed every function and dissected its sense: from the exposure time, to the blow-up, to the lenses, to the use of photography. His attitude is "operational" with regard to the analysis and the completeness of the logical and practical ideas. He reveals his need: "It may be that at the base of these digressions of mine there is a need to shine a light on my own game, something which is typical of the self-taught who having started in the dark, want to make everything clear and visible."[6]

Between these two ends of the creative muddle – the complicity with the artists and the theoretical analysis of photographic language – that gave him such great notoriety, Mulas was also called on to bring his magic touch to various other fields. In theatre, his set designs for Berg's *Wozzek* and Britten's *Turn of the Screw* were unforgettable. In fashion, he brought in so many innovative ideas that entire generations were needed to catch up with them. The most important fashion designers have benefited from his interpretation, which was slightly intellectual, but always filled in with a magnificent lightness that ennobled the clothes through images that told far more.

Mulas also tested himself in advertising photography in the vivid 1960s. Typically, he took his own approach, using architecture as an evocative place where people do not actually appear in the photograph. Often he would also take up the challenge of industrial photography as well as other jobs as wide-ranged as the various facets of photography itself.

The photographer Ugo Mulas is a very peculiar figure. He was an intellectual in the broadest and most sincere sense of the word, who during his both extremely brief and prolific career, knew how to explore new territories and provide a deep and illuminated account of them, step by step, thought by thought, shot by shot. "... So at a certain point I began operations by myself... to see what it felt like to face a job alone, how it is to look for nothing except the truth, to find it only in oneself, and to understand what this profession is, to analyze every single operation, take it apart like you can do with a camera, to get to know it."[7]

[Enrica Viganò]

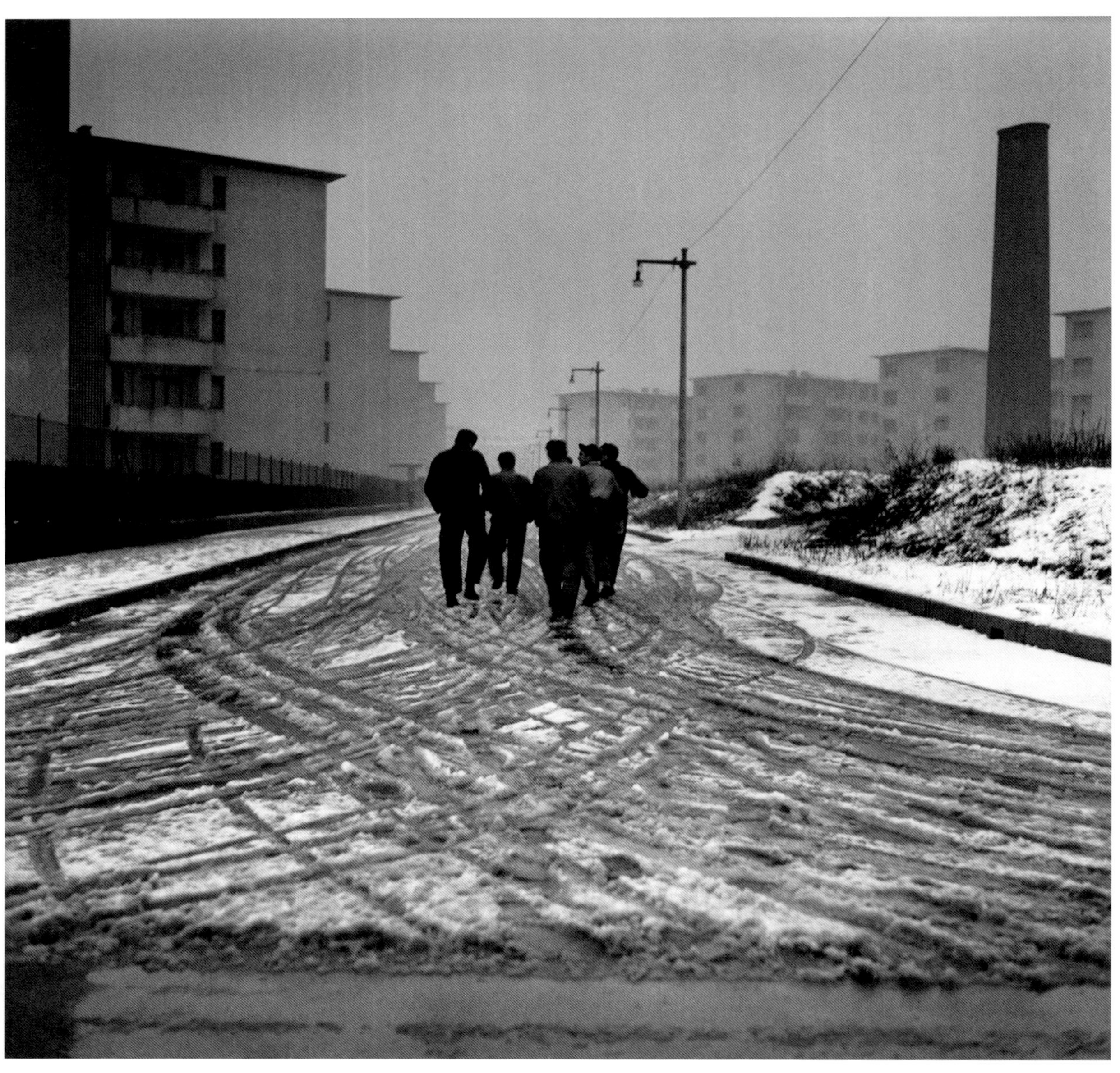

*Milan*, 1953-54
Courtesy Archivio Ugo Mulas

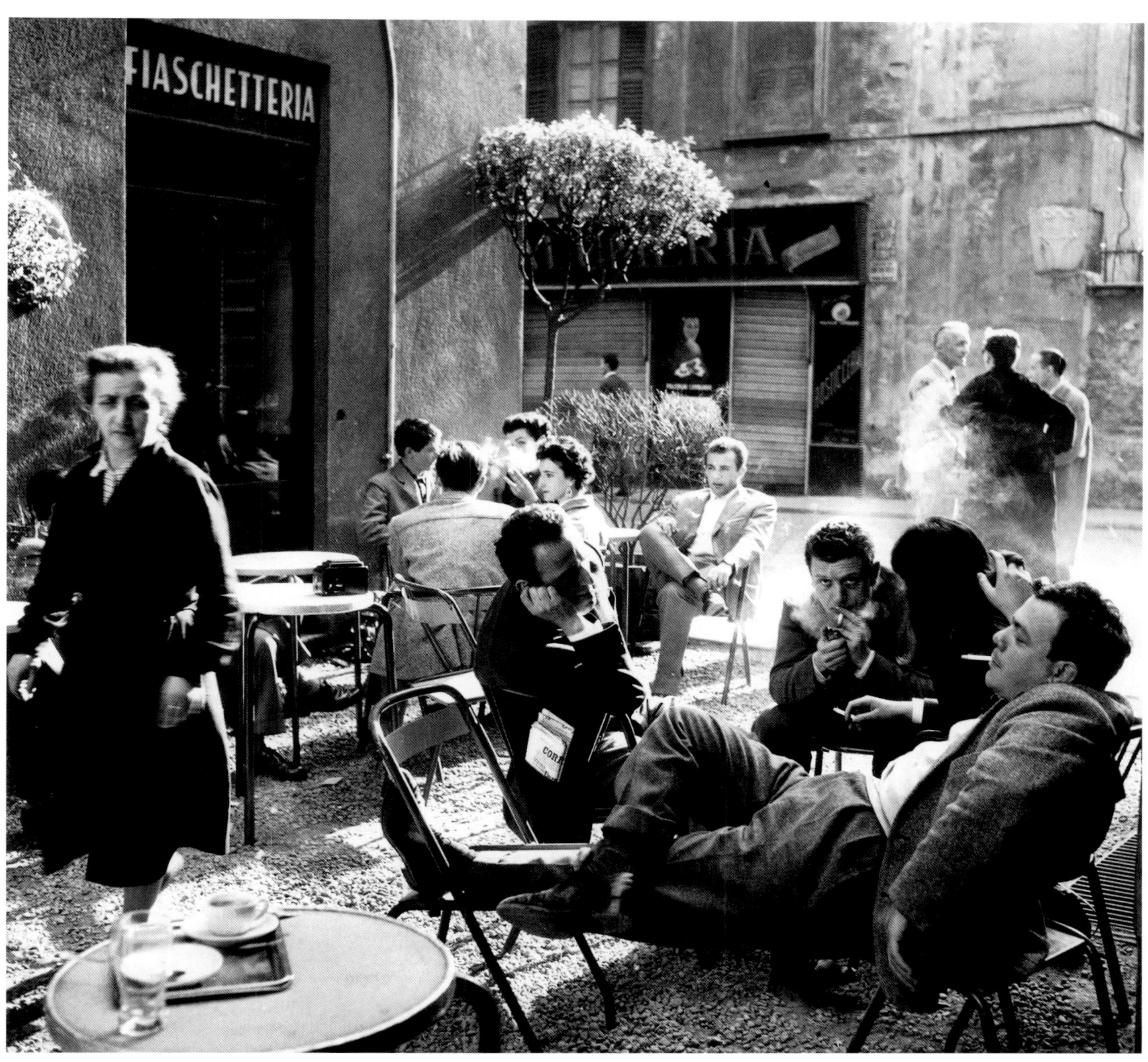


*Lina Mainini, Alfa Castaldi, Arturo Carmassi & Cesare Peverelli. Jamaica Bar, Milan*, 1953-54
Courtesy Archivio Ugo Mulas

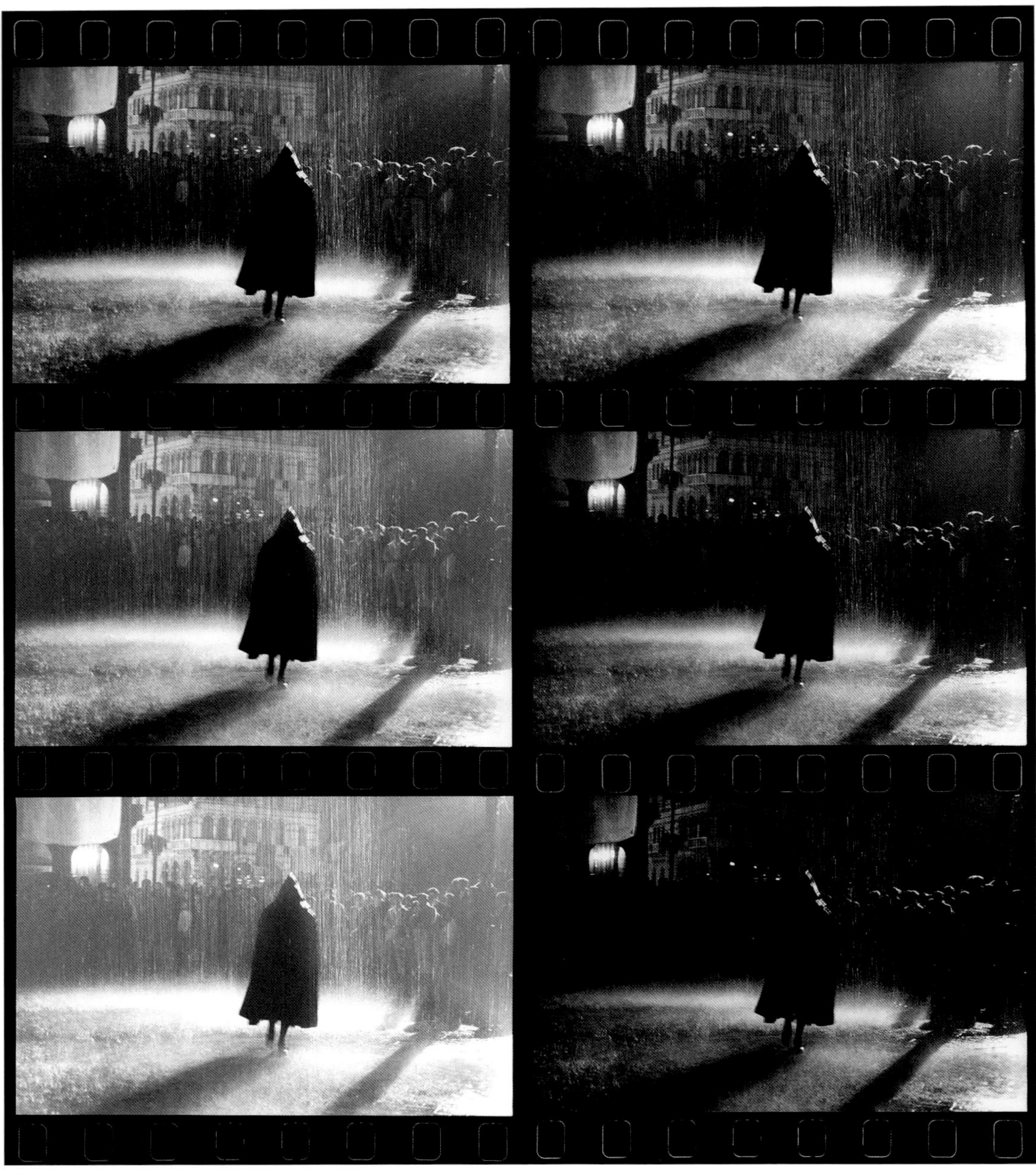

*Urban Landscape, Como*, 1969
Courtesy Archivio Ugo Mulas

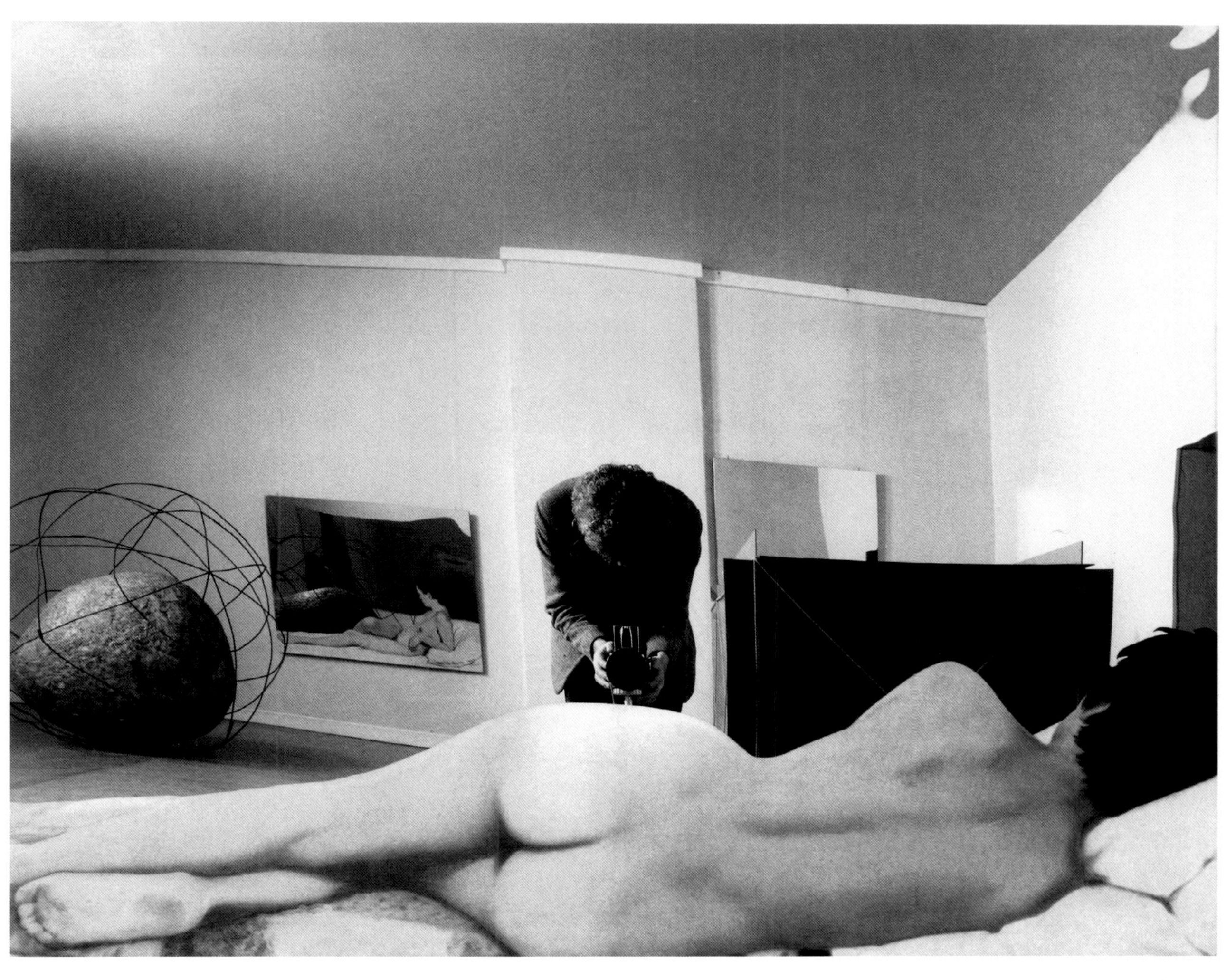

*Ugo Mulas self-portrait, reflected on Michelangelo Pistoletto's work "Vitalità del negativo", Rome,* 1970
Courtesy Archivio Ugo Mulas

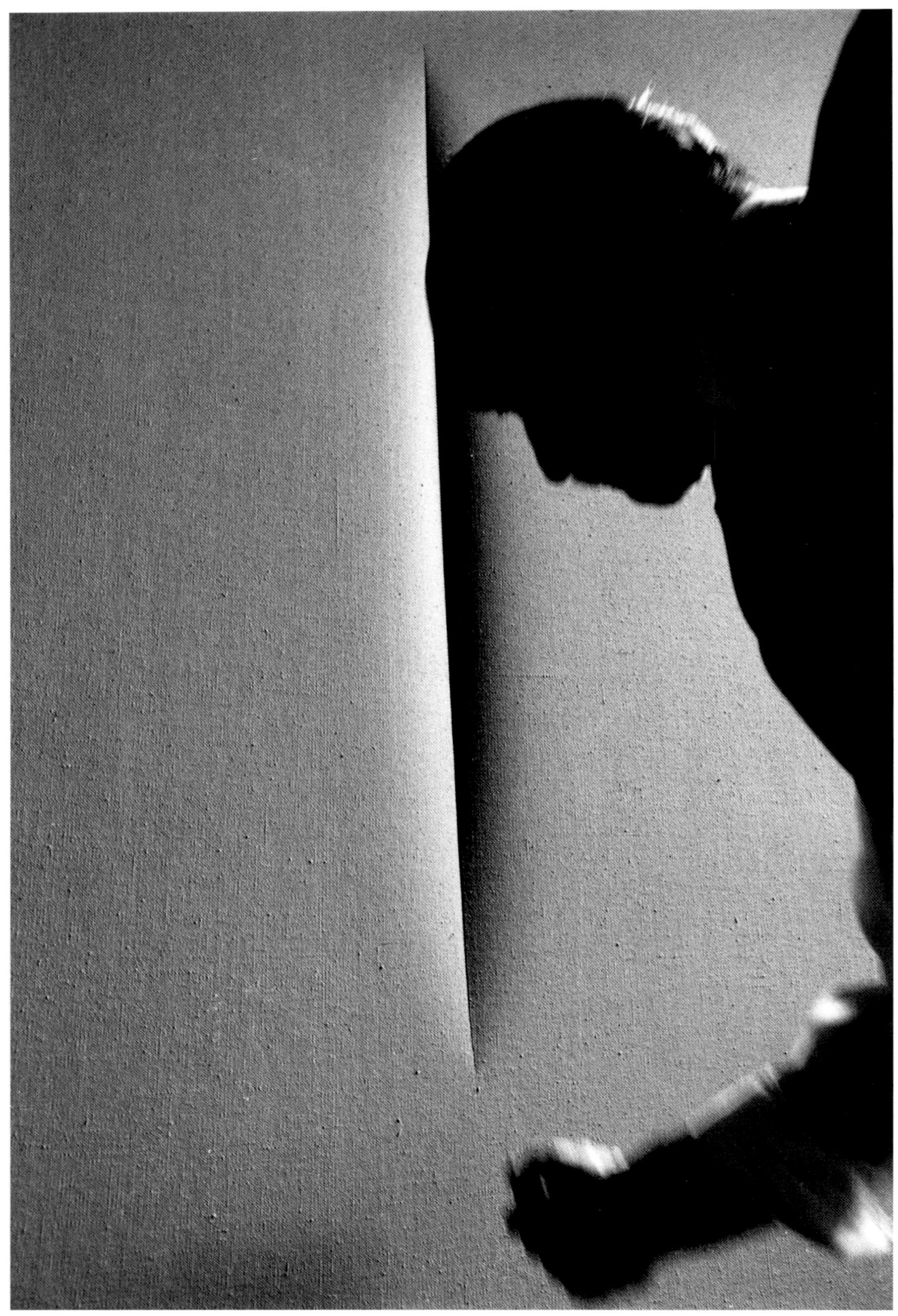

*Lucio Fontana, Milan*, 1964
Courtesy Archivio Ugo Mulas

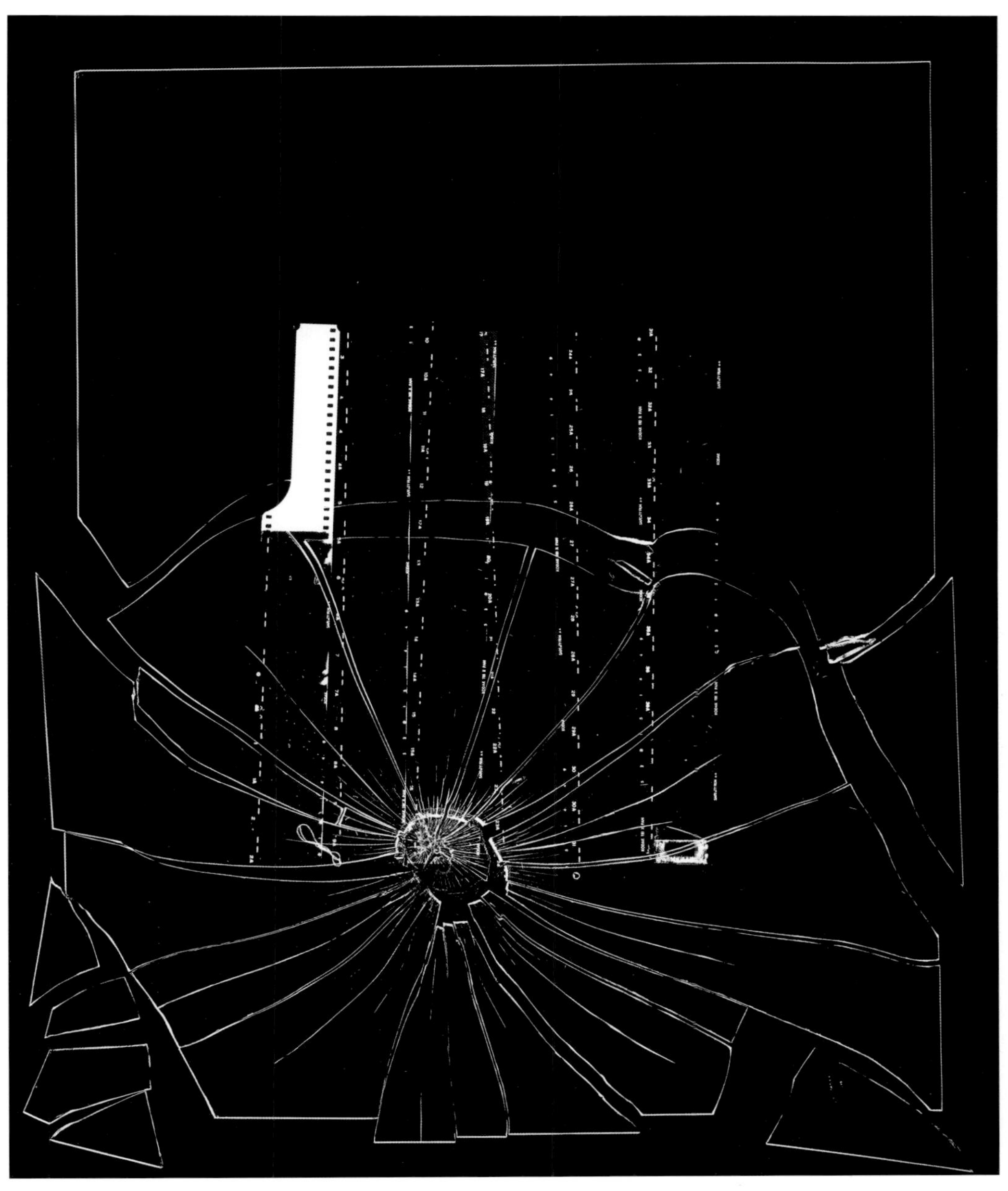

*End of the series Verifiche. For Marcel Duchamp*, 1970
Courtesy Archivio Ugo Mulas

# Cristóbal Hara

## Documents and Everyday Life

Cristobal Hara (Madrid, 1946) has been constructing a very peculiar imaginary since the 1970s, focused on places and situations that are, in some way, paradigmatic of the Spanish vernacular geography. In small villages and a few cities, Hara has scrutinized very diverse topics of the daily experience: episodes and characters, streets and public spaces, rituals and everyday events, expressions of the sacred and the profane, animals (mostly horses, bulls and stray dogs), manifestations around death and sexuality. These are images connected with fundamental and essential themes of the Spanish reality, which he reconfigures in this way through a disconcerting *phenomenology of everyday life.*

Cristobal Hara's trajectory was initially more closely related to the tradition of black and white reportage photography. But one should not rush into judging his creative affiliations, simply because Cristobal Hara does justice to one of the most valued and exceptional qualities that one should expect in an author: the creative and ethical capacity to construct a singular universe in order to establish a unique and genuine idiosyncratic domain. This is also the reason why Cristobal Hara has defined, at his own pace, a solitary and personal path that is almost impossible to classify.

In 1985, Cristobal Hara shifted into colour photography. And when he did it, he chose the most widespread films, the ones that can be bought in any store, or even the supermarket. This kind of film allows for a more saturated colour spectrum, which he considered suitable to work on his eminently informal, simple and circumstantial style. As a matter of fact, one should recognise that the apology of the informal (on the edge of the snapshot aesthetics), which can frequently be identified in the work of Cristobal Hara, should not be mistaken for a lack of commitment or the adherence to an aesthetics of randomness. Truth is, that in this case, informality is conscious and has been submitted to a careful and refined sense of construction and composition of the image (sometimes subtly revealing his pictorial culture and interest in cinema) but always in the sense of its simplest and most "familiar" manifestation. Thus, it is a lucid and deliberate look, attentive to the justice and justness of the image, which does not yield to the technical and aesthetical mannerisms of "good photography."

The work of Cristobal Hara arises from an attentive and prolonged experience of observation, in an anthropological manner, in which the photographer attempts to understand the routines, the movements and the connective signs between the people and between these and the places they go to and live in. However, despite their documental character, his photographs are not limited to the description of specific themes and matters; these are images that instruct the expectation of mobilizing comprehension into grey zones forcing the viewers into scrutinizing the(ir) possible meanings of the image. This is also the reason why the places are more or less unrecognisable, almost abstract (and yet indisputably part of the Spanish vernacular imaginary), and the characters are ambiguous, nameless, closer to typologies of people than to real individuals.

In this context, these images are very far from the genre of photojournalism, although sometimes reminiscent of this socio-professional branch of photography. And they are very different because

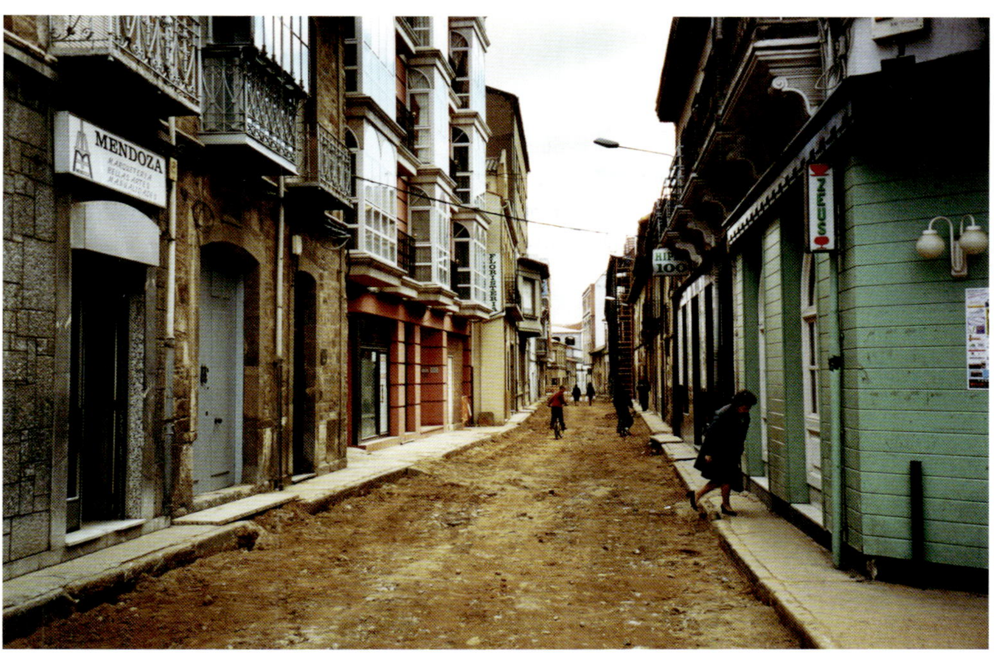


Cristobal Hara marshals the real into an expanded time, into a zone in which the most unexpected instants and the most elaborated images demand for a certain duration – a duration that states the possibility of the image to be, besides an experience of the eye, an experience of thought. This duality has a correspondence with one of the most interesting features of Hara's work: the oscillation between what is concrete and what is ambiguous, between the descriptive and the metaphorical.

This communicational game is relevant because it creates the possibility for the images to be presented not as simple *fait-divers* of daily life but, on the contrary, that this gaze over the more earthly life should be a privileged way of determining a speculative documentation. It is a photographic *pathos* that does not seek the spectacular and extraordinary (in fact, refusing it), but that builds up from an experiential basis of the small moments that compose the heart and the precariousness of life (and photography). When faced with these images by Cristobal Hara, we get the impression that only the photography media is able to open with such strangeness and productivity this imaginative and reflexive confrontation between image and reality, between art and society, between high culture and popular culture. This is the spectrum of photography.

[Sérgio Mah]

*La Bañeza*, 2004

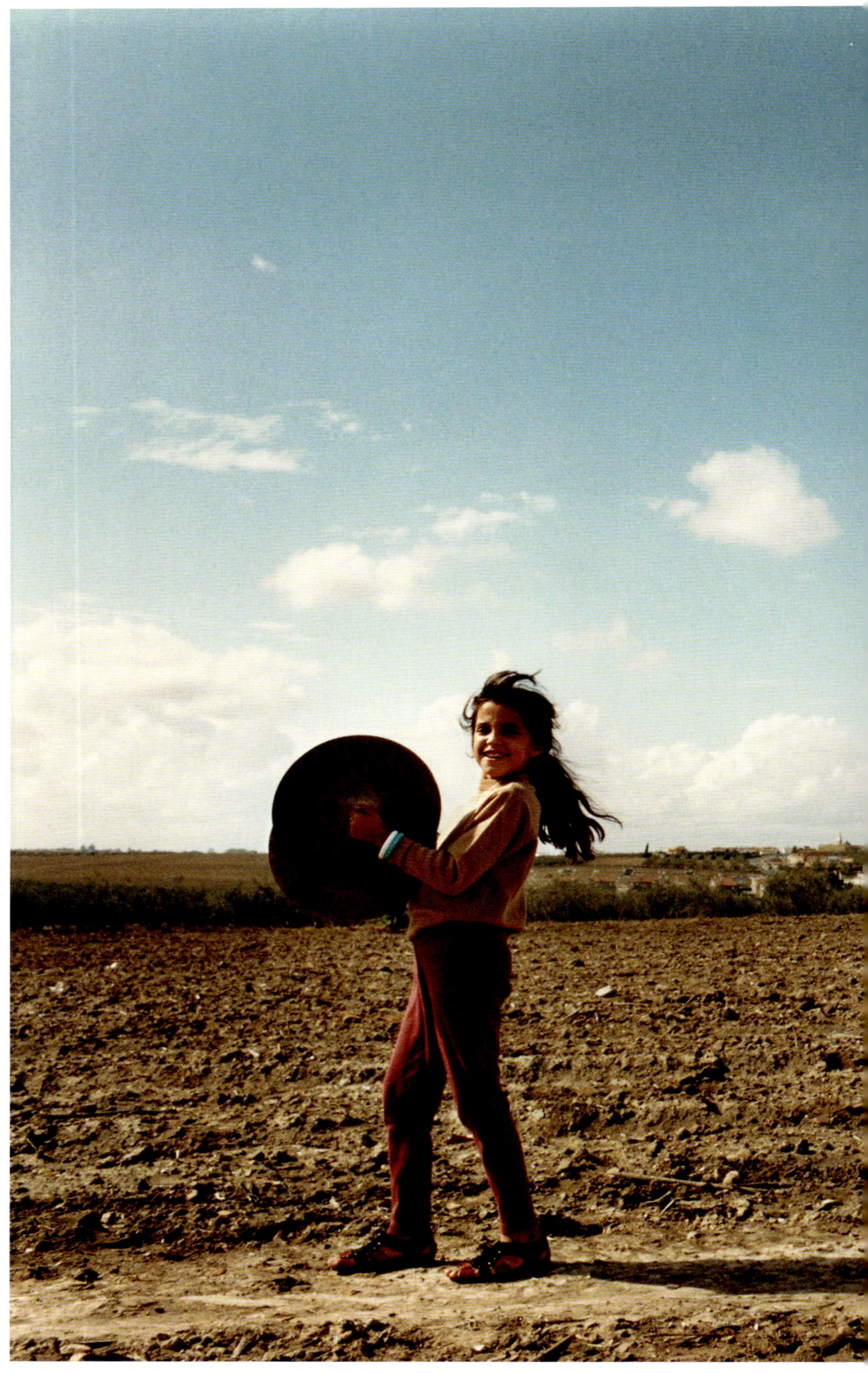

*Valencina de la Concepción*, 1993

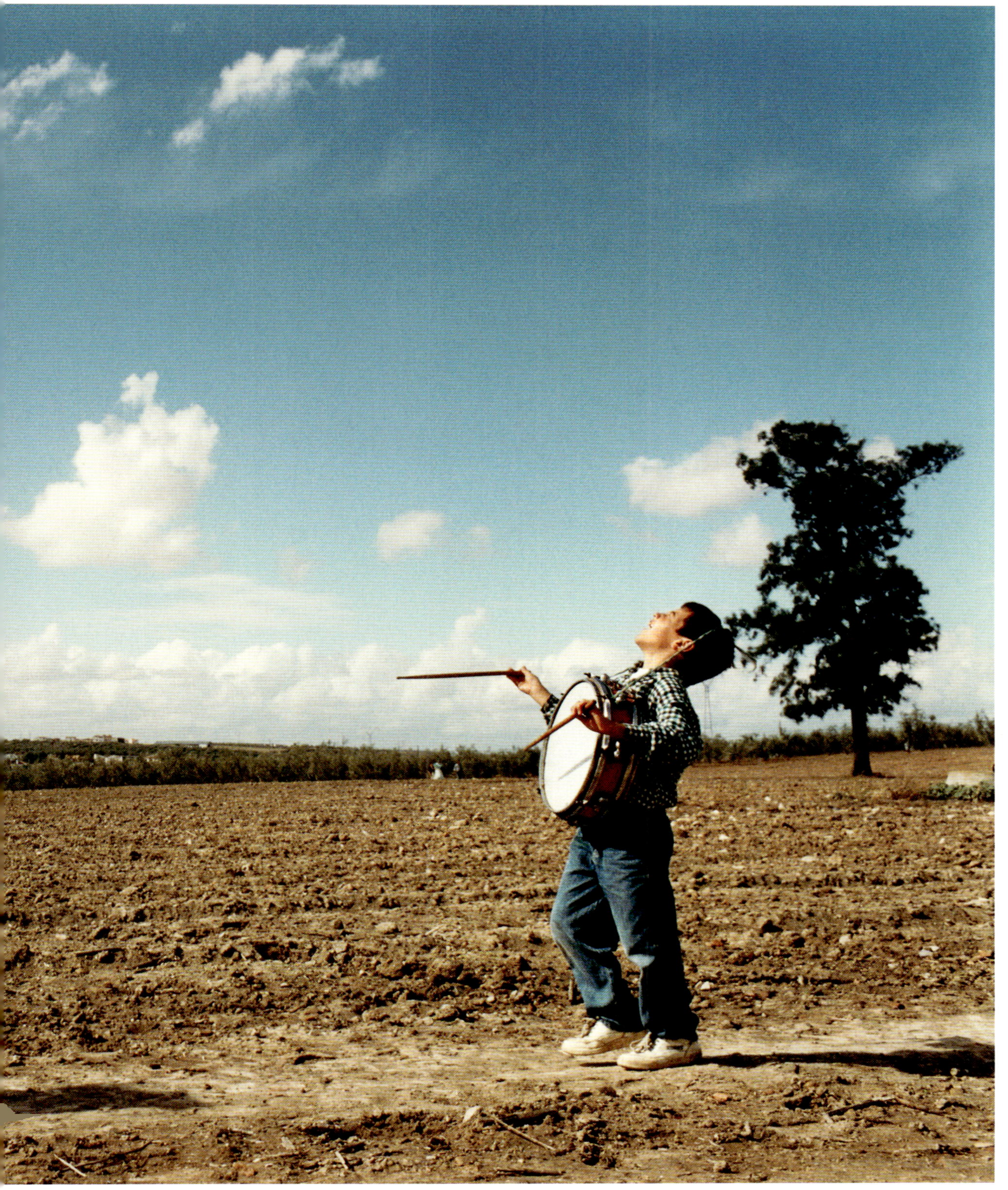

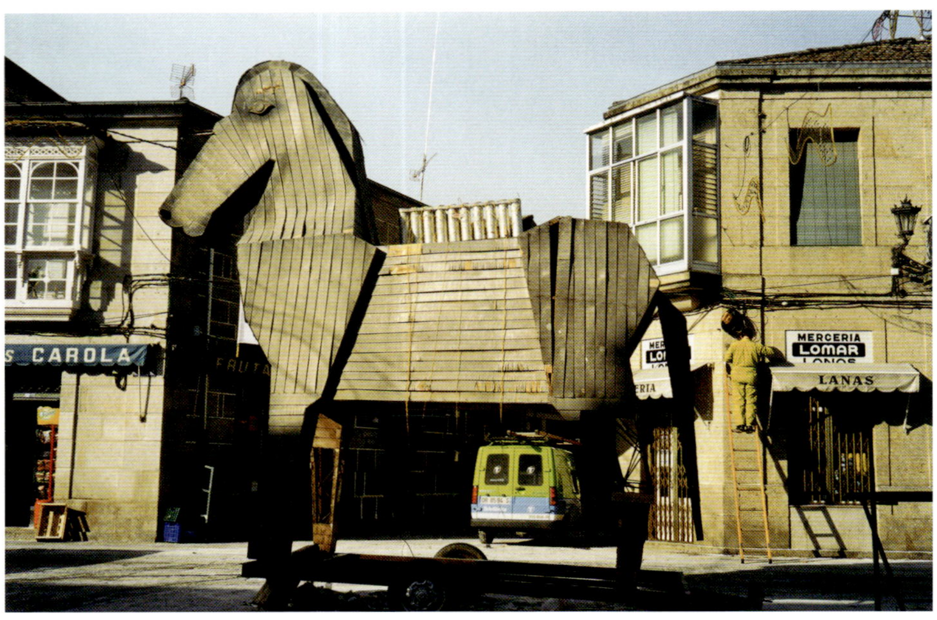


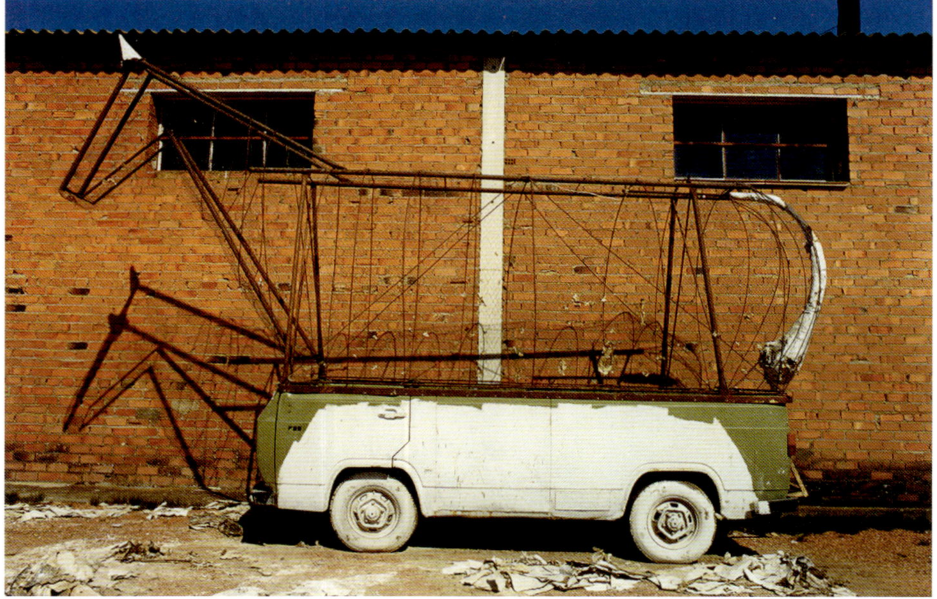

*Verín*, 2000


*Fuentesecas*, 2001

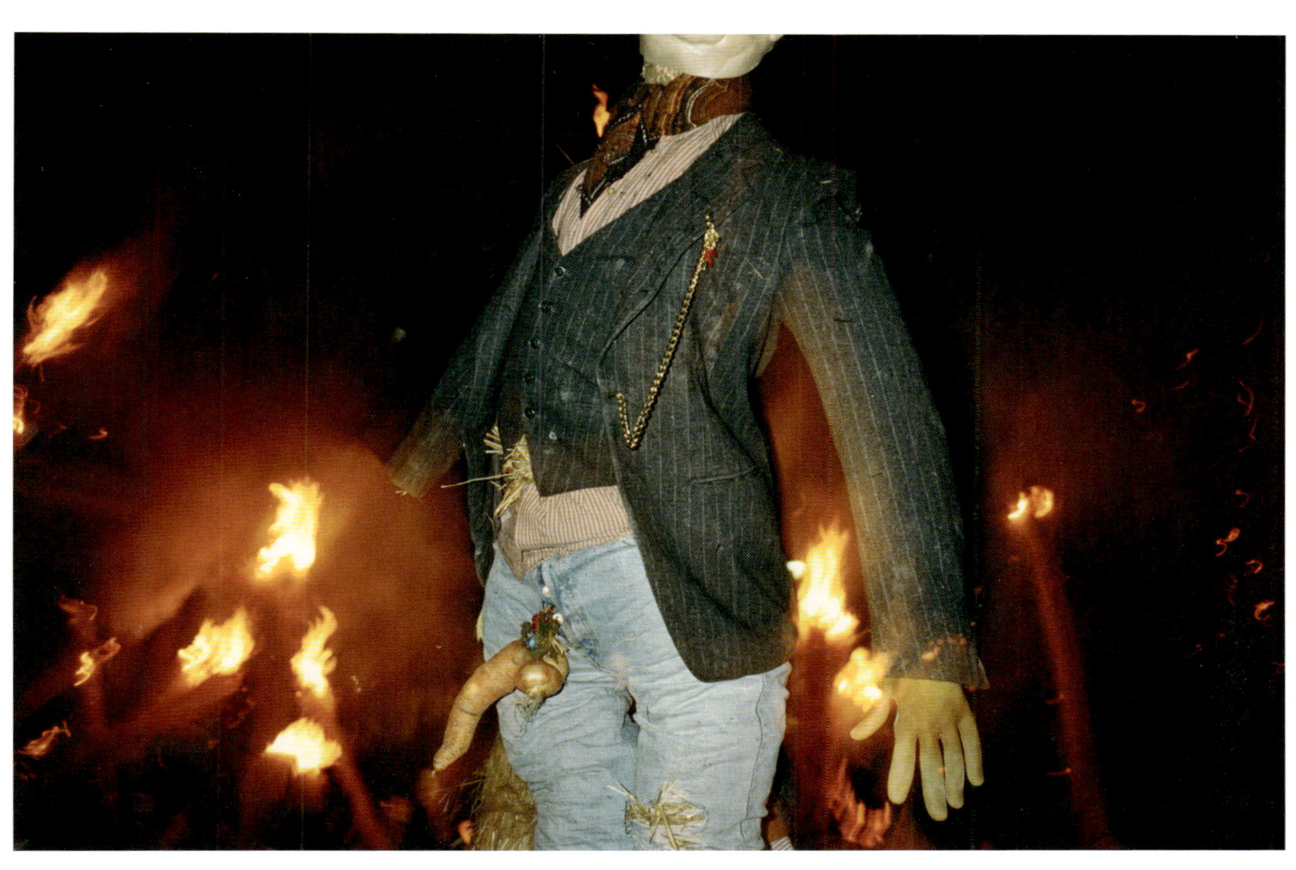

*Oimbra*, 1997

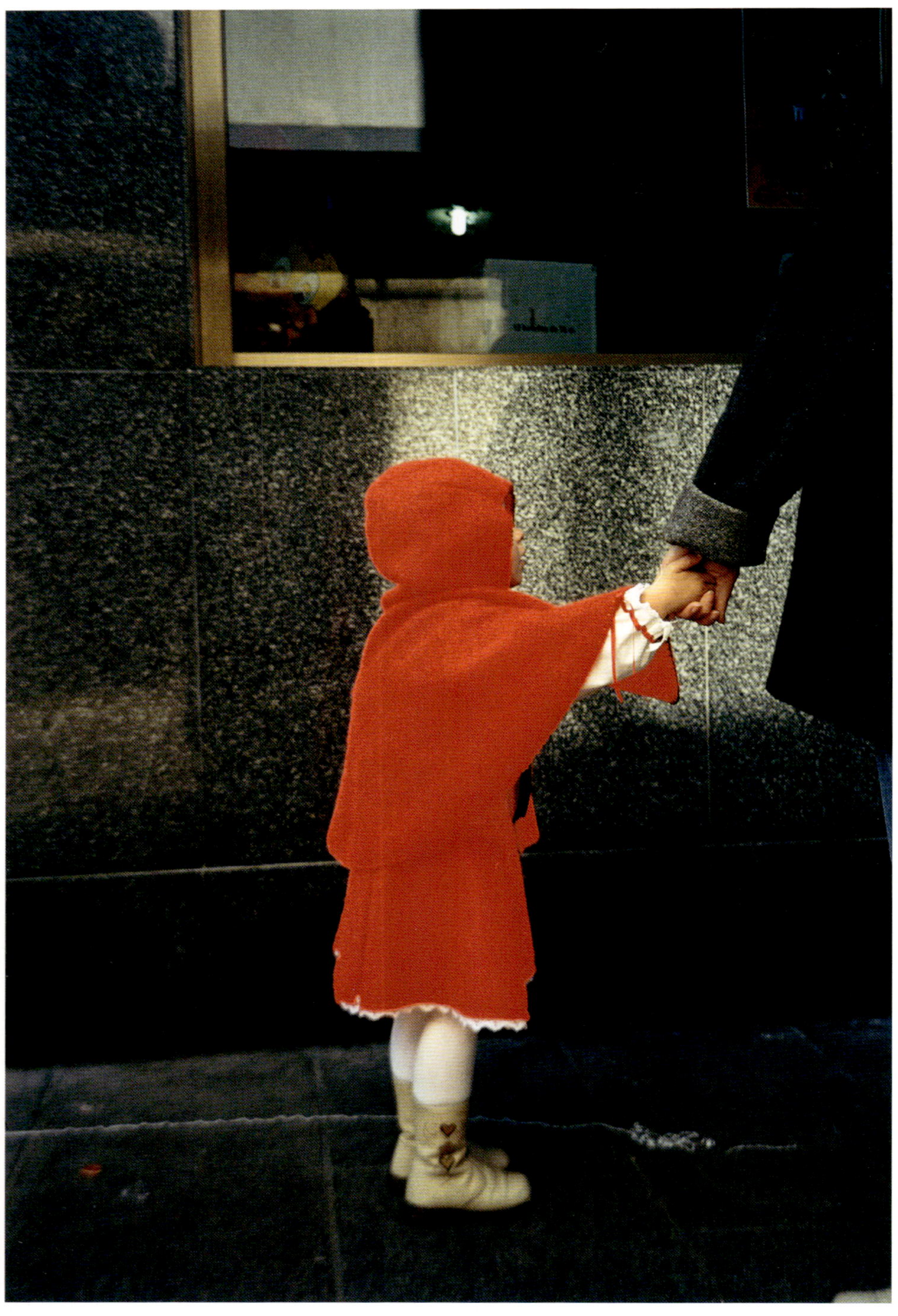

*Xinxo de Lima*, 2005


*El Corpiño*, 1995

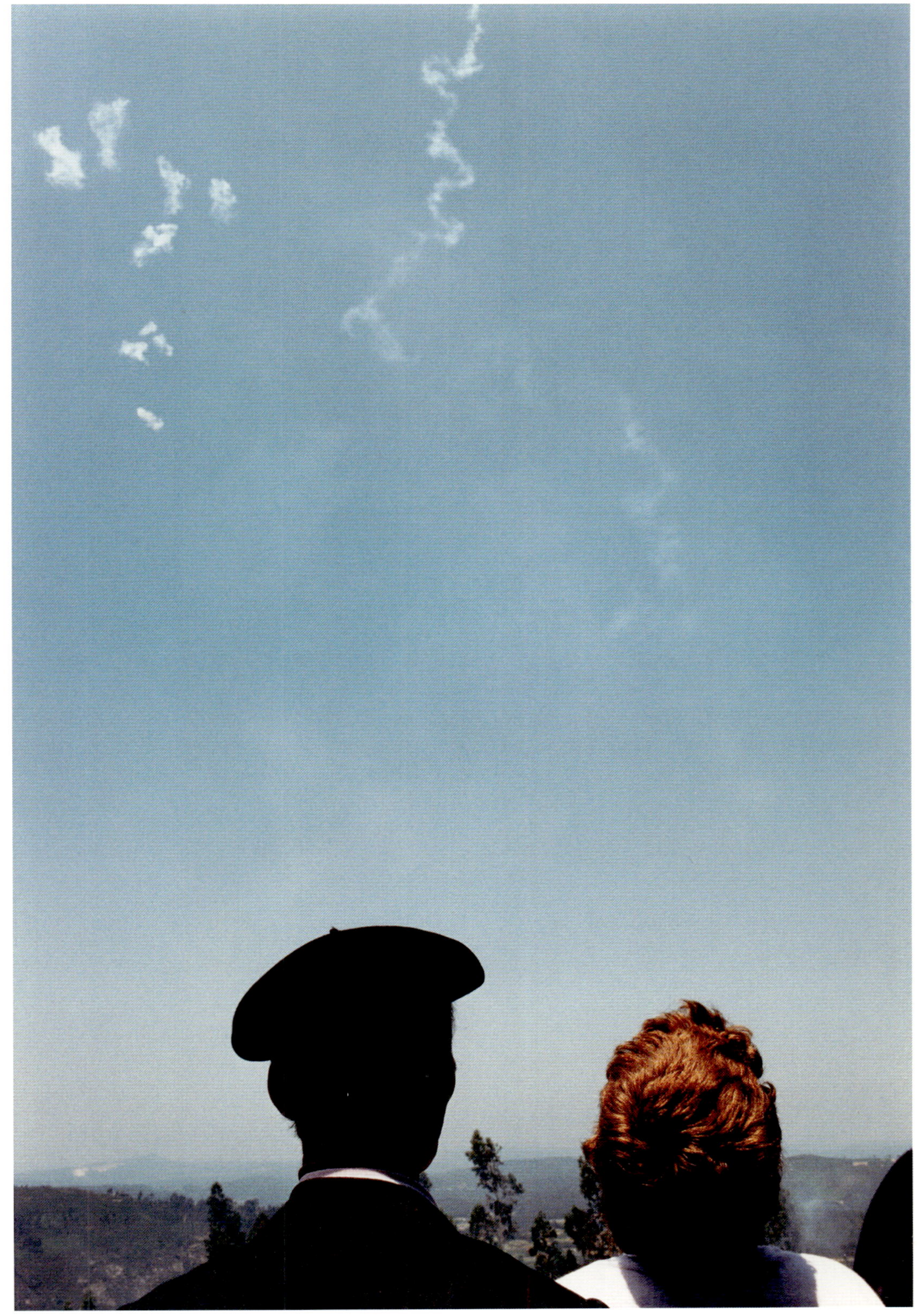

## Bartolomé Ros. Borders of Africa

### A Plausible Epic

Born in Cartagena, Murcia in 1906, Bartolomé Ros lived in Ceuta from 1918 until the mid-nineteen fifties. He learned photography in this city and began to work documenting civil and military society. His professional oeuvre is both a testimony to daily life in the Spanish protectorate as reflected in his portraits of the bourgeoisie of Ceuta and the postcards he published with urban motifs and picturesque views of Morocco, and a graphic chronicle of Spanish military presence in the western part of northern Africa. Ros worked for the army in this geographical area photographing military acts and facilities, an activity that he later extended with his contributions to the local and national press.

One of the most surprising facts in Ros's biography is his precocious intelligence and early passion for entrepreneurial challenges. Born to a humble family in Cartagena's Los Dolores district, Bartolomé Ros began to work when he was barely ten years old doing the accounting for his Uncle Alfonso. As historian José Luís Gómez Barceló explains in his very thorough reconstruction of the photographer's life published by the Ministry of Defence in 2005, young Bartolomé had left public school after his teacher notified his parents that he no longer had anything left to teach him. His attraction for photography dated from this time, although he was unable to learn the trade until he began to work as an apprentice in the Calatayud photographic studio in Ceuta, the city to which his family had moved in search of a better future. Having mastered the rudiments of the medium and after obtaining a small loan, the young Ros purchased his first photographic equipment and the materials to install his own laboratory at the age of fourteen. Very soon he began to freelance and went out to look for clients in the city's military facilities and even in the Llano de las Damas bullring, where he photographed the spectators. As the bullfight progressed, Ros used to develop and print these shots in his brand new home laboratory and return to the bullring in time to put the portraits up for sale before the bullfight ended. A short time later, he rented premises with his father, Prudencio Ros, where he offered photographs and collections of postcards of a costumbrist nature to the public. Installed in his own photography shop, he made numerous albums on Morocco and Ceuta and reached an agreement with Hauser Menet, a prestigious company of photographers and publishers, to print and distribute his editions of postcards.

Before coming of age, Bartolomé Ros established another agreement with Agfa, a company producing photosensitive material, to distribute their products. Because of his age, however, the contract had to be signed by his father. In 1921, at the age of fifteen, he published his first photograph in the *Mundo Gráfico* magazine, which paved the way for him to work as a photojournalist in Ceuta and occasionally publish work in the *ABC* newspaper and the *Blanco y Negro* magazine. During the following years, he signed a collaboration agreement with Ceuta photojournalist Ángel Rubio to do press assignments. Together with Rubio, he was invited to participate in a photo essay on Spain published in the *National Geographic Magazine* in 1929. That same year he created Casa Ros in Ceuta, a company that would later spread throughout the entire zone of the Spanish protectorate in Morocco and Tangier. Subsequently, during the Spanish Civil War, he provided material both to photographers and hospitals in the Iberian Peninsula. Thanks to his network of contacts, he could make penicillin reach the doctors of the intervention service at no profit to himself. In 1963 he founded the Ros Fotocolor photographic laboratories in Madrid. This laboratory, which served all of Spain, remained a family company until its sale in 2000.

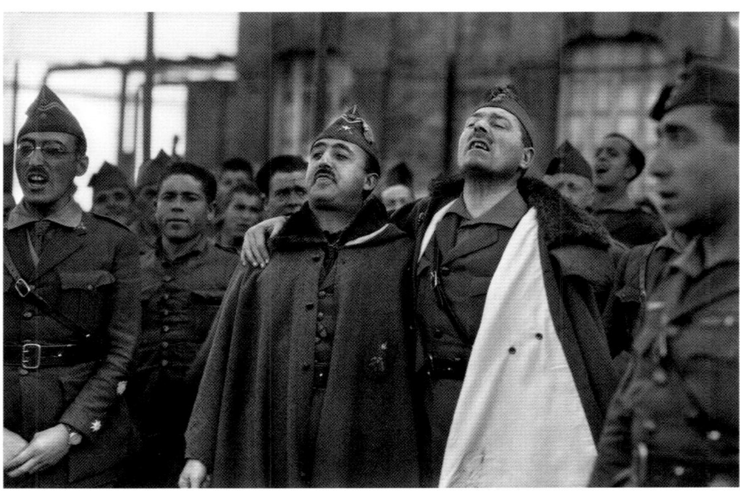

The photographic legacy of Bartolomé Ros covers a historical period that began in the final years of the Moroccan war and the beginning of the General Primo de Rivera dictatorship, which ended that conflict. His camera recorded visits by illustrious figures of the era, such as the arrival of Alfonso XIII and his family in the Spanish protectorate and the change of command in the Spanish Foreign Legion, which passed from a young Francisco Franco, recently promoted to general at the age of thirty-three, to José Millán-Astray who took charge of the Legion in 1926. Ros was a privileged witness to the moments preceding the Spanish army's uprising in Morocco against the Second Republic. His chronicle of this period has left exceptional moments for history, but also includes scenes of the daily life of anonymous soldiers, recorded with the exquisite formal meticulousness and documentary responsibility that characterised European photographers of the era. These are images free of artistic aspirations; they describe and document the troops at their daily tasks in order to illustrate the pages of *África Revista de Tropas Coloniales*, a monthly publication founded in 1926 by the military men Gonzalo Queipo de Llano, Francisco Franco and Antonio Martín de la Escalera, among others. The sobriety of these images contrasted with the propagandistic fervour of the texts, providing a counterpoint of verisimilitude to the epic narrative prose that prevailed in the faction that was later going to carry out the coup d'etat that began the Spanish Civil War.

The exhibition and book on Bartolomé Ros presented at Madrid's Museum of Contemporary Art seek to highlight the refined nature of his photographic work and the gaze of a man of liberal convictions who lived through the most tumultuous times in the history of twentieth-century Spain.

[Alejandro Castellote]

*Franco and Millán Astray Arm and Arm while Singing Legionary Songs, 1926*
Courtesy Archivo Familiar Ros Amador

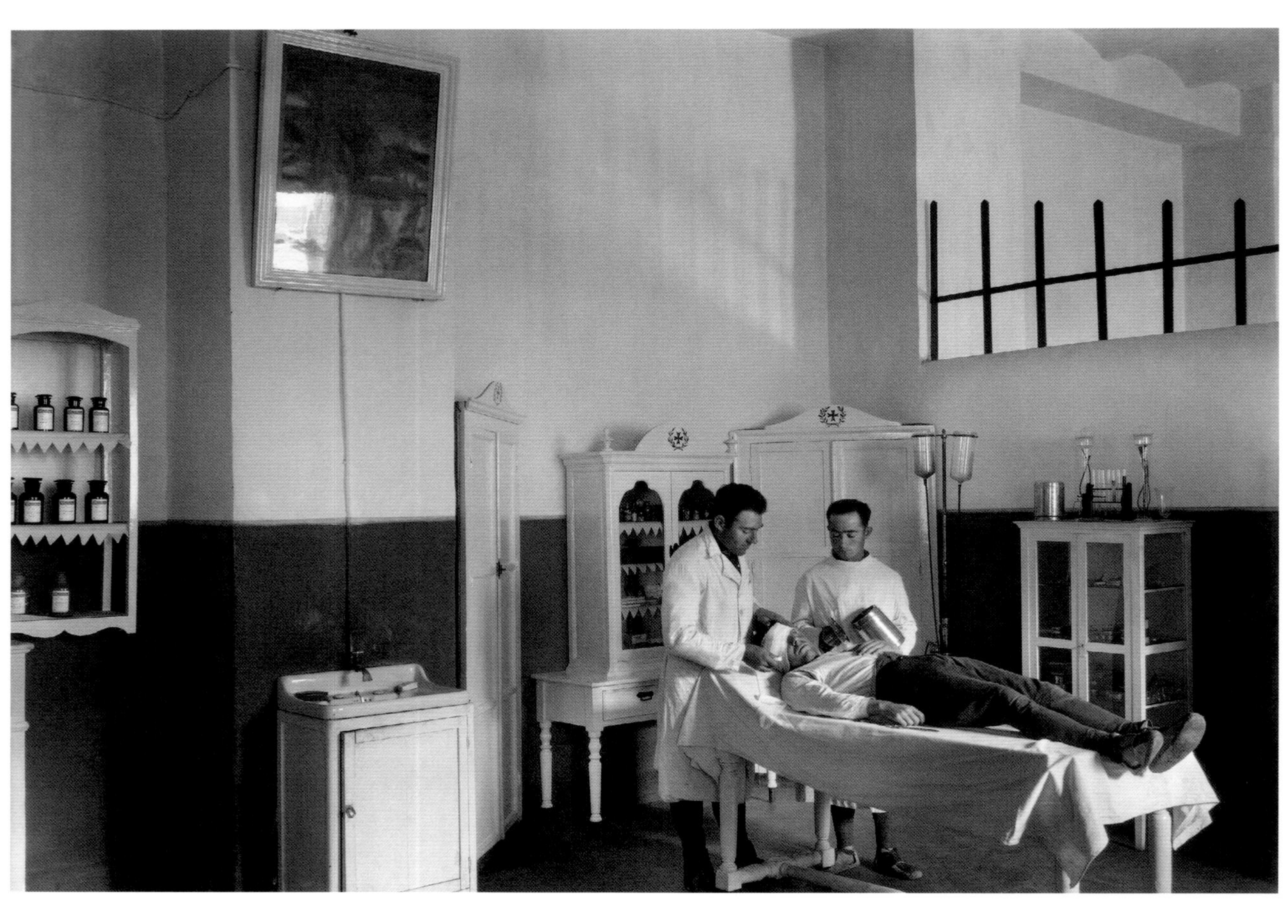

*Ceuta's Military Hospital Ward. Ca. 1927*
Courtesy Archivo Familiar Ros Amador

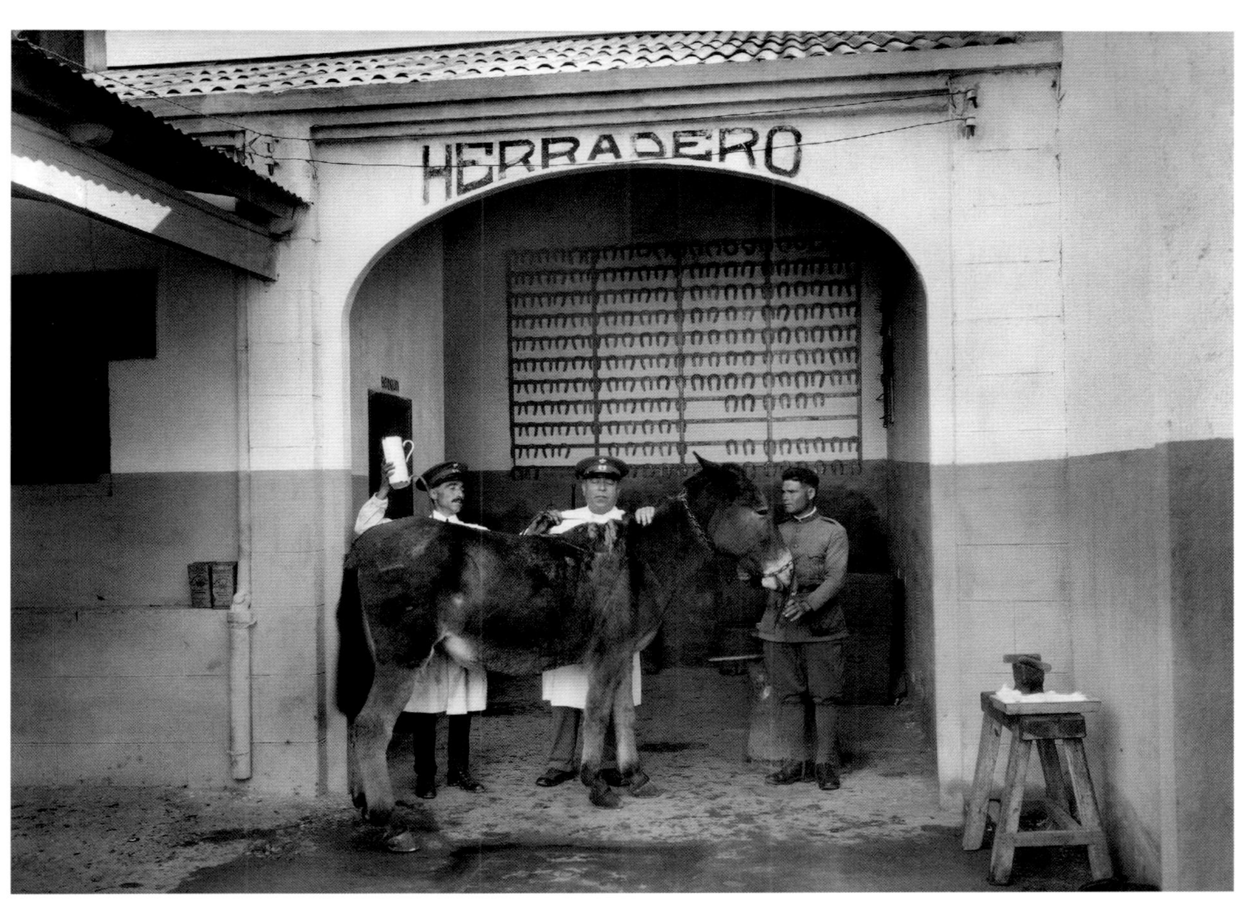


*Ceuta. Farriery and Animal Ward. González Tablas Regular Army Barracks. Circa 1924*
Courtesy Archivo Familiar Ros Amador

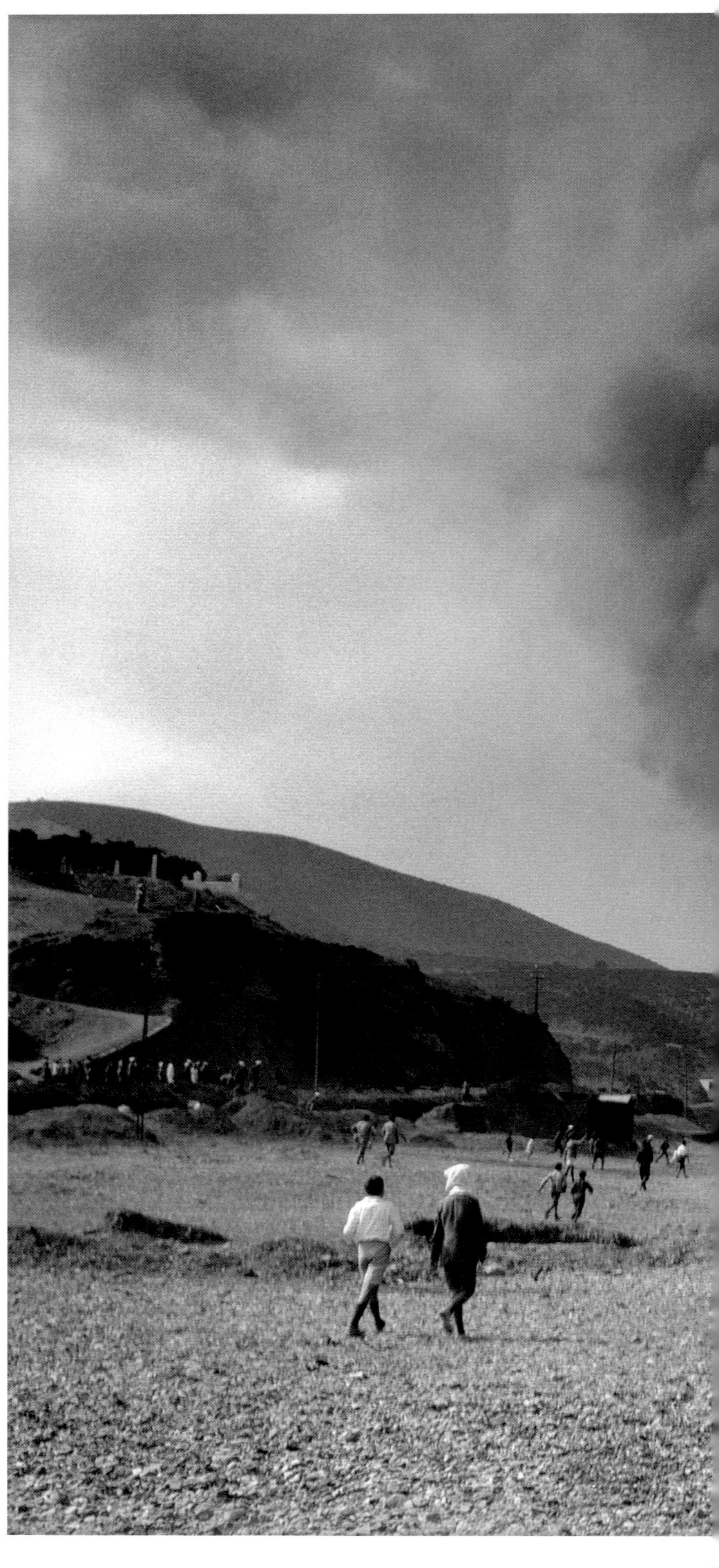

*Ceuta, Fire at Calamocarro Beach. Circa 1924*
Courtesy Archivo Familiar Ros Amador

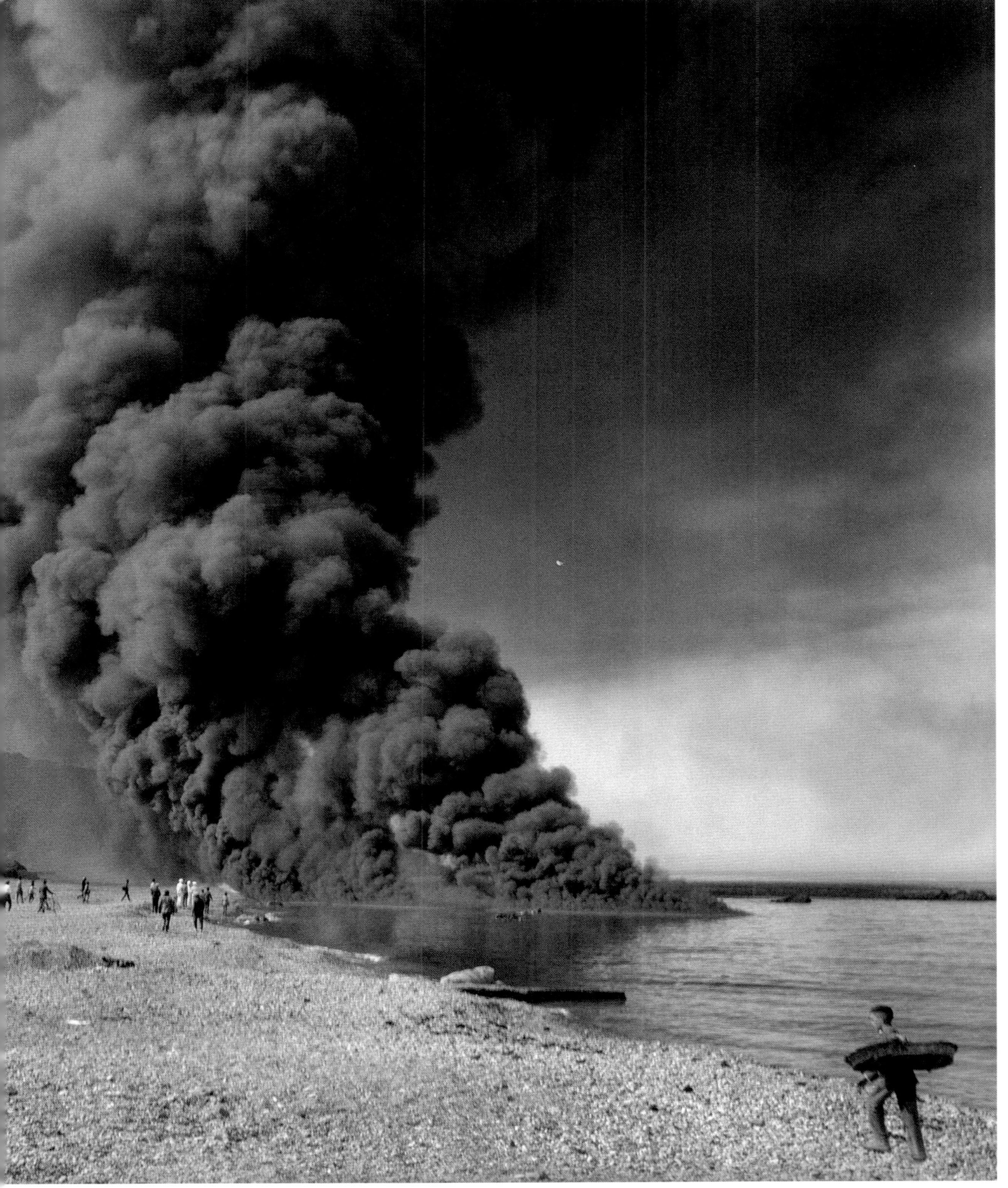

# Annie Leibovitz

**Annie Leibovitz. A Photographer's Life: 1990 – 2005**

My mother and father took photographs and made eight-millimeter home movies when I was growing up, but I didn't start taking pictures myself until the late 1960s, when I was studying at the San Francisco Art Institute. Personal reportage was a prominent element of the curriculum then. You were supposed to photograph things that meant something to you. One of the most meaningful pictures to me is Robert Frank's portrait of his wife and kids in the car when the sun is coming up. They've pulled over to the side of the road and may even have slept there. That reminds me so much of my family. My father was in the Air Force, and every time he was transferred to a new base we jumped into the car and drove there. We lived together in cars. When young photographers ask me what they should do, I always tell them to stay close to home.

When I worked for *Rolling Stone* in the 1970s, I was called a rock 'n' roll photographer. I began calling myself a portrait photographer because it lent a kind of dignity to shooting well-known people. But I'm not a great studio portraitist. At best, my studio photographs are graphic. I can always fall back on composition. When you have a subject who projects himself well, an actor or some other kind of entertainer, you can get an interesting picture, but I don't like trying to make something happen in the studio. There are truly intelligent photographers who work in the studio, but it's not for me. Richard Avedon's genius was that he was a great communicator. He pulled things out of his subjects. But I observe. Avedon knew how to talk to people. What to talk to them about. As soon as you engage someone, their face changes. They become animated. They forget about being photographed. Their minds become occupied and they look more interesting. But I'm so busy looking, I can't talk. I never developed that gift. I have the same problem with my children. I know I have to be more involved, to interact more, but I love just looking at them.

I hadn't realized how much Avedon meant to me until he died. He set a great example with his magazine work. He rode both horses. It didn't seem like he was a commercial photographer. He was an artist. I took his portrait for *Vanity Fair* when he had that last big show at the Metropolitan Museum of Art. He was nervous, perhaps about appearing old and frail — he was seventy-nine and had been ill — and I turned to him and said, "Don't worry." You go into a situation like that thinking that you want to be Avedon, to expose him the way he would very likely expose you. And then you don't. Afterward he sent me a note saying, "Thank you for taking care of me."

My pictures are helped by an environment. I love the street. I love going to someone's house, seeing what's on their walls, what chair they sit in. I like to see how they live. Most of the photographs of my family were taken at gatherings around a dining table or a pool or beside the ocean. After my father retired from the Air Force, my parents lived in Silver Spring, Maryland, a suburb of Washington, D.C., but they always had a house at the beach. My father built a shack in Ocean City, Maryland, with his own hands. And they had a place in St. Thomas for a few years. When they got older they decided to spend the winters in Sarasota, Florida, and they rented a house there while they looked for something to buy. My mother would wake up and put her bathing suit on.

Extracts from the text by Annie Liebovitz in
*A Photographer's Life: 1990 – 2005*, edited by Lunwerg.

When I edited a collection of my work from 1970-1990 for a book, I found that my favorite pictures were early ones taken when I was doing reportage. The pictures from the 1975 Rolling Stones tour were particularly strong, probably because I spent so much time traveling with the band. The very last photographs we put in that book were taken over a period of weeks in Florida in the summer of 1990, when I worked with Mikhail Baryshnikov and Mark Morris and a group of dancers, documenting their preparation for the first season of the White Oak Dance Project. It seemed like a return to the kind of work I had been doing in the beginning, but I wasn't able to go back to reportage in a completely pure way. I knew too much by then. Too much about how a picture can be set up, how you can manipulate a picture, when it should be taken. I'm not a journalist. I have a more powerful voice as a photographer if I express a point of view.

[Annie Leibovitz]

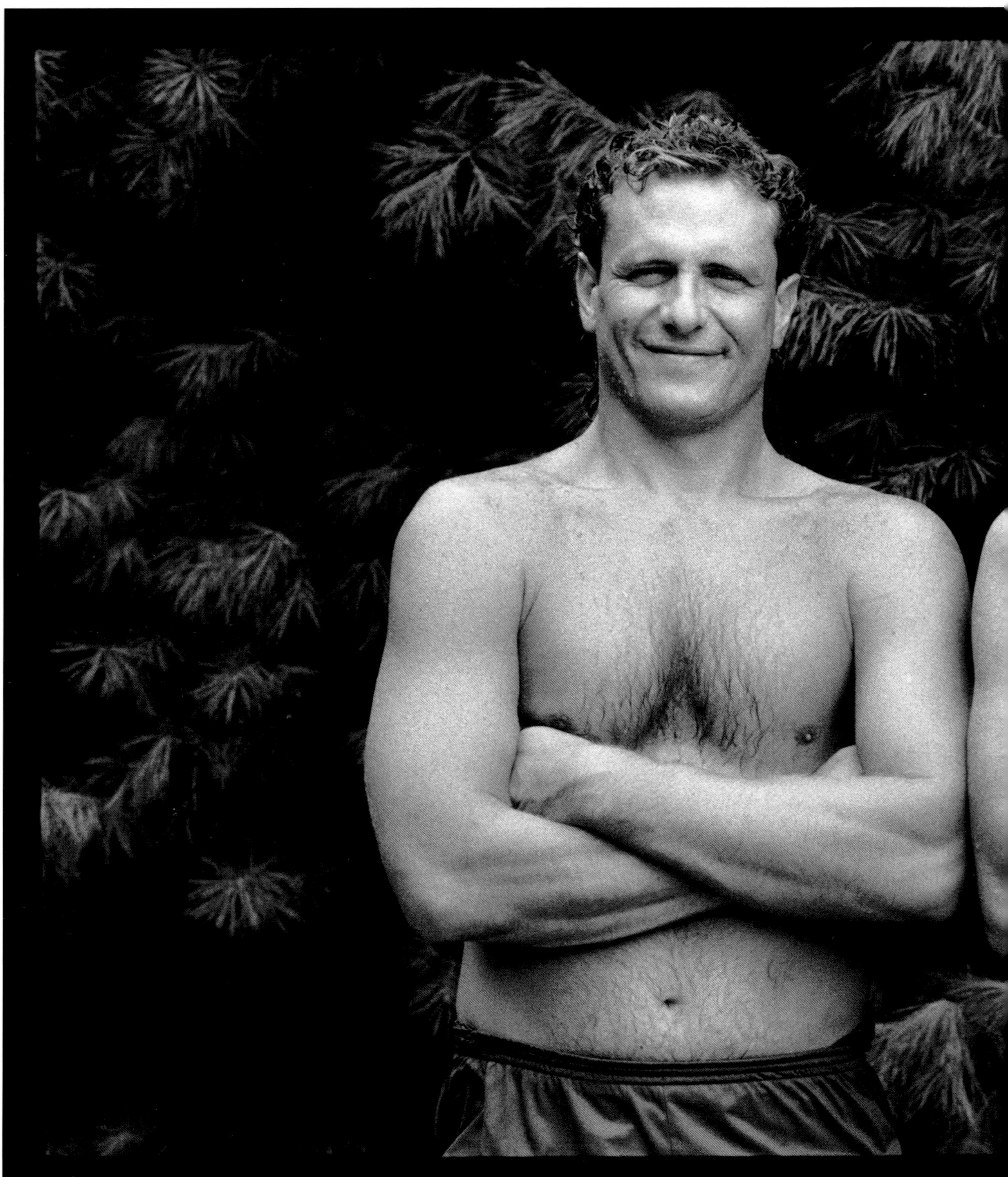

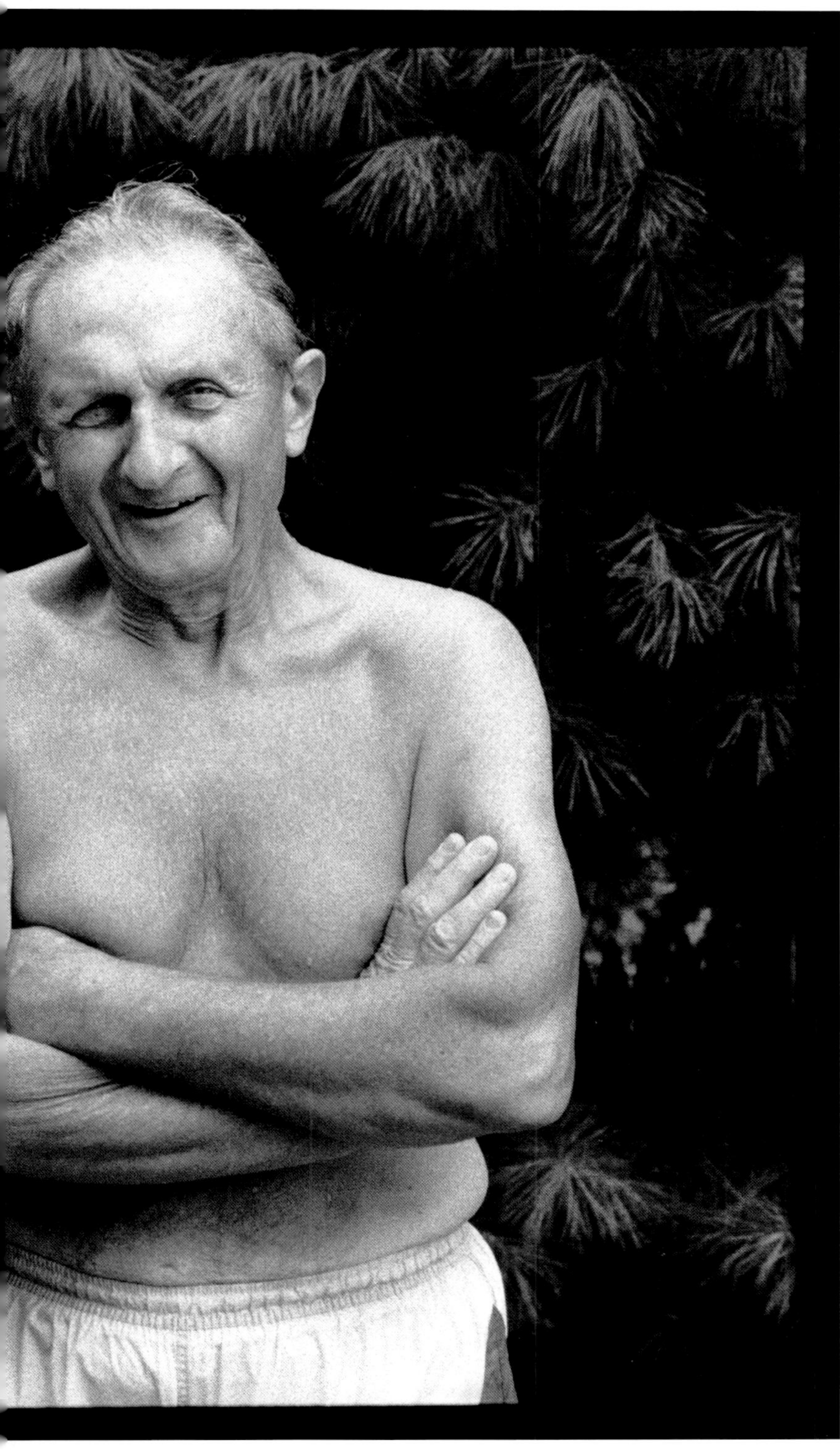

*My Brother Philip and My Father, Silver Spring, Maryland,* 1988
Photography © Annie Leibovitz (Contact Press Images)
From *Annie Leibovitz: A Photographer's Life, 1990-2005*

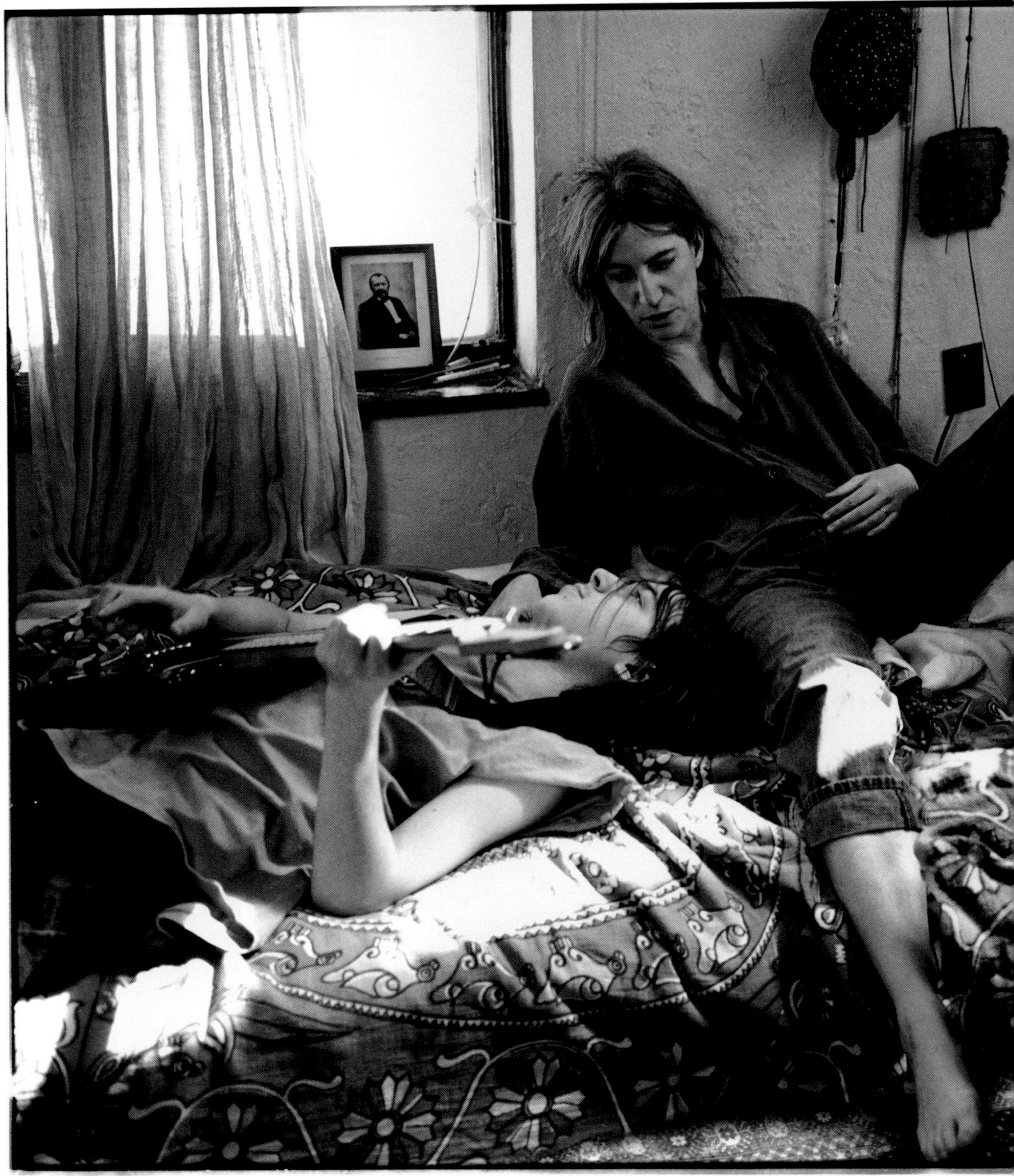

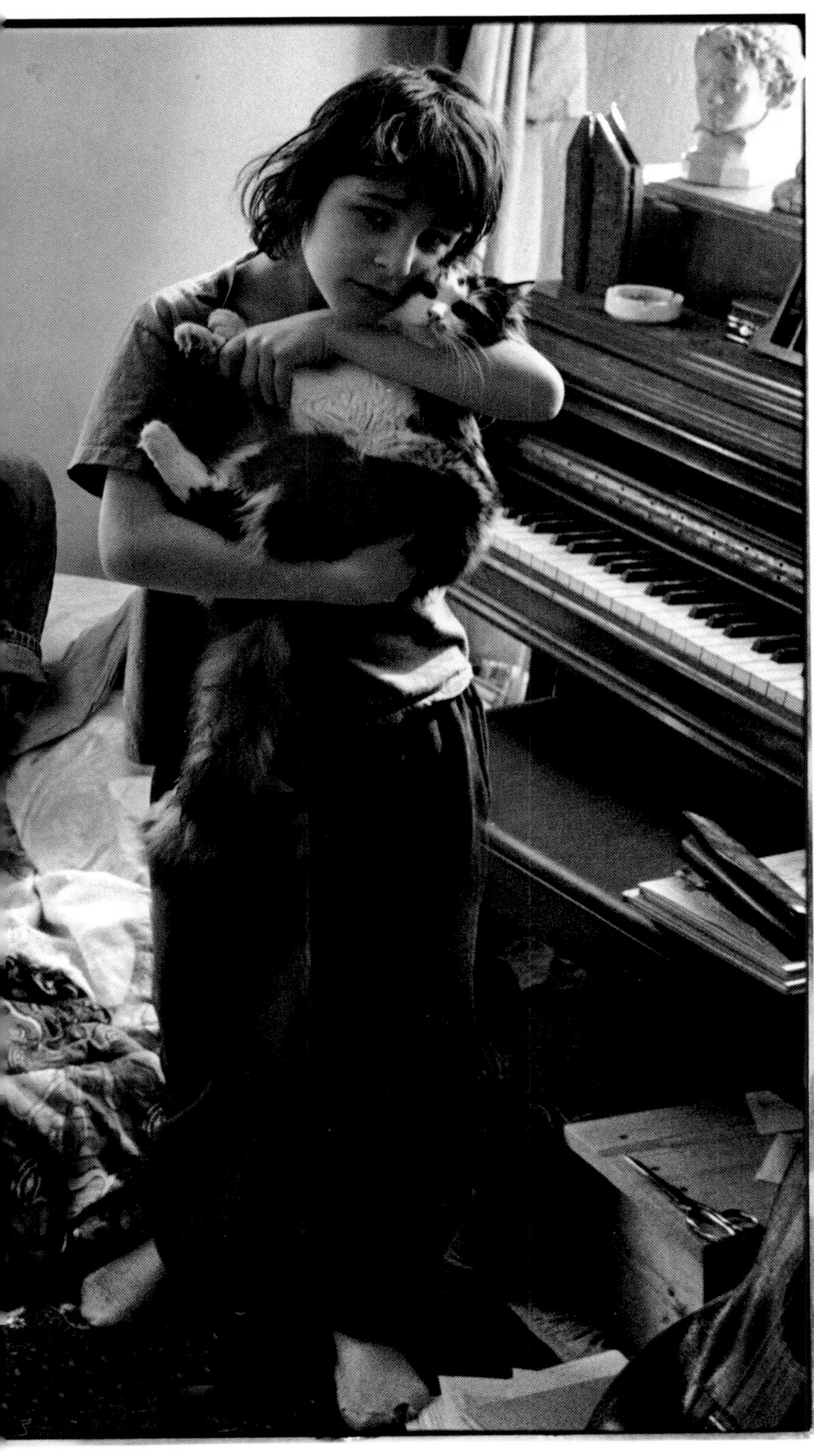

*Patti Smith with Her Children, Jackson and Jesse, St. Clair Shores, Michigan*, 1996
Photography © Annie Leibovitz (Contact Press Images)
Courtesy Vanity Fair
From *Annie Leibovitz: A Photographer's Life, 1990-2005*

# A Group Exhibition. Resilience

## Adaptation and Resistance

"Resilience: 1. Phys. The ability of a solid to recover its original shape and size when the system of forces causing its deformation ceases."
*The Essential Dictionary of Sciences of the Royal Academy of Exact, Physical and Natural Sciences*

*Resiliencia (Resilience)* presents the work of 10 young artists who participated in the 2009 edition of Descubrimientos PHE in Latin America.

A jury designated by PHotoEspaña selected 40 projects to take part in the portfolio reviews in Mexico City and Lima from a total of 342 by photographers living in the region. This edition represents a heterodox overview of contemporary photographic work in which all styles and themes fit.

Creation processes in Latin America emerge during full political, economic and social effervescence. Most of the works offered deal from various perspectives with the capacity for adaptation and improvement of a society that has been affected by continuous fluctuations; a need for adjustment that not only involves the referents for the projects presented, but also conditions creators and their models of representation.

We live in an environment saturated with images, and artists are obliged to investigate new forms of conceptualisation in order to highlight their projects amidst an ocean of possibilities.

We present the work of professionals who in addition to having the interest to show the changes taking place in their surroundings also reflect on the role of images in our society and use all means available to present their creations. In this way, customary paradigms are questioned and formats are adapted to new visual codes in a time of continuous mutation.

Dante Busquets and Pavka Segura show everyday images of Ciudad Satélite and Villa Coapa, two outlying neighbourhoods in Mexico City that have been integrated into the large Mexican metropolis over the last decade. Their residents belong to a middle class that feels particularly affected by the country's economic variations and resists losing its distinguishing traits. The *Two Million Homes for Mexico* project by Livia Corona, introduces us to the state-subsidised "living solutions" created during the government's previous six-year term and represents with fine irony the way government policies influences the private lives of inhabitants.

Óscar Fernando Gómez and Mark Powell capture with originality scenes and figures from Mexican streets, Gómez from his taxi in the city of Monterrey and Powell while strolling through the streets of Mexico City.

The images by Ramiro Chaves take us to Miramar (Argentina), a small village flooded after the rise of the Mar Chiquita Lagoon. The author's metaphorical metalanguage guides us through unusual areas loaded with nostalgia and conflicting feelings. Along this same line, but with a very different aesthetic, the Peruvian artist Ana Cecilia Gonzales Vigil photographs the reconstruction of villages damaged by the 2007 earthquake in the south of Peru. Under very difficult conditions, the region's inhabitants struggle to pull through and rebuild their daily lives.

Tomás Munita explores the daily reality of an island community in Peru that produces guano, a natural fertilizer of animal origin that after having lost its commercial value for several decades is now being used again due to environmental policies.

**Photographs by Livia Corona, Ramiro Chaves, Mark Powell, Dante Busquets, Nicola Frioli, Óscar Fernando Gómez, Pavka Segura, Tomás Munita, Morfi Jiménez & Ana Cecilia Gonzales Vigil**

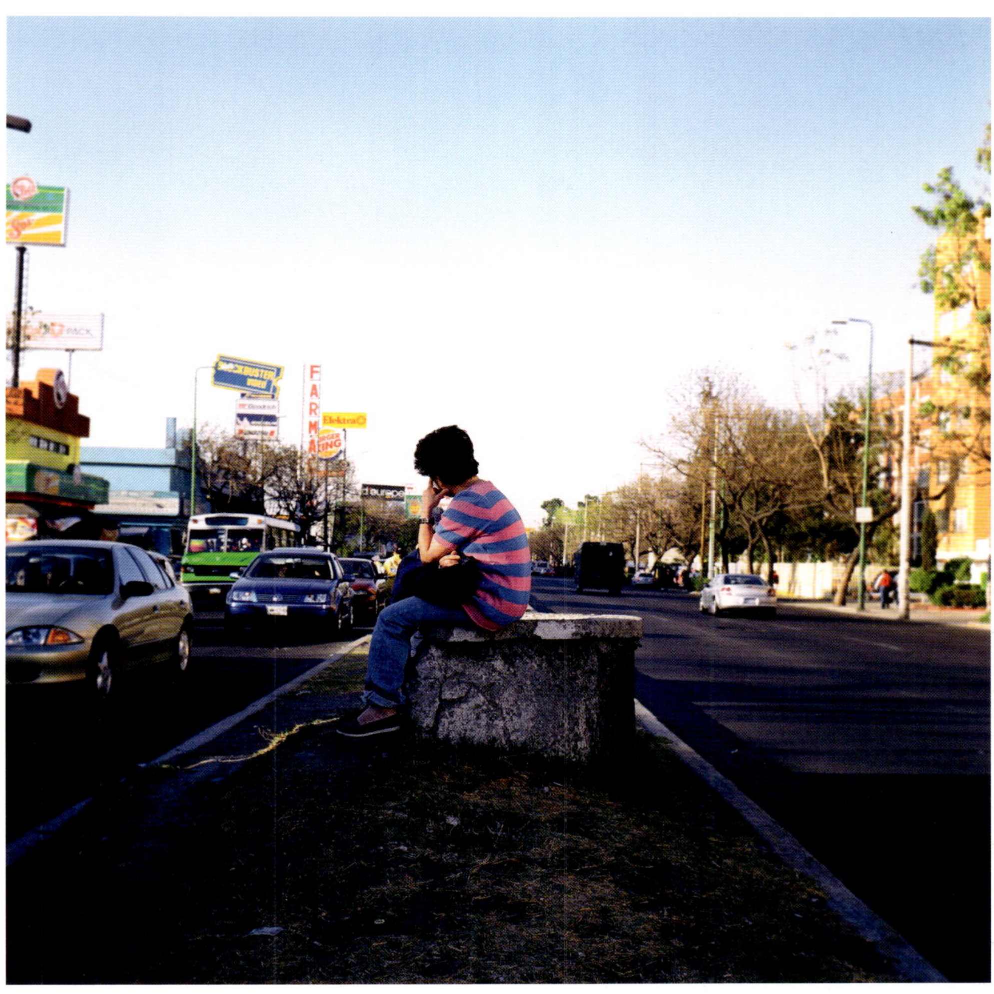


Morfi Jiménez generates magical artificial images portraying people from the interior of Peru, and with a very personal aesthetic submerges us in the Andean world, generating an interesting friction between documentary and fiction.

Finally, Nicola *Okin* Frioli portrays Central American immigrants who have seen their expectations drastically frustrated in the south of Mexico.

This is a varied tour of contemporary photographic creation in Latin America. All the projects selected show particular aspects that affect local problems.

The "Resilience" concept that provides the title for this exhibition quantifies the capacity for regeneration of a body after an impact and confirms this continuous acclimatisation.

[Claudi Carreras]

**Pavka Segura**
*Untitled.* From the series *Pioneeros*, 2006
© Pavka Segura

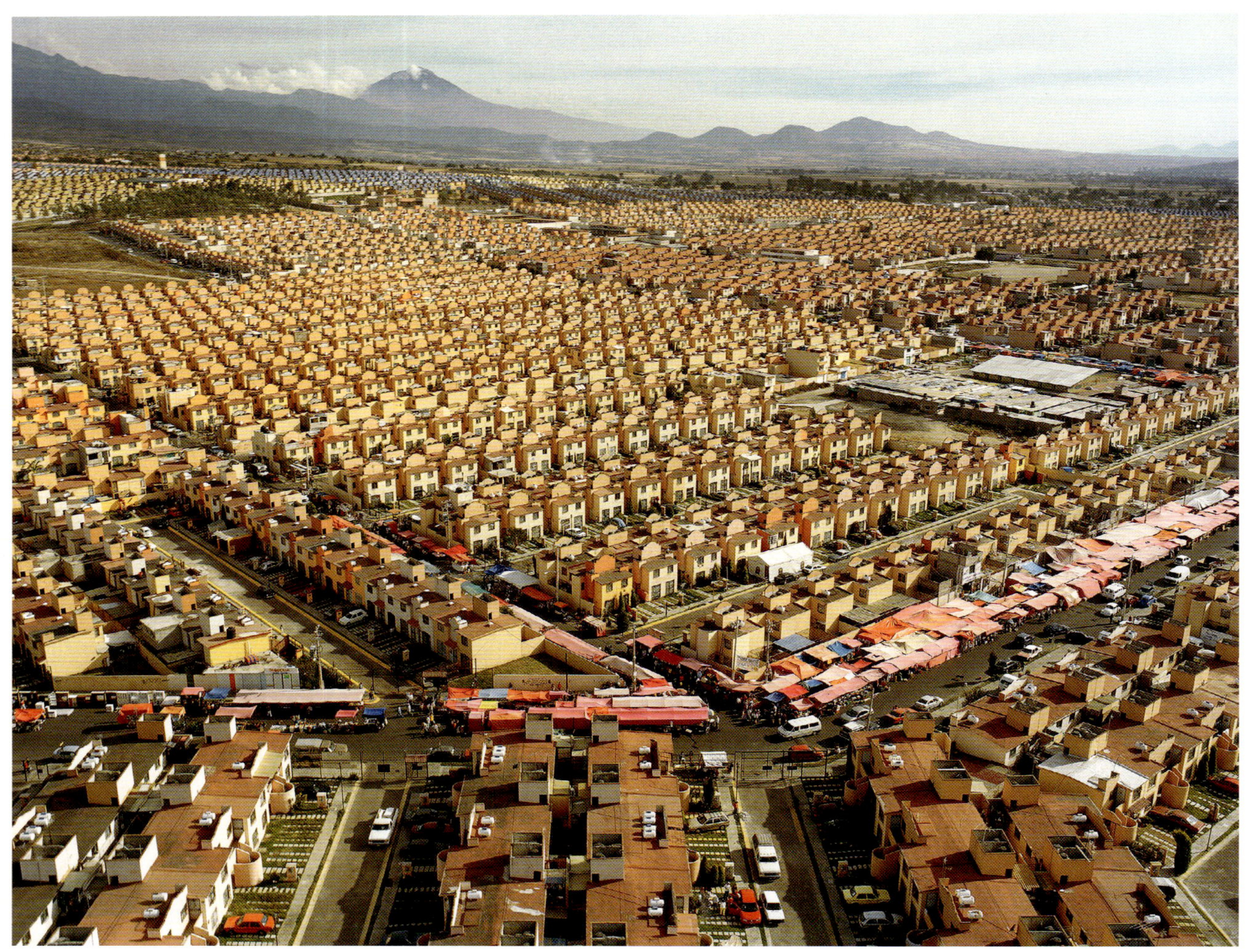

**Livia Corona**
From the series *Two Million Homes for Mexico*, 2008

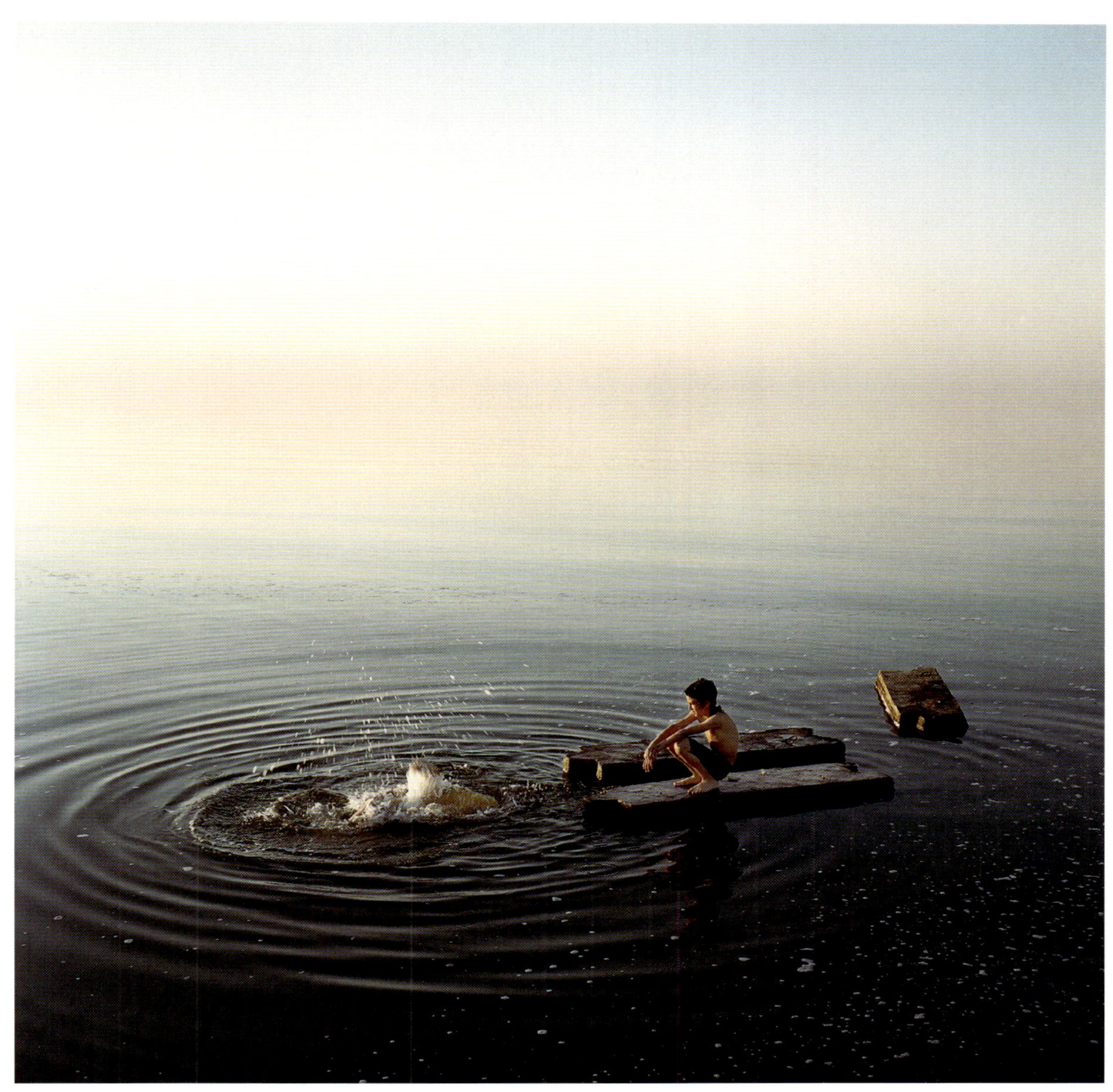

**Ramiro Chaves**
*Two children*. From the series *Miramar*, 2008

OFFICIAL SECTION

Ugo Mulas
BBVA / Sala de Exposiciones de Azca

Mauro Restiffe. *Mirante*
Casa de América

Jindřich Štyrský. *On the Needles of these Days*
Círculo de Bellas Artes / Sala Goya

Zhao Liang. *City Scene*
Círculo de Bellas Artes / Sala Minerva

Patrick Faigenbaum. *Photographies 1974-2008*
Círculo de Bellas Artes / Sala Picasso

Annie Leibovitz. *A Photographer's Life: 1990 - 2005*
Comunidad de Madrid / Sala Alcalá 31

Sergey Bratkov. *Glory Days*
Comunidad de Madrid / Sala Canal de Isabel II

A Group Exhibition. Descubrimientos PHE09
Comunidad de Madrid / Complejo el Águila

Yann Gross. *Horizonville*
Comunidad de Madrid / Complejo el Águila

Pedro Costa
Filmoteca Española-Cine Doré

Gerhard Richter. *Overpainted Photographs*
Fundación Telefónica

A Group Exhibition. *Resilience*
Instituto Cervantes

Íñigo Manglano-Ovalle. *Nocturne... (in real-time)*
Matadero Madrid / Abierto x Obras

*The Best Photography Books of the Year*
Matadero Madrid / Central de Diseño

Pedro Costa. *Back Home. Video works*
Matadero Madrid / Nave 16

Dorothea Lange. *The Crucial Years*
Museo Colecciones ICO

Cristóbal Hara
Museu Colecção Berardo (Lisbon, Portugal)

Mabel Palacín
Museu Colecção Berardo (Lisbon, Portugal)

Bartolomé Ros. *Borders of Africa*
Museo de Arte Contemporáneo de Madrid

*The Atlas Group (1989-2004). A Project by Walid Raad*
Museo Nacional Centro de Arte Reina Sofía

Larry Sultan & Mike Mandel. *Evidence*
Real Jardín Botánico - CSIC

Sara Ramo
Real Jardín Botánico - CSIC

A Group Exhibition. *70s. Photography and Daily Life*
Teatro Fernán Gómez. Centro de Arte / Fundación Banco Santander

PHE09

Director
Claude Bussac

Artistic Director
Sérgio Mah

General Coordinator
Luis Posada

Head of Promotion and Marketing
Sergio Mantilla

Head of Exhibitions
Marta García Haro

Exhibitions
Pilar Blanco
Sofia Nunes
Carmen Riestra

Coordinator of Educational and Professional Programs
Emily Adams

Educational and Professional Programs
Jaime González
Gonzalo Monge

Production
Ana Morales

Coordinador of PHotoEspaña en la Calle
Leticia Díez

Picture Editor
Julio César González

Travel
Pablo de Bergia

Public Relations
Gemma de los Mártires

Director of Communication
Álvaro Matías

Head of Press
Myriam González

Press in Spain
Judith Herrero
Mariana Urquijo

International Press
María Peláez

Creative Direction
Nadie. The creative think tank

Accounting
Verónica Martín

WWW.PHE.ES

Technical Director
Francisco Fernández

Web Coordinator
Inés Ruiz del Árbol

ORGANIZED BY

LA FABRICA

Verónica 13
28014 Madrid. Spain
T + 34 913 601 320
F + 34 913 601 322
info@lafabrica.com
www.lafabrica.com

La Fábrica Associates
Alberto Anaut
Alberto Fesser

General Director
Agustín García Benavente

Director of Exhibitions
Oliva María Rubio

Director of Accounting
María José Alonso

CATALOGUE

Published by
La Fábrica Editorial

Production
Paloma Castellanos

Coordination
Luisa Lucuix

Copyediting
Emilio Ruiz Mateo
Susan Coombs



Translations
Herrán Coombs
John Elliott
Tamara Gil Somoza
Ramón González Férriz
Carlos Vitale
Alan Waite
Luísa Yokochi
Art in Translation

Graphic design
gráfica futura

Printing
Brizzolis

Reproductions
Cromotex

ISBN
978-84-92498-80-2

Depósito legal
M-22212-2009

Impreso en España

Cover illustration
**David Goldblatt**
*Child Minder, Joubert Park, Johannesburg.* From the series *Particulars*, 1975
Courtesy of the artist; Michael Stevenson Gallery, Cape Town; Elba Benítez Gallery, Madrid


Back cover illustration
**Gerhard Richter**
*19.2.92.* Detail
Courtesy Isabel & David Breskin Collection , San Francisco. Published in *Gerhard Richter. Overpainted Photographs.* Hatje Cantz Verlag, Ostfildern, 2008


Front flyleaves
**Mauro Restiffe**
*Red Light Portrait #19*, 2006
Courtesy Coleçao Sérgio Carvalho, Brasília


Frontispiece
**Dorothea Lange**
*Wife of a migratory laborer with three children. Near Childress, Texas. Nettie Featherston*, June 1938
Courtesy Library of Congress, Prints & Photographs Division, FSA/OWI Collection LC-USF34- 018294-C


Pages 4-5
**Walid Raad / The Atlas Group**
*We Decided to Let Them Say, "We Are Convenced", Twice*, 2002
Courtesy Galerie Sfeir-Semler, Hamburg, Beirut / Anthony Reynolds Gallery, London


Page 27
**Viktor Kolář**
From the series *Ostrava*, 1980
Courtesy of the artist


Colophon
**Larry Sultan & Mike Mandel**
Untitled. From the series *Evidence*, 1977
Courtesy Galerie Thomas Zander, Cologne


Back flyleaves
**Sara Ramo**
*Added*, 1993-2008
Courtesy Fortes Vilaça Gallery, São Paulo


ACKNOWLEDGMENTS

Archives of American Art, Smithsonian Institution; Archivio Ugo Mulas; Benny Levenson; Bernd & Christa Rosenblum; Bernhard Moser; Christopher Apap; Claus A. Wille; Czech Center, Madrid; Dieter Giesing; Dietmar Elger; Edward Jaeger-Booth; Élia Pijolet; Erwin Hake; Eva Felten; Galeria Casa Triângulo, São Paulo, Brasil; Galerie de France, Paris, France; Galeria Fortes Vilaça, São Paulo, Brasil; Galeria Mario Sequeira, Braga, Portugal; Galerie Sfeir-Semler, Hamburg/Beirut; Gerhard Richter; Hans-Ulrich Obrist; Hartmut Griepentrog; Heiner Oettli; Heinz Teichmann & Heidi Pfanzelt; Hubert Becker; Inhotim, Brumadinho, Minas Gerais, Brasil; Konstanze Ell; L.A. Galerie, Lothar Albrecht, Frankfurt, Germany; Manfred Leve; Mauro Restiffe; Meg Partridge; Münchener Rückversicherungs-Gesellschaft; Museum of Contemporary Photography at Columbia College Chicago; Museum of Decorative Arts in Prague; Norbert Arns; Oakland Museum of California; Patrick Faigenbaum; Pedro Barbosa; Peter Metzger; Rainer Jacobs & Dorit Jacobs; Regina Gallery, Moscow; Rosa Ros; Sérgio Carvalho; Susanne Ehrenfried; Sylviane De Decker; Temari Anstalt; The Bancroft Library. University of California, Berkeley; The Library of Congress, Washington; Thomas Wientgen; USA Embassy; Van den Valentyn Foundation; Walid Raad; Wolfgang & Astrid Troschke.

We also thank all the artists and curators who have participated in the projects for their invaluable collaboration.

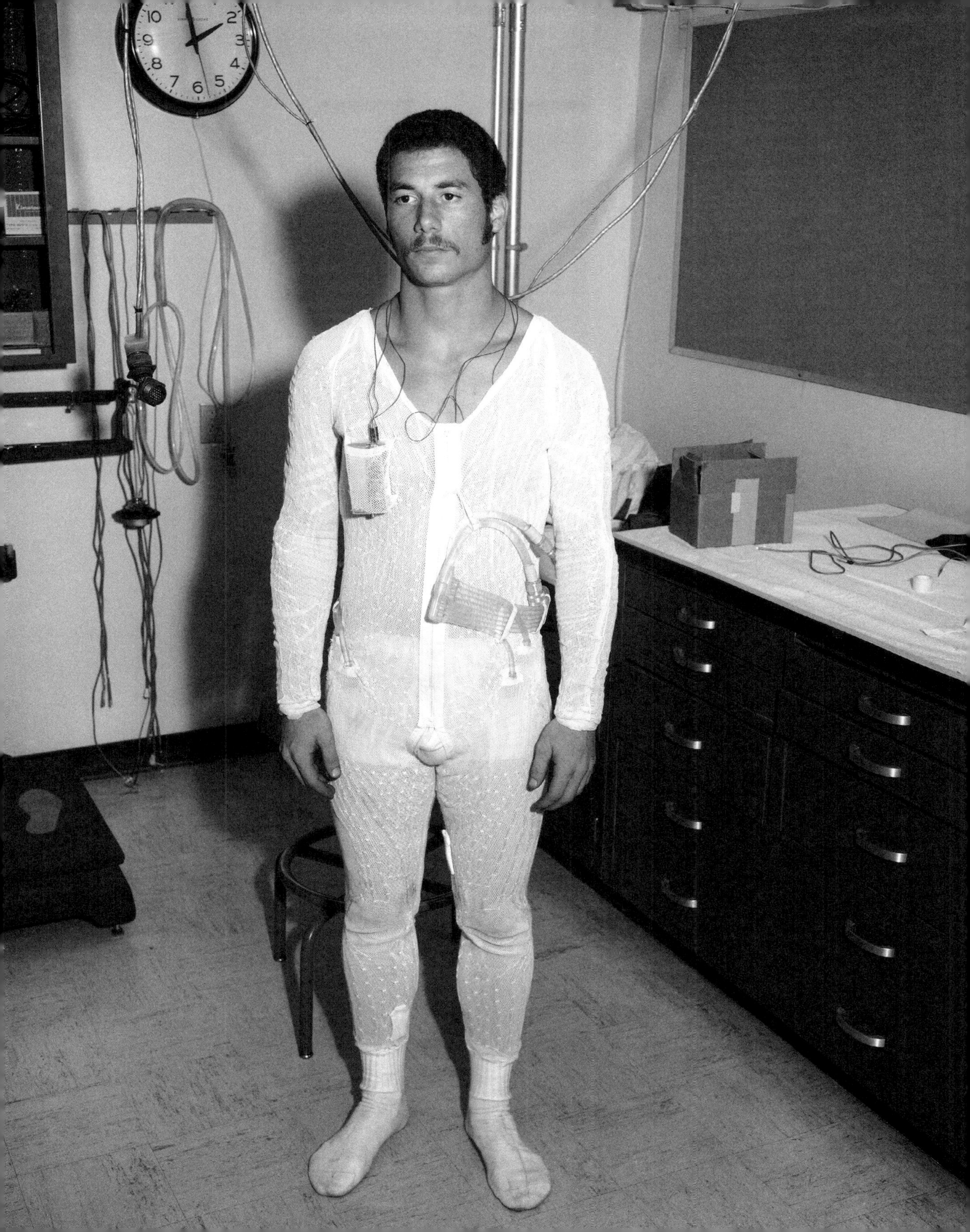

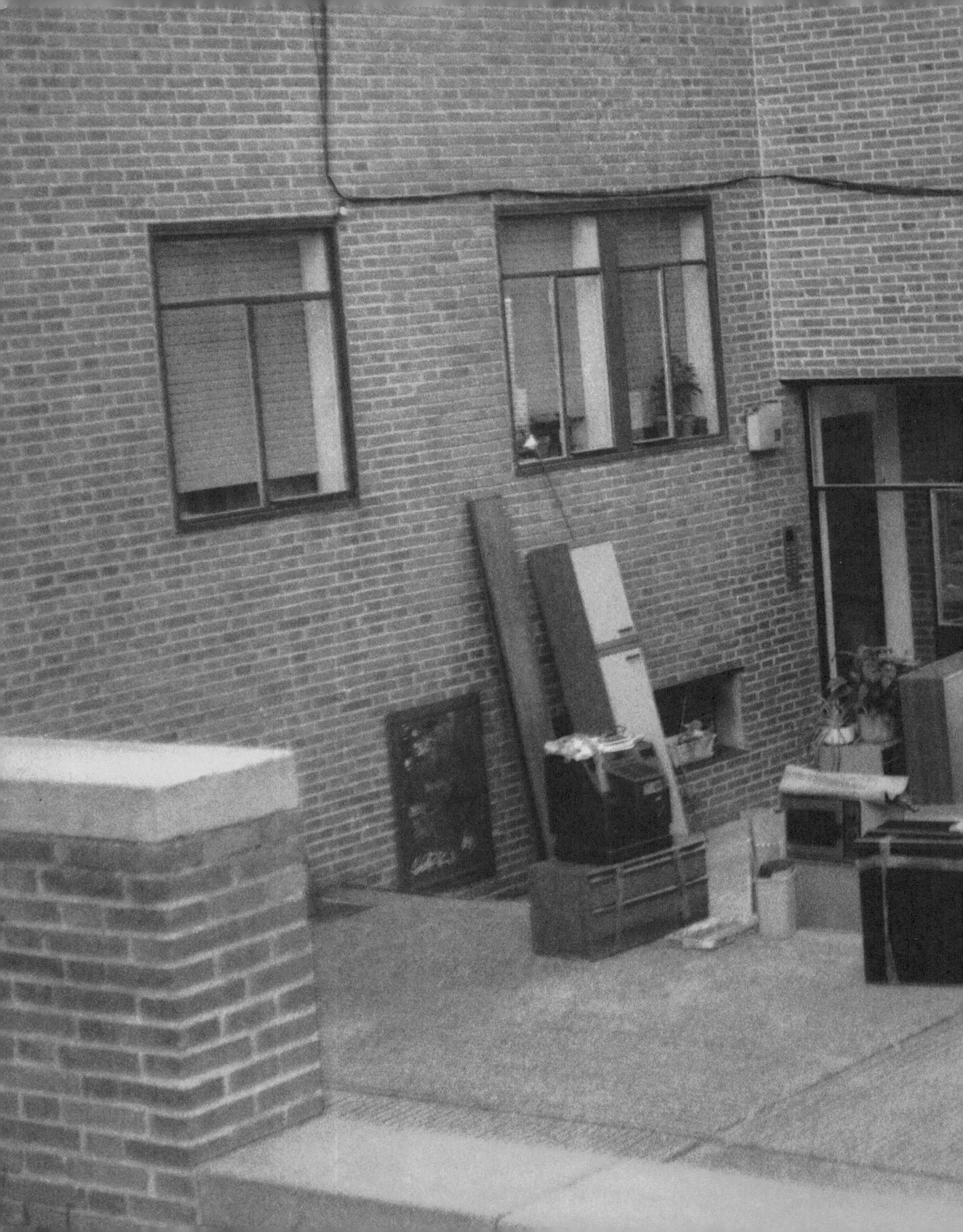